LIFE
An Owner's
Manual

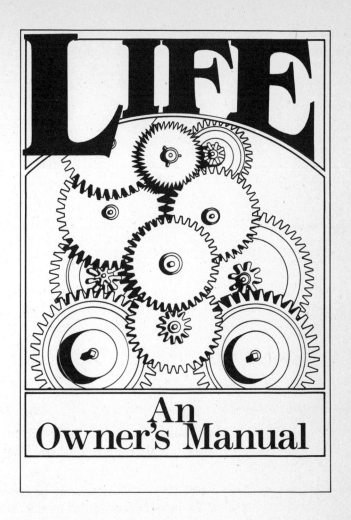

LIFE

An Owner's Manual

Alice Slaikeu Lawhead

CROSSWAY BOOKS • WESTCHESTER, ILLINOIS
A DIVISION OF GOOD NEWS PUBLISHERS

Life: An Owner's Manual.

Copyright © 1986 by Alice Slaikeu Lawhead. Published by Crossway Books, a division of Good News Publishers, Westchester, Illinois 60153.

Book Design by Karen L. Mulder.

First printing, 1986

Printed in the United States of America

Library of Congress Catalog Card Number 85-72912

ISBN 0-89107-375-2

TABLE OF CONTENTS

LIST OF SPECIAL CHARTS

INTRODUCTION

If I were picking up a book entitled *Life: An Owner's Manual*, I'd be very interested to know what the author of such a book might have to recommend herself as an authority on such a broad subject. Anticipating that same curiosity in others, I will now set forth the range of experiences in my own life which, I believe, suit me to the task:

- —Got fired from the best job I ever had;
- —Moved nine times in ten years;
- —To date, have owned four cars (one was a Vega), three sets of living room furniture, two bikes, twelve phones, and over two hundred fish;
- —Was turned down for credit when I needed it most;
- —Know how to throw a great party;
- —Have an adult relationship with my mother;
- —Have been working full-time at some kind of paying job since the age of eighteen;
- —Paid off a $2,500 school loan;
- —Have had membership in four churches, three health clubs, three community organizations, and held borrowers' cards with five libraries since living on my own;
- —Once had a savings account—with real money in it;
- —Know the polite thing to do immediately after spilling bean dip on my host's Haitian cotton sofa;

—Read fifty books a year, attend fourteen movies a year, buy fifteen record albums a year and watch about one and a half hours of television per day
—Have successfully balanced my checkbook for the past 162 months;
—Have visited most major American cities, a couple of dozen rural communities, and a handful of foreign countries;
—Have been robbed three times;
—Have fired my doctor;
—Have an up-to-date will;
—Have both sold and bought insurance;
—Attended my ten-year high school reunion;
—Have been on about 258 dates (but who's counting?);
—Have failed when I wanted desperately to succeed, and have succeeded in some very unlikely endeavors.

If the above resumé has satisfied you as to my qualifications, we can now proceed with this book about life.

All I ask is that you keep in mind the title of the book while you read, believing that you really do own your life; now that you're on your own, you have full responsibility for how you conduct yourself and your affairs. And if you'd like a little help making it on your own, well, that's what I'm here for.

Part I:
People in Your Life

1.

PARENTS

Richard hangs up the telephone receiver. It's his mother: she and Dad are coming by to drop off some books of his that they borrowed. Richard begins policing his apartment, preparing for their visit. Never mind the sugar grit on the kitchen floor or the dust bunnies on the stairway. First things first: all empty beer cans are placed in a brown paper bag; the bag is rolled up, deposited in the trash bin outside, and covered over with newspapers. Any stray beer in the refrigerator is transferred to the bottom drawer of his bureau. His roommate's ashtray—his one and only ashtray—is emptied into the toilet (toilet is flushed—twice) and hidden under the kitchen sink, behind the bag of sprouting potatoes. The dog-eared copy of *How to Pick Up Girls* is removed from the bookcase and shoved into the record cabinet behind a stack of old 45s.

Deidre answers the doorbell. It's her mother, in tears.

"Your father is such a cruel man, Deidre," explains her mother as she kisses her on the cheek. "I'm going to leave him this time for sure. If it hadn't been for you and Roger I would have left him years ago. But you're out of the nest, of course, and Roger doesn't care to give me the time of day, so I don't know why I should even bother to hold on. When I think of all I've given that man, I could just kill him."

Deidre takes her mother's coat, gets herself some ice tea ("No, darling, I couldn't drink it, I'm so upset") and settles down for a long heart-to-heart with her mom.

After spending a crisp fall morning pheasant hunting with his father, Steve is presented with a gift.

"Here, son, you can get more use out of this than I can."

"What's this? It looks like the chamois shirt I gave you for your birthday!"

"It is, son. Doggone it, Steve, you shouldn't be spending money on me like that. You've got your own life to live. We're about the same size. If it's a little short for you in the sleeves, you can return it for your size. Did you keep the sales receipt?"

"Dad, I gave you that shirt! It's a present!"

"When your dad needs you to buy him clothes, he'll tell you."

Kristin comes home from work, exhausted. She throws her portfolio on the kitchen table, sorts through her mail—junk, junk, junk—pulls a handful of grapes out of the refrigerator, and ambles to her room where she flops on the bed and stares at the ceiling.

Her bed is made, although she didn't make it. The clothes in her closet are cleaned and pressed, but she didn't wash or iron them. Dinner is in the oven and it smells good—Kristin doesn't know much about cooking. "Living at home has its advantages," she muses.

A knock at the door. The door opens. "Kris, honey, do you have a minute to go over this roofing estimate for me? I don't understand this charge for removal of the old roof; the whole thing seems like more than I can afford."

"It also has its disadvantages," Kristin mumbles to herself as she gives her mother a vacant look. "Why can't she leave me alone and let me live my own life?"

Russ uses his fork to capture the last bits of food on his plate. He is stalling, hoping that the conversation destined to take place this evening will not come about. Next week he'll graduate from college; he has already informed his parents that he has applied to the graduate school of journalism.

"So, Russ, it's finally here. You're going to graduate from

college. The first of my kids to get a degree. You're making me a proud man, boy."

"Thanks, Dad."

"And this journalism thing. You think that's the right thing to do?"

"Yeah, I do, Dad. I just hope I get accepted."

"Of course you'll get accepted. No one could turn you down—you're a real self-starter, a bright, independent guy who knows how to get what he wants!"

"Thanks, Dad."

"Of course, if you were going into law, I'd be able to throw enough business your way during the first year that you'd be right up there with F. Lee Bailey and all those other rich lawyers! Isn't that right, Mildred?"

"Right, Dennis."

"Right, Dad."

Now here you are, in the serious business of establishing your independence, becoming your own person, figuring out what your talents are and developing life proficiencies, and look who's holding you back: Mom and Dad, that's who. Why can't they find that right mix of support and hands-off that you need to make it on your own? Why are they acting like children? Why can't they treat you like an adult?

When you were a little kid, you knew how to behave like a child and your parents knew how to behave like parents. You were sick, they took you to the doctor; you were tired, they sent you to bed; you got hurt, they comforted you; you misbehaved, they punished.

But at some point—probably *this* point in your life—your relationship with your parents must change. If it doesn't, you won't grow up and neither will they. Remember Norman Bates in *Psycho*? There's a guy who never did grow up, who continued to be Mama's little boy—even though Mama was dead (sorry, I gave away the ending).

Extreme cases of this are easy to recognize. But what about your case? Are you and your parents working to develop an adult relationship? Are they encouraging you to grow and gain independence? Are you starting to look after yourself, doing things the hard way even when it would be easier to ask Mom and Dad for help?

Or are your parents clinging to you for dear life? Do they pout when you don't take their advice, make excuses to involve themselves in your personal affairs, and use guilt to control you? Are you afraid to confront them on important issues, agreeing with them when you should be standing up to them, and letting them bail you out of the messes you get yourself into?

This is a book designed to help you become independent. All the sympathy here is for you. So there are no platitudes like the ones you got from your high school guidance counselor, Uncle Ned, or the night manager at Burger King. You already know that parents are people, too, that they were young once, that if you'd act like an adult you'd get treated like one, blah, blah, blah.

But the fact of the matter is that if you've got problems with your folks, it's going to be *your* responsibility and yours alone to work through the difficulties and eventually relate to them adult-to-adult.

"Look, they're the ones who want me to be a little kid; it's their problem and they should make the first move. They're making my life miserable in a million ways, and I'm sick of it."

You can say that until you're blue in the face, but it won't do one bit of good. You're not a kid anymore—you're an adult. An adult doesn't wait for other people to solve his problems—he solves them himself or herself. If you own your life, you own your problems and figure out how to work through them. So your parents are the cause of it all. Big deal. What are *you* going to do? Are you going to change what you can, or gripe about everything beyond your control?

The only person you can change is yourself. Your parents are their own people; they make their own decisions. You make yours. This is not to say that they are beyond hope—they probably aren't. But wishing won't make it so. The best you can do is to make changes in your own life that will inspire them to look at their lives for areas of possible growth.

"I Don't Need 'Em"

Oh yeah? You think you don't need your parents? Well, you don't need them to pay your tuition anymore, or to house you (maybe), or to put Band-Aids on your boo-boos, but you still need your parents.

Let me count the ways:

(1) You need your parents because they tie you to the rest of

your family. They are the link between you and your grandparents, and all your ancient ancestors. They are the parents of your siblings. They are the branch of your family tree that your twig is growing on.

(2) You need your parents because you love them. A frustrated relationship with your parents, whom you love, is just like any other frustrated love affair—miserable and tortured. Love demands communication, acts of kindness, mutual understanding, support, and intimacy. Because you love your parents, you will be troubled and unhappy when your relationship with them is bad.

(3) You need your parents because you have unfinished business with them. Maybe you're angry at them for the way they treated you, or your brother, or your best friend, or each other. Or you feel a debt of gratitude for all they've done for you. Or you're burning with curiosity about them—what makes these people tick? The loose ends of your relationship keep it alive and vital.

(4) Your parents are a part of your personal history, and you need them for that reason. They have known you since you existed. You've shared all the important experiences of life together. They are a part of you. Like it or not, you are dependent upon them because so much of them lives in you. All the time you see yourself doing what Mom or Dad would do—or maybe the opposite. But whether you are like them or determined *not* to be like them, they are influencing your behavior. They always will.

You need your parents. But you need them in a different way than you used to. You need to begin relating to them adult-to-adult. There's still a lot of child left in both of you—that's normal, natural, good. Sometimes your folks behave like little children who are afraid to be left with a babysitter—they don't want you to leave. They kick and scream and holler.

You behave like a kid, too. You look to them for answers to questions you should be answering yourself. You panic at the prospect of navigating through life on your own. The more you behave like children—on both sides—the more problems you'll have.

But the more you can relate to each other as adults, the better your relationship will be. It will take years, even in the best of situations, to go from parent-to-child to adult-to-adult. Your folks may be uncooperative. You may be unwilling. But, believe me, it's the only healthy way to live.

Stop the Music

Did you catch the common denominator that connected each of the opening parent/child scenarios? The thread is this: each parent and each child was locked into an old routine, unwilling or afraid to change the song-and-dance that had been going on for years.

Richard mechanically performed the get-ready-for-Mom-and-Dad drill; he hid the beer, the ashtray, his favorite book. He hasn't been communicating with his parents, and if he keeps this up he never will. Apparently he's willing to sacrifice openness (with its attendant disappointments, arguments, and recriminations) for "peace" in the family.

Deidre has had to listen to her mother gripe about her dad more than once. She knows what her mother will say before she says it. Her mother knows that Deidre is a dependable and ever-present shoulder to cry on—this is why she drops in unannounced and thinks nothing of laying a guilt trip on her daughter ("If it hadn't been for you and Roger, I would have left him years ago"). Deidre's mother isn't paying attention to what she is saying; and she has talked so long that Deidre doesn't hear her anymore.

Steve's dad doesn't want to be on the receiving end of a father-son relationship. He won't even accept a birthday present from Steve, harping back to old times when it was Daddy who gave presents to little Stevie. He feels threatened by Steve's adulthood—"When your dad needs you to buy him clothes, he'll tell you."

Kristin feigns a desire for autonomy in her life, but is unwilling to pay the price for it. She resents it when her mother asks for help with a problem ("Why can't she leave me alone . . ."), but allows her parents to provide her room and board, make her bed, and wash her clothes; and she generally imposes on their hospitality. She's in a rut, but it's a safe, comfortable rut. Leaving it will be hard to do.

Russ's father is proud of his son. He likes Russ's success in school. But he gives him a double message—he's saying to Russ, "Be independent; do as I say." Russ is in a no-win situation, the classic double-bind. If he pursues his ambition to be a journalist, his father will always be critical of him for failing to become a rich lawyer; if he becomes a lawyer as his father wants him to do, he will sacrifice the initiative his father supposedly admires in him.

You undoubtedly perceive your parents as the cause of your strained relationship and believe that things will improve when they see the error of their ways and start treating you as they should. Great.

You can wait around for that to happen (see you later), or you can take action on your own. If you are willing to concentrate mainly on yourself and your own ability to change and grow (and pray that your parents will follow suit), try these ways of dealing with your parents.

If you want to be treated like an adult, act like one. Do your own laundry, clean your own apartment (or room), pay your own bills, and make your own decisions.

If you live at home and you have a paying job, you should be paying for your room and board—a fair price. If you can afford it, have your own phone line installed, do your own laundry, and share in household chores to show that you are carrying your own weight.

Most people, after they are off on their own, have the humiliating experience of having to ask their folks for money. If you find yourself in this position, don't lose respect for yourself—it happens all the time. But don't let it get to be a habit, either. Live within your means, and determine to make it on your own. Loans should be paid back as agreed; gifts should be accepted gratefully. It's usually better to face financial difficulties on your own than to run to Dad every time your bank balance dips.

Talk to your parents as you would to any rational adult. This means that you deal with facts, bypassing emotional issues that are straining your relationship.

For example, you have decided to move out and get your own apartment, even though you know your parents are dead set against it. You can have a long harangue with them, "Why won't you let me have some independence? Do you want me to be a baby all my life? You were younger than I am when you moved out of your parents' house. Quit telling me that things were different then. I can too support myself on my salary!"

Such arguments are useless; they accomplish nothing. If you've really made up your mind, discuss your decision as rationally as possible. "Well, this is it. I've signed a lease for an apartment downtown, and some friends are coming over to help me move out Friday afternoon. I known you think I'm making a mistake, but it will be my mistake to make. Of course, I'd like your help, but either way Friday is my last day."

It may seem cold and heartless, but it can get you through the screams and tears and down to the facts of the situation.

Take the initiative. Let's say you have a mother who drops in, unexpectedly and unannounced, with greater frequency than you'd like. The best way to solve this problem is to call her up one day and say, "You know, Mom, I really would like to get together with you and have a nice evening together. I'm tied up all the rest of this week, but I have next Thursday evening free and wonder if you could come over for dessert around, say, 8:00?" Your mother feels loved and welcome, and you have let her know that you are a busy person whose life is disrupted by her chance visits. By setting your meeting rather late on a weeknight, you have an excuse to make the visit short and sweet—you have to get up early the next morning for work. When you take the initiative, you gain equality.

Try a change of venue if you're in a rut. Your dad always invites you out to lunch on a weekday and always gets on your case about being a hairdresser instead of a forklift operator at the warehouse. Whenever you get an invitation to lunch, you know what's going to happen. You're in a rut.

So, suggest a different activity. Decline the lunch invitation and follow up with a suggestion that you go bowling Saturday afternoon. If shopping trips with your mother invariably end in a suggestion that you lose thirty pounds and marry a rich doctor who can buy you some really nice duds, take her to a Tupperware party instead. Invite your parents to your place rather than going to their house all the time. Avoid places and situations that have historically been bad for you and your parents.

Take a risk. Leave the latest issue of *Cosmopolitan* on the coffee table and see what your mom says. Break your "Hi-how-are-you-I'm-fine-you-look-awful" litany with an unexpected response. "How am I? I'm not great, but I'm dealing with my loneliness. How are you?" Bring up a taboo subject (religion, politics, Aunt Wilhelmina's hairdo) in casual conversation. Invite your parents to a party. Let them meet your friends that they've been so critical of. You never remember your Dad's birthday—so send him a card at some odd time of the year thanking him for being a good father. Tell your mom that you love her.

Do something unexpected and different. Sure, there could be fireworks. But, more importantly, there could be change. If you've been keeping secrets, start telling them. Your parents may be disappointed—deeply disappointed. But you've got to wonder how long you're going to be able to keep up the charade. These are your parents—they're a part of your life you can't deny. If you're like other children, you'll find a tremendous sense of relief when you come clean with them, even if there are some tears along the way.

Challenge the assumptions you've cherished about your parents. Resolve to quit underestimating your parents ("My dad's just a bum," "My mother loves to nag," "My parents always liked Ralph better than me"). Have you always believed that your parents didn't have your best interests at heart ("They want me to fail," "They've never liked Jennifer," "I know my mother didn't really want children")? Maybe you're wrong. Maybe your parents have been responding to your cues. Change the cues, and you might change their behavior.

Quit blaming your parents for everything. It's hard for you to love and have a relationship with someone whom you perceive as the ultimate cause of everything that's wrong in your life and the world in general. So your dad fought in Vietnam; that doesn't mean he is responsible for the whole fiasco. Your mother never told you about sex and you had to learn the hard way? Join the club. If your father hadn't been an alcoholic, you wouldn't have been ashamed to bring friends home from school, and you could have had an allowance like other kids. Water over the dam.

You're only going to get bitter if you place all the blame with your parents. Life's tough. They're human. You don't have to agree with everything that your folks did and are. But if you're serious about putting together a life of your own and being all that you can be, you'll come to grips with your parents' fallibility *and* your own responsibility for your own life. The longer you blame your parents, the longer it will take to become a whole person. Forgive—if not for their sake, for your own.

A memorable episode of "The Cosby Show" dealt with drugs. Claire, the mother, picked up son Theo's schoolbook and a joint dropped out. Theo denied owning it and later found out that a friend had hidden his stash in the book so a teacher wouldn't catch him with it.

Dad (played by Cosby) had a talk with Theo about drugs. He said (approximately), "Son, as long as you live in this house, as long as you eat our food, as long as you are a member of this family, you don't do drugs. And when you get older, when you move out of the house and have a place of your own and a life of your own—*you still don't do drugs!*"

That's parents. They're yours for life. You're never absolutely free from them. But who wants to be? You want to love your parents, and want to be loved by them. No matter what's gone on up until now, you can begin working to have a better relationship, a relationship that is based on mutual respect, one adult to another.

2.

ROOMMATES

Previously your roommates were chosen for you. You shared a room with Lucille because she was your sister; you were assigned to Debi by the college housing office.

Well, things are looking up! You can now have a roommate of your own choice! No more forced pairing. You are your own boss from now on. *You* decide if you want/need a roommate . . . and then pick the lucky person from a pool of qualified candidates. Isn't life grand?

(Read no further if you have already decided against sharing accommodations. And may I take this opportunity to congratulate you on your material prosperity and resistance to loneliness.)

First Step: Finding a Roommate

Ideally, you'd like to find a roommate who's about your age, shares your interests, and is rarely home. Someone wealthy and generous would be nice; someone with a cute brother or sister; someone who knows how to cook and loves to clean house; someone sympathetic and supportive; someone who never gets sick, who keeps no pets and is learning how to play no musical instruments; someone who bathes daily and owns a lot of fine furniture.

If you know someone like that, skip on to the Third Step. On the other hand, if you have no one waiting in the wings, you have a big job ahead of you. You will pick your roommate from the vast pool of known, semi-known, or completely unknown people who also cannot afford $625 a month for a one-bedroom apartment. But how to make contact?

Start with word-of-mouth—that's the best. Let your co-workers, parents, cousins, and friends know that you're looking for a roomie and ask if they know anyone else in a similar position. Call up old acquaintances and solicit them as roommates or leads to roommates.

If that doesn't work, post a notice on the bulletin board at work, the student union, the laundromat, or corner grocery store. If you can, weed out the crazies in your notice.

"Wanted: Friendly, employed, nonsmoking straight male roommate to share two-bedroom apartment with same. Must be able to pay $240/month rent + utilities and have own bedroom furniture. Bassoonists, snake-handlers, and slobs need not apply."

Give your phone number, but not your name or address.

You can also place (or respond to) advertisements in the newspaper. Stay clear of personal ads in large metropolitan newspapers—really, your chances of finding a good roommate this way are slim, and your chances of making contact with a goon are pretty good. A better bet is a school paper (even if you're not a student you can advertise in the university rag), a special interest periodical (some denominational magazines are possibilities; also fraternity letters and hobby magazines), or the local newspaper in a smaller city or town.

If all else fails, you can try a professional agency that specializes in matching people who need roommates. In some cases, this should be the first place you try. As a matter of fact, if your city is large enough to have such an agency (or many of them) there's a good reason for it—finding roommates any other way could be a waste of time and dangerous to boot. Remember, this is a person you're going to live with. He or she will have free access to everything you value—including your life—and living with someone who borrows your cashmere sweater without asking might end up to be the least of your concerns.

We'll assume now that your search has netted you a roommate *candidate*. What next?

Second Step: Interviewing a Roommate

A roommate should be interviewed at least as thoroughly as an employee. This person will be *living* with you, for goodness sake. Know as much in advance as you can.

The initial interview should take place in a public place, preferably a restaurant. You will be observing this person closely—not only what he says, but how he acts. Here are some things to watch for:

- What kind of food does he order? Meat and potatoes? Quiche? Peanut-butter-and-mayo? Does he send it back to the chef for replacement?

- Does he eat like a pig at the trough? Or does he pick at his food? Leave the crusts?

- Does he display any disgusting habits, like grinding his cigarette butt into the salad, picking his nose, or harassing the waitress?

- Is his personal appearance good? More importantly, is he about your size? Do you like what he's wearing? Would it look good on you?

- Is he boring? Humorous? Fascinating? Does he listen as well as he talks?

- Does he try to stiff you for the check, or does he pay for it with his American Express Gold Card?

As the interview progresses, you should explain what you have in mind in terms of the apartment and how living arrangements would be worked out. You should let the candidate know if you've already got a place, or if one needs to be found—or if you're more interested in moving in with him.

If all is going well, begin sharing important information that he needs to know: what kind of work you do (it makes a difference if you're a nine-to-fiver or a respiratory therapist who works the graveyard shift at the hospital); how much rent you can afford (include utilities); how much furniture you own; what pets, if any, you plan to bring to the arrangement; special needs, such as a heated garage for your Corvette, a diabetic diet, or peace-and-quiet in the evenings so you can study for the bar.

Be as honest with him as you want him to be with you. During this initial interview, you should come clean on anything that you suspect may cause problems later. Better to have the interview terminate *sans* roommate than walk blindly into a doomed living arrangement.

If all goes well, exchange references with each other and make plans to get in touch again. If the candidate has no references or doesn't want to give you any, then you should take this as an automatic disqualification. Pay for your food and leave—it's over.

If you do get references, that's obviously a good sign—he probably has nothing to hide. But check anyway. Contact every reference; the list should ideally include one former roommate (if available), a former landlord (if applicable), a friend who has spent a lot of live-in time with the candidate (his football buddy who used to room with him at away-games), a business reference (employer will do), and anybody else who can vouch for his sterling character and trustworthiness *from experience*.

After you've checked his references and he's checked yours, make a decision. TRUST YOUR INTUITION. If everything seems copacetic but you don't *feel* right about it, go with your feelings. In the end, feelings have the last word. If everybody's happy, proceed to the next step.

Third Step: Assessing the Apartment

A lot is said about how to get a good apartment later in the book (see pages 118 to 129). For now, it will suffice to highlight the features of an apartment well-suited for cohabitation.

If possible, there should be a separate bedroom for each person. Sometimes this is not possible. In New York City, Chicago, and Washington, D.C., it is not unheard-of for two or more people to share a one-room efficiency apartment. That's because costs are high, apartments are scarce, and expectations are low. Still, it's best if each person has a room of her own where she can go and shut the door and have privacy. If there is only one bedroom but two people, the bedroom can be shared; but it is often better if one person sleeps in the living room on a daybed or sofabed. The living-room sleeper should be the one who keeps the most erratic hours, likes to fix herself late-night snacks, and enjoys falling asleep in front of the television. The light sleeper who works nights should, by all rights, have the bedroom.

There should be adequate closets and shelving for all room-

mates. Bathroom shelving is important—take a look at the medicine cabinet and/or linen closet: will it hold everybody's deodor-
ant and cotton swabs? Maybe you should ask the landlord if it
would be okay to put up some temporary shelving. What about
closets? A lot of roommate squabbles center around closet
space—check it out ahead of time.

Most apartment-sharers agree that adequate space is more
important than luxury features. The kitchen may have a built-in
microwave oven—nice, nice, very nice—but a refrigerator of
adequate size is more important. The bathroom walls are covered
with flocked red-and-black wallpaper? Such aesthetic aberrations
are easily tolerated by roommates who each have a nice big five-
foot closet in which to hang their Ocean Pacific collections.

Fourth Step: Logistical Matters

Roommate relationships are fraught with disagreements and accusations on the most minor points. Richard drank all the milk
and didn't replace it; JoDee is accused of making a $23.45 long-
distance call she hasn't paid for; it's Alan's turn to clean the
bathroom and he *still* hasn't done it. Picky, picky, picky.

Let's deal with money matters first. If you are the person with
the apartment, it is your job to decide who pays what. If you are
living in someone else's apartment, he decides. In most cases,
you'll just split all expenses 50-50 (or 33⅓-33⅓-33⅓ or 25-25-
25-25—depending on how many roomies you have)—except
that extra charges may be levied in the following situations:

- the person who gets the biggest bedroom (or the only bedroom) pays more.

- the person who is at home all day and/or takes three twenty-minute showers each day and/or has a window air conditioner in his bedroom pays extra on the utilities.

- the person who owns most of the furniture and major appliances pays less.

- the person who does all the shopping and cooking and cleaning (although who would want to, I don't know) gets a break.

Before moving in, all roomies should be clear on what the prorated monthly expense is going to be. One person should take responsibility for handling all matters financial—and if this is an unpopular job he may be reimbursed by the group accordingly. As an example:

Ann: Works at home, runs plant lights all day, never cooks, keeps the place clean, has the largest bedroom.......60%
Lee: Rarely home, does most of the cooking, sleeps on the couch in the living room, organizes finances..........40%

Five days before the beginning of the month (or whenever the rent is due), all roommates ante up their share of the rent. They may also pay the prorated portion of utilities at this time, if utilities are billed separately. I would further suggest that a "kitty" be kept, into which each roommate contributes a modest cash amount on a regular basis. This money can be kept in a cookie jar for common expenses—such as paying the paper carrier, buying small household items, or paying for household repairs.

Food expenses can be handled in a number of ways. You may be in a roommate situation because you want a sense of fellowship and community with the person/people you are living with. In such a case, you'll probably pitch in equally for food and make a point of preparing and eating meals together. If one person wants to orchestrate the shopping and cooking, that's fine; usually, though, it works best to share shopping and cooking responsibilities equally. You may be on your own for breakfast and lunch, and do an every-other-night routine for dinner. Maybe it's enough to plan on a communal meal only once, twice, or three times a week, on evenings that are convenient for everybody.

But if your eating habits and standards are completely alien to those of your roommate, it should be every man for himself. Each person pays for her own food, which is kept in her own cupboard and on her own refrigerator shelf. Each roommate shops and cooks for herself. (To keep it from getting crazy, specify certain items as community property—salt and pepper, condiments, paper napkins, flour—and pay for these out of the kitty.) If you must borrow from your roommate's larder, replace *immediately*. No exceptions.

If one person eats most meals at home, while another eats out a lot, you can try a proration of rations. Post a list (in the kitchen) with each roommate's name on it, and use this to record which meals were eaten at home by whom. At the end of the month, charge for food expense accordingly. Under this scheme, shopping and cooking are done cooperatively, with each person contributing equally to a fund that pays for food. But at the end of the month, based on actual meals eaten, there will be refunds for light eaters and an extra levy for chow hounds.

Here's an example of how the chart might look:

	Janie	Dana	Stephanie
Breakfast	ℍℍ ℍℍ ℍℍ ℍℍ ℍℍ ℍℍ	ℍℍ 111	ℍℍ ℍℍ ℍℍ ℍℍ 1
Lunch		ℍℍ ℍℍ ℍℍ ℍℍ ℍℍ	ℍℍ
Dinner	ℍℍ ℍℍ ℍℍ ℍℍ ℍℍ ℍℍ	ℍℍ ℍℍ ℍℍ ℍℍ 11	ℍℍ ℍℍ

Let's assume that each roommate chipped in $100 at the beginning of the month for food, and that the total of $300 pretty much covered expenses.

Here is what each roommate consumed:

Janie: 30 breakfasts, 0 lunches, 30 dinners (Janie is always home for meals, never goes out, eats lunch at the company cafeteria every day.)

Dana: 8 breakfasts, 25 lunches, 22 dinners (Dana rarely eats breakfast, nearly always fixes a lunch to take to work with her, and is usually home for dinner.)

Steph: 21 breakfasts, 5 lunches, 10 dinners (Stephanie eats breakfast regularly, sometimes fixes herself a lunch to take to work, and rarely participates in the evening meal.)

Based on experience, the roommates may decide that it costs about twice as much to provide an evening meal as it does to provide breakfast or lunch. So breakfast and lunch have a value of 1 and dinner has a value of 2. Multiply each meal eaten by its value, and adding them together, a factor is reached for each roommate, thus:

Janie: $(30 \times 1) + (30 \times 2) = 90$
Dana: $(8 \times 1) + (25 \times 1) + (22 \times 2) = 77$
Steph: $(21 \times 1) + (5 \times 1) + (10 \times 2) = 46$

The total number of points is 213 which, divided into $300, equals $1.41; breakfast and lunch are working out to about $1.41 each, and dinner is twice that: $2.82. So here's what everyone pays:

Janie: $90 \times \$1.41 = \$126.90$
Dana: $77 \times \$1.41 = \$108.57$
Steph: $46 \times \$1.41 = \$\ 64.86$
$300.33 (Close enough!)

Each roommate has already paid $100 for groceries. The rest is simple: Janie gives Stephanie $26.90 and Dana gives Stephanie $8.57.

This is obviously a little bit of work to figure out, and there are other systems that work just as well. But if one person eats a lot more than another, or one roommate is rarely home for meals, it is important to adopt some kind of system whereby people are paying for approximately what they are eating. Otherwise, resentment is likely to build up with those who aren't getting their fair share.

Life will also be smoother if each roommate has his/her own telephone. Consider how much money you're saving already by sharing the main expense of housing, surely you can afford your own phone line. It's enough that you have to share a bathroom—sharing a phone carries things too far. With your own phone, you can talk when you like for as long as you like without being accused of blocking an important business call; you can be absolutely sure that you are paying for your own long-distance calls, and *only yours*; you can get the style and accessories you want (stripped-down dial phone or poshed-up computer phone). Roommates will determine whether or not they want to answer each other's phone and take messages when one or the other is absent or soaking in the tub.

Logistic matters can be adequately addressed only if you are communicating with your roommate on expectations and performance. For this reason you should set aside a half-hour or so each week for a house meeting. Make it a fixed time each week and keep the appointment. (This has the added benefit of segregating business matters from social matters, which is good.) Topics of discussion may include:

- any plans you have that might affect the other roommate(s), such as a Christmas party or weekend guest.

- gripes—too much noise at night, no-shows at dinner, personal feuds, etc.

- proposed changes in any previous arrangements ("The window air conditioner is broken now, and I'm not getting it fixed, so I shouldn't have to pay extra on the utilities any more").

- financial problems ("The kitty is low—everybody ante up"), including insolvencies of any roommates.

- possibilities ("That three-bedroom apartment upstairs is going to be vacant at the end of the month. Should we try for it?").

Fifth Step: Dealing with Problems

The best way to handle problems is on an as-they-happen basis. Each roommate must have a willingness to deal with minor difficulties the same way they would handle major catastrophes— immediately! Little things get to be big things if they aren't brought out in the open and discussed on an ongoing basis.

The weekly house meeting will help facilitate the communication needed to air grievances. If someone is "in charge"—say, the person who holds the mortgage on the house or the one who organized the apartment—that person may be called upon to arbitrate disputes. "Look, Carol, I know you think that if you're doing the cleaning you should pay less, but you've got to remember that Sissy cooks almost every night, and I own the furniture, so I still think we should call it even."

If three or more people are sharing the apartment, you have the opportunity to put disagreements to a democratic vote. "Okay, all those in favor of wallpapering the dining room raise your hands." Beware: some decisions should not be decided by a majority, but must have 100 percent approval—for example, a new roommate shouldn't be taken on unless *everyone* is in favor of her. Nor should financial responsibilities be significantly altered unless all parties are willing and able to support them.

Some problems are personal. For one reason or another, you simply do not like your roommate. She bugs you. She doesn't respect your privacy, but guards her own. She tells your most intimate secrets to large groups of people. She borrows your clothes without asking and returns them the worse for wear. She can't hold a job and hasn't paid her share of the rent for two months. She is argumentative; she is devious. She eats all the time; she exercises all the time; she whistles under her breath all the time; she entertains guests all the time. You can't stand her for another minute.

"To find a friend one must close one eye—to keep him, two."
Norman Douglas

Well, it's time to go back to the initial interview. No matter how disgusting she is, make an appointment to meet on neutral turf—a restaurant, again—and discuss the problems that you are having. "What problems?" she may say. "There are problems," you assure her, and insist on the meeting.

Once you've ordered, it's time to begin your discussion. Stay away from emotion-laden statements and inflammatory accusations. Start with the facts.

"Lisa, I have been dissatisfied with our living situation for the past two months. Here's what's bothering me: You seem uninterested in housekeeping, so I end up doing all the cleaning. Your last rent check bounced, and I still haven't gotten the money for this month's rent. You've been having parties without consulting me on *my* plans, and last Saturday night you let three of your friends spend the night—and two of them slept in my bed! I think that these are serious problems."

Even seemingly untenable situations can be worked out if

both (or all) roommates are committed to making it work. In this way, it's just like a marriage. It's unlike a marriage in that you're probably not in love with your roommate, you have no legal responsibilities (beyond the lease) that cannot be easily resolved, and society will not frown upon you if you split up. And there will be no children to consider. But if you want or need to stay roommates, you can work it out.

Nevertheless, for this or other reasons you will eventually come to a parting of the ways, which is the

Sixth Step: Parting Company

He gets transferred, she graduates, you can afford your own place. Or you're both sick of each other. It's time to dissolve the living relationship and go your separate ways.

Always keep it in the back of your mind, right from the start, that roomies are *not* forever; this is a temporary arrangement. Do *not* make any major purchases with your roommate(s), such as pooling funds to buy a new stereo. When it's time to say farewell, one person will have to come up with the cash to buy the other person's share—and who's going to do that? Stay away from joint purchases that will cause problems later on.

There's always the minor stuff—the table lamp you bought with funds from the kitty, the cleaning supplies and equipment that belong to both of you, or the wobbly coffee table that a mutual friend gave you when she joined the Army. What are you going to do about that?

You could each bid on items that you want, and then divide evenly the proceeds of your little auction. Or you could have a lottery, placing chits in a hat identifying all jointly-owned property and giving each to the lucky one who draws it out. How about doing it the way you picked a soccer team in grade school?

"I choose the carpet sweeper."

"Okay, then I want the SKI KANSAS poster."

"Good. I'll take the Boston fern."

"The miracle mop."

And so on. Flip a coin to see who goes first.

If you can part company amicably, that's obviously best. Who knows? You may need to use each other for a reference later. If you part company enemies . . . that happens sometimes. Living with another human being (or several) is very demanding. It takes a lot of work. Don't feel like you're a failure at life just because you didn't get along with your roommate—even if you're pretty sure that you were the cause of the split. You'll learn something from it, and next time it will be better.

Hey, some of the funniest movies, plays, books, and television shows are based on the wild, wonderful, existentially rich experiences of sharing living quarters with another person. Where would we be without Oscar Madison and Felix Unger? *The Good-Bye Girl?* Kate and Allie? Snoopy and Woodstock? Good or bad, you'll probably laugh about it later.

3.

FRIENDS

I, the possessor of one friend with whom I have maintained a close relationship since second grade (even though she lives now in Mexico), and who have not even seen, much less ascertained the whereabouts of, my absolutely very best friend in high school, will now share my thoughts on the subject of friends—old and new—and what it means to have adult friendships.

You've Got a Friend

Why is it that old friends inspire musical sentimentality? It's got to be easier to sing about old friends than maintain an old friendship. As I think back on the friends of my past, I realize that even the simplest of maintenance steps—a phone call, a letter, a visit—have proven impossible to accomplish where old friends are concerned.

Oh well, they've probably changed; I've changed. I've even changed my name, and a lot of them have too—more than once.

There's also the uncomfortable matter of being confronted with one's infamy when meeting up with an acquaintance from the past. "Dori, how are you? Char, this is Dori—we went to junior high together. Dori was the one I told you about who vomited all over her desk in algebra class." Who needs it? Old friends knew you when you wore stupid clothes, lived in a stupid house, and told stupid jokes. No one likes to have the embarrassments of his or her past resurrected.

I'd be the last one to advocate a life in which all old friendships are maintained. Some of them simply aren't worth it. Others involve too much pain. In still others the point is moot; the childhood friend lives in some unknown locale, has changed his or her life to the extent that there is no longer any common ground on which to relate, or has no interest in seeing you again.

Nevertheless, it certainly is a shame when a good friendship starves to death for want of basic nourishment. When you move, or change jobs, or graduate from school—or when a friend of yours does these things—you have a choice to make: you can either continue the friendship or let it go by the side of the road. If you decide not to decide, then the decision is made by default: lack of attention inevitably means an end.

Maybe you feel the need to continue a relationship with a friend who is changing his life, or you're changing yours, and don't want to lose touch. Or maybe you'd like to see old what's-his-face again, the boy you used to hang around with when you were a kid. You have any number of good reasons for feeling this way: you miss the good times, you want to be connected to your past, and what's-his-face owes you money. Whatever your motivation, it's rarely too late to reestablish contact.

Communication is obviously the first step. Write a letter. Call on the phone. Visit. When you write or call or visit, do more than relate the events that have transpired since your last communiqué. "I've moved out of my folks' house and have an apartment of my own. I paid off my car last month." If you want to make contact, then say something important. "I've been thinking about all those plans we used to make, about what we'd be when we grew up, and I decided that the first step in growing up is moving out, so last December I got my own apartment. It was hard to make the break with my folks, but I don't regret it. And things are going okay financially, I guess. I finally got my car paid off, and I'm thinking of saving the money I used to spend on payments. If I can set aside $150 a month for the next three years, maybe I will have enough to take a sabbatical and do some traveling. It's what we always talked about, remember?"

Individual letters and calls and visits are time-consuming and can be expensive As an alternative, you might make plans to do a mass mailing to friends. Usually people do this at Christmas— they send holiday greetings, and enclose a little letter telling what happened during the year. This isn't such a bad thing. It can be done at any time of the year, though. How about in February? July? Write out a letter that will contain most of the news and musings that your friends would be interested in. Duplicate it, and then add a personal note as you wish. It may be a bit forced, but it's probably better than nothing. (An updated address book is vital for maintaining friendships by mail.)

How about a reunion? You don't have to wait until your high school or college reunion; you can organize your own. Have it in a convenient place ("hometown" is often best) and at a convenient time (over a holiday or during the summer). Reunions are a lot of work—there's no doubt about that. But they're also a lot of fun. I've had some experience with nonschool reunions, and have been surprised at how far people will come, and what trouble they'll take to be with people they really like and miss seeing.

When reuniting with old friends, you must remember this: even though your friendship is based on the way you were, you must be the way you are. You're a different person than you were ten, five, or even one year ago. So is your friend. You've changed and will continue to change. Sometimes this means that the friendship will suffer.

That can be hard to accept. The temptation is to pretend that everything is the way it was back when. But, in the long run, it will be better to let a friendship slowly fade than to keep it alive on a false basis.

Let's say that Fred and Jon were college friends. They shared a room in their fraternity house, both majored in architecture, dated the same girls, partied together, and were best friends for four years. They graduated; Fred moved to Denver, Jon stayed in Phoenix. Fred got married and had three children; Jon remained single. Fred's idea of a good time is going to a Broncos game with the guys from work and partying afterwards; Jon has grown into a serious kind of person who spends a lot of time reading, watching television, and writing a novel that he hopes to publish someday.

Both Fred and Jon think back to college days and have great memories of that time. They think about each other, too, and wish they could have a friendship like that again. But the fact of the matter is that they've changed; if they were meeting each other for the first time today, they probably wouldn't be attracted to one another.

They may choose to make an effort to revive their friendship.

If they do, it will be better for them to be who they are now in that friendship than to revert back to when they were fraternity brothers in Phoenix. That time is gone. If the friendship doesn't click the way it once did, at least they'll have the fond memories of it without having the stress of pretending that neither one of them has changed.

If all this talk of old friends sounds melancholy, that's because it invariably is. Old friends, just like old songs, bring back waves of nostalgia—usually to some time that we imagine to have been better than now. Or our old friend may have been the only oasis of happiness during a very unhappy time. Friendships that span the years are often bittersweet, but sweet nonetheless. Not every friendship will endure, but those that have the promise of a lifetime friendship deserve some care and nurture.

New Kid in Town

Old friends are great, but everyone needs to continue to make new friends, or life can get stale. The same old crowd gets boring without the infusion of new blood. And if you're in a new job in a new city, old friends aren't an option.

When moving to a new city, finding out where people are is every bit as difficult as getting a new bank, learning the street arrangement, and apartment hunting. You may see people every day—thousands of them—but where can you find someone with your interests, who is interested in spending time with you?

Look in the likeliest places:

Church: Especially one that has an active fellowship group for people of your age and circumstances (young married couples group, singles group, college and career group, etc.). You won't meet people if you're just warming a pew.
School: Take an evening class at the local junior college, university, or adult education program. That class will attract other people like you.
Clubs: Check the newspaper club notices: chess, poetry writing, modern dance, or philately—you can always find an established club that's looking for members.
Work: Most people count on their job to provide them with social opportunities and, eventually, friends. Make it a point to learn names and show your friendliness. Join the company softball team, or volunteer to assist with the United

Way drive, or work on projects that will put you in touch with new people.

Neighbors: Although it doesn't always hold true that a person who happens to live next to you will be someone you like, it doesn't hurt to cultivate neighbors as friends. With any luck, you'll end up like Rob and Laura, Jerry and Millie; Lucy and Ricky, Fred and Ethel; the Drysdales and the Clampets!

Volunteer work: Aside from the personal satisfaction you'll get from doing volunteer work of any kind, you'll probably meet some of the nicest people in your community. Your city may have a volunteer bureau, or notices in the paper of needed volunteers. You may also contact group homes, hospitals, nursing homes, etc. directly to see what help is needed.

Community organizations: Involvement with neighborhood associations, political campaigns, community improvement groups (such as the Junior League or Jaycees) is an excellent way to meet people.

Some places are not good for finding friends. The most obvious places *not* to look are bars. I have never met another person with serious friend-potential in a bar, and I've never known personally anyone who did. The conviviality of "Cheers" notwithstanding, bars are crummy places to meet people, even if the bars promote themselves as social clubs. For one thing, it can be dangerous hooking up with someone—male or female—that you've met at a bar. And then you've always got to wonder, "What are they doing here, anyway? Why aren't they at church/work/school/a club meeting/a private party/whatever?"

There are hundreds of quirky ways to make friends. One guy I know is best friends with the fellow who shared his hospital room when he had a hernia operation; a couple met their best friends when they were both looking at a house each couple was interested in; two young women who kept running into each other at the grocery store and adjacent laundromat ended up sharing an apartment and becoming close friends. Be open to the possibilities!

Once you've found some friends, introduce them to each other, and ask them to return the favor. Nothing is sillier than hogging a good friend. If you meet a fascinating person at work who would hit it off great with a friend from church, introduce them to each other. Now you are three. Your good example will encourage the guy at work to invite you when he's having his bowling team over for a victory celebration—at the party you meet someone who goes to your church; you've seen her, but were never introduced.

In sharing friends you'll lose exclusivity, but you'll gain much more. This week, some good friends are moving to Minneapolis. Last Sunday they had a going-away party, and as part of the festivities there was a ceremony in which they presented a Certificate of Friendship to us, deeding over their best friends. Ah, the circle will be unbroken. Our good friends are gone, but the gap will be filled somewhat by their other friends.

You can create occasions that are conducive to establishing good friendships. When was the last time you had a party? Or went to one? Quit being so busy, and socialize more! Make it a point to call a friend today just to talk, or to find out how things are going—did she get the job? Is his brother still planning to visit? Is the romance still hot?

One of the best ways to enrich a friendship is to work with your friends. Nothing lets you get to know a person like tackling a project together. When my dad used to visit his folks, who lived on a farm, he always wanted to spend time working with his father. He knew that they were closer when they were pitching hay, milking cows, and mending the fence than when they were sitting in the living room telling each other what they'd been up to for the past year.

If you or someone you know needs to paint their apartment, give their car a tuneup, put in a new lawn, move, or bake six cakes for a reception . . . see if it can't be done together. The work goes faster, and the relationship improves.

You are in the process of building experiences, making memories for the future. Think ahead forty years from now. Will you have good times to look back on, good times that you shared with your friend? Will the two of you be able to laugh about the time that you wasted thirteen strokes getting out of a sand trap, or dropped the chest of drawers down the stairs, or washed thirty-five windows in one afternoon, or stayed up until 2:30 A.M. playing Trivial Pursuit? If you want those kinds of memories later, you have to create them now. Even the snafus, disagreements, and disappointments work to enrich your life with a friend.

The Matter of Manners

It's too bad that the word *manners,* in addition to meaning polite ways of social behavior, also connotes snobbish affectations. Let us, then, distinguish between *protocol* and *consideration.*

Protocol is a tricky business. You probably know that the U.S. government employs a staff of people whose specialty is knowing whether or not the First Lady should curtsy to the Queen, where the forks should be at a state dinner, and who walks in front of and who walks behind the President when he ambles casually through the Rose Garden.

Every human endeavor possesses certain expectations for specific protocol. At a business lunch, the salesperson pays for the potential client's meal; a vice-president has a corner office while a supervisor gets a mere divider by his desk; if you receive a Christmas gift from your boss you are expected to reciprocate—with a less expensive gift.

Weddings have a specific protocol: friends of the bride on one side of the church, friends of the groom on the other; guests don't wear white out of deference to the bride; if a person is invited to a wedding shower, they must also be invited to the wedding.

The complexities of protocol have been expounded on by such etiquette gurus as Emily Post, Amy Vanderbilt and Miss Manners herself, Judith Martin (see pages 328 to 330 for some of Miss Manners' better advice). Volumes have been written about what to do if you simply cannot swallow the meat you've been chewing for the past two and a half minutes, how to go Dutch on a date, and whether or not to shake hands with gloves on. I find the whole subject rather fascinating, especially to the extent that it explains our cultural heritage. Have you ever wondered why a man escorts a woman on the street by walking close to the curb? In the old days, this was so that chamber pots dumped out of upper-story windows would land on the gent, not the lady. It's considered impolite to use a knife to cut the lettuce of a green salad into manageable mouthfuls, a throwback to the time when knife blades were made of sterling silver, and the vinegar in the salad dressing would have corroded the hostess's flatware.

I heartily suggest that those who are interested in social custom latch onto a good book of etiquette and use it as a guide to acceptable behavior. Many people are uncomfortable in social situations simply because they don't know how to act. This is easily solved by becoming familiar with expectations. Obviously, one can enjoy the food and company at a fancy dinner if freed from the tyranny of worrying whether or not it's okay to pick up an olive with one's fingers.

More to the point, though, where manners are concerned, is the matter of consideration. Men walking close to the curb, and the taboo against using knives on a green salad, are perfect examples of social customs that have developed around simple consideration for another person—one's lady friend and hostess, respectively. (Flash! The experts have decided that since most people no longer throw excrement out of their windows, and knife blades are almost always stainless steel, the ban has been lifted; men may now walk where they choose, and a polite guest may use fork *and* knife to subjugate an unwieldy piece of endive.)

A person who is considerate will not go far wrong where manners are concerned. Maybe some of the protocol will suffer, but the intent will invariably come shining though. Let's take an example:

You get an invitation to a friend's graduation party. It looks like this:

You are invited to a party
To celebrate Kristine's graduation.
Please join us for a barbecue
At 4056 Delaney, May 27th at 5:00 p.m.
Mrs. Walter Dinsdale

R.S.V.P.

While there is some ambiguity in this invitation (the type of dress is not specifically noted, nor whether or not guests should bring gifts) it doesn't take Charlotte Ford to figure the basics. For one thing, you let Mrs. Dinsdale know whether you're coming or not. R.S.V.P. means she wants to know. If *you* were serving dinner to a lot of people, wouldn't you? Consideration for Mrs. Dinsdale, not something you read in a big fat book on etiquette, tells you this, and also tells you to let her know as soon as possible.

Should you bring Kristine a present? Probably. It's customary to reward graduates with a gift. If you're unsure, ask others who have been invited. Wait a minute—don't assume you know who's been invited. It wouldn't be *considerate* to take a chance on assuming that someone else is coming when she isn't. When you call (or write) to Mrs. Dinsdale, you may ask her if so-and-so has been invited, since you plan to share transportation or buy a gift jointly. That call alone may give you a clue to whether or not you're expected to bring a gift.

What will you get Kristine? Out of consideration for her, you'll think about what she's doing after graduation. Going for a Ph.D.? Starting a new job? Facing unemployment? Your gift will reflect her plans.

Dress is usually casual at a barbecue. But if you dress like a slob it sends a message: "I don't care enough about you, your party, or your achievement to wash my hair or put on a clean shirt. So much for you, Kristine."

At a party, you remember who's being honored. You show deference to Kristine. You express your appreciation to Mrs. Dinsdale, thanking her for the invitation. You don't leave without speaking to your hostess and the guest of honor. And the next day, if it seems the considerate thing to do, you call Mrs. Dinsdale to thank her for the good time, or send a note of appreciation.

These are the basics on considerate behavior. Also sandwiched in are a number of protocol issues—can chicken be eaten with the fingers at a barbecque or is it strictly a knife-and-fork operation; should I introduce myself to her cousin or wait to be introduced; would it be polite to help out in the kitchen or not?—but they are not nearly as important as simple and sincere consideration for the hostess, the honoree, and the other guests.

Cynical, conceited, and selfish people lack the motivation to display good manners. They may know how to conduct a letter-perfect introduction and be tireless in their attention to their dinner napkins, but their attitude will pervade all their actions, showing that they behave not out of consideration, but out of a wish to show their superiority and separate themselves from those who are less socially refined.

An Englishman who emigrated to America and lives in New York City was explaining the difference between Americans and the English. London, he said, is known as the most civilized city in the world; New York has no such reputation. His observation was this: in London, people are polite to those they dislike so as to keep them at a distance, whereas in New York City, people are only polite to those they like.

I've been to London *and* to New York City, and I can't say I agree totally with this assessment. But it does illustrate the point: attention to protocol, concern with etiquette, and the cultivation of manners may either be used to create distance between you and others or to show deference to those you care for.

Part II:
Gainful
Employment

4.

WORKING

Anyone who wants to live on his own, and who lacks a personal fortune, needs a job. We're going to talk about making the most of an existing job (for those who have one), finding gainful employment, writing resumés, suffering through interviews . . . the whole banana.

Your First Job

Perhaps you are now working in your first serious job. Sure, you had part-time jobs when you were in school, but these days your paycheck is going toward more than record albums and sneakers (i.e., food, rent, gas). This makes your present job your first serious job.

This job may not be what you have trained for, what you are educated for, or what you want to do for the rest of your life. That's okay. Your first job isn't everything. It also isn't nothing. What you are doing now will become, at the very least, an employment reference and a line or two on your resume. So, in everything you do on this job, you've got to think toward the future and how you're going to explain it to your future employers.

As you're hosing down the cages at the city dog pound, ruminate on how this might be described later: "Was responsible for maintaining suitable housing for forty-eight wards of the city government." You're driving an ice cream truck this summer? "Spent three months in dairy retailing; increased sales 23 percent over previous year" (thank goodness it was an especially hot summer).

Don't be too concerned if, for one reason or another, you're stuck in a stupid job. It won't be your last job. And it can be minimized as a part of your employment history (more on this later). Do your best to concentrate on the positive aspects of it. And take comfort in the knowledge that most employers are sympathetic to the job plight of the young, and will look more favorably on someone who has been working—even at a crummy job—than on someone who has been hanging around the house for fourteen months waiting for IBM to call.

HIGHEST-PRESSURE JOBS IN THE UNITED STATES

1. Manual laborer
2. Secretary
3. Inspector
4. Waitress-waiter
5. Clinical lab technician
6. Farm owner
7. Miner
8. Office manager
9. House painter
10. Manager-administrator
11. Foreman
12. Machine operator

LOWEST-PRESSURE JOBS IN THE UNITED STATES

1. Clothing sewer
2. Checker, examiner of products

3. Stockroom worker

4. Craftsman

5. Maid

6. Heavy-equipment operator

7. Farm laborer

8. Freight handler

9. Child-care worker

10. Packer, wrapper in shipping

11. College or university professor

12. Personnel, labor relations

13. Auctioneer-huckster

(From *Occupational Stress*, U.S. Department of Health, Education and Welfare, National Institute for Occupational Safety and Health, 1978.)

Perhaps this is you: you are working at a fairly good job, but it's not one you like. Maybe you've got a job on the line at Chrysler. Lots of people would jump at your job—it's a sought-after position. But you eventually want to go into the lawn-and-garden business, doing contract work for residential customers. Or you're an English teacher in a high school—a hard job to get—but you'd rather work in business. When you look for other work, an employer may wonder why you're changing jobs—after all, you have a perfectly good position. If you're now in a field that's highly specialized and carries with it a great deal of prestige, and you'd like to move into a less-skilled, less prestigious (but, to you, more satisfying) field, employers will *really* be suspicious. They'll say, "Look, you'll never make as much trimming shrubs as you do at Chrysler. What gives?" or "You say you want to work in business, but you'll have to start as an administrative clerk. You'll probably get bored with it, and go back to teaching, and then where will I be?" Your protestations that you want to work outdoors, or that you truly don't mind starting at the bottom, may fall on deaf ears.

TYPICAL JOBS RATED ACCORDING TO BOREDOM

	Boredom Rating*
1. Assembler (work paced by machine)	207
2. Relief worker on assembly line	175
3. Forklift-truck driver	170
4. Machine tender	169
5. Assembler (working at own pace)	160
6. Monitor of continuous flow goods	122
7. Accountant	107
8. Engineer	100
9. Tool and die maker	96
10. Computer programmer	96
11. Electronic technician	87
12. Delivery service courier	86
13. Blue-collar supervisor	85
14. White-collar supervisor	72
15. Scientist	66
16. Administrator	66
17. Train dispatcher	64
18. Policeman	63
19. Air traffic controller (large airport)	59
20. Air traffic controller (small airport)	52
21. Professor with administrative duties	51
22. Professor	49
23. Physician	48

*Based on average of 100
(Institute for Social Research, University of Michigan)

This is why I say that while your first job isn't everything, it's not nothing, either. What you're doing now can work to your advantage or disadvantage. Some of this has to do with the job itself, but happily more of it has to do with how you present yourself.

Do keep in mind that this job will be discussed with your next employer. Lying about what you do is no good, so you should concentrate on making your job *now* take you in the direction you want to go later. An English teacher who wants to work in business could sponsor the DECA club, or work with Junior Achievement after school. He could try to arrange to teach a class in business writing. Or spend summers interning (giving free work) at a local business. By highlighting the aspects of a job that point toward your ultimate goal, you can keep the nonapplicable components in shadow.

Sometimes job titles help. One of my first jobs was working for a large corporation in their insurance department. I stayed with the company for a while, showed some aptitude, and was promoted a couple of times within that department. I soon became aware that I was becoming a very marketable commodity in the insurance field. The only problem was that, promotions notwithstanding, I didn't want to work in insurance for the rest of my life. But I realized that the longer I stayed in insurance, the harder it would be to break out of it.

At one point I was given a promotion that put me in charge of the company's insurance-related employee benefit programs— life insurance, medical and dental insurance, disability insurance. It was a new position, and there was no title for the job. My boss and I talked it over; what should I be called? He came up with two choices: "Life and Health Manager" and "Employee Benefits Manager."

There was no doubt in my mind. I chose "Employee Benefits Manager." Why? At the time I was interested in the personnel field. "Life and Health Manager," on my resumé, would indicate to potential employers that I was an insurance professional (the manager designation cinched that) through and through. I'd have a hard time getting hired for anything else. But "Employee Benefits Manager" made it look as if I were more involved in the personnel aspect of my job than I was.

In any case, do the best you can in every job you hold. Your summer as a carhop at the A & W may not mean much to you, but it will become critically important if your boss there is handing out bad references, saying you were late to work, lazy on the job, and always griping about the pay. That's the kind of worker *nobody* wants to hire, no matter what.

So here's your plan for this first job:

1. Play up the good parts of it.

2. Change it in whatever way you can so it works toward your goal.

3. Do it as well as you can.

The Job Search

You're looking for a job—the best one you can get. If you're lucky, maybe you'll get the job of your dreams: in your chosen field, working for a good employer, a challenging and interesting position. Where are you going to look for this job?

Newspaper advertisements. This is mentioned first only because it's the most obvious—it certainly is not the best place to find employment. Why? For one thing, most of the people who need workers are not advertising in the newspaper. A newspaper ad means scores, hundreds, possibly thousands of applicants who may or may not be qualified for the opening. Weeding through the applications, letters, and resumés is a daunting task.

Many jobs that are in the paper are, alas, not really available. Some companies, and most government agencies, are required (by company policy or law) to publicly advertise all job openings. Very often it is the case that an applicant has already been selected for a position, but the company is obligated to keep the ad running for a certain period of time anyway. The decision's been made; the ad is a formality.

Many ads are ridiculous come-ons. "Housewives, make $30-$50 an hour working 20 hours per week. No experience necessary. No direct sales. Call 555-4567." Now, really, does that look like a serious job opening?

Even the most honest employers, because of space restrictions, tend to give sketchy and consequently misleading job descriptions in their newspaper ads. You could spend a lot of time responding to an ad for a job that you're completely under- or over- or unqualified for.

If you live in a small town or city (about 200,000 or less) you may have some luck answering newspaper ads. Otherwise, they're not your best bet.

Personal network. A much better place to start your job search is with your friends, relatives, business associates, and others in your personal network. If you are looking for a job, let it be known. Tell as many people as you can without having it get back to your present employer (if you've already got a job).

If you are interested in a particular field, try to make contact with people you know who are already working in that field. Ask a friend to introduce you to someone who has a job like the one you'd like. (I get a lot of calls from friends of friends who would like to write.) You may learn more about the job, and also get a lead on a vacant position—or both.

Coworkers who have moved on to bigger and better things are a valuable connection. Sometimes a person who is hired away from one firm by a competitor will be expected to hire away his or her "team." This very thing happened in one company I worked for several years ago. The board of directors hired a new president for the firm, and within six months the new president had added five vice-presidents to the company—all people he had worked with in his previous position.

Your parents and their friends can help out, and will usually be glad to do so. I remember going over to my mother's house one morning after completing an interview with a local paving company. An employment agency had sent me over to apply for an accounting assistant position. A friend of my mother's was at her house that morning, and heard about my interview. Good news! He was good friends with the president of the paving company. He offered to call him and put in a good word for me. He did; I got the job. That sort of help should never be scorned, assuming you are qualified for the job.

Placement offices. Your college (or possibly high school) has a placement office. It may be no good—this is often the case, unfortunately. But in a good placement office, your transcript, resumé, and references will be kept on file to be sent out to employers at your request. You will also be provided with access to job leads; businesses that need college (or high school) graduates often contact school placement offices for applicants. Keep an eye on the bulletin board where notices are posted, or check the files regularly. Apply for the jobs that you seem qualified for and/or interested in.

Employment agencies. Either private or government-sponsored employment agencies can be very helpful. They assess your qualifications (through your resumé, your references, your education, and your skills—for which they may issue tests) and then try to match you with their employer-clients.

Government agencies make no charge for this service—either to you or to the employer. The drawbacks of government agencies is that they tend to have hundreds of openings for dishwashers and precious few for brain surgeons; in other words, if you're looking for a professional position, you won't fare as well as someone who is a clerk-typist or warehouse worker. I got one good job through a state employment agency, though, so I do recommend that you try them.

Private agencies offer more possibilities. For one thing, they are sometimes specialized—one may handle only office workers, one insurance and banking positions, another chemists and engineers, etc. The employment counselors work on commission, which makes them eager. And because the agencies make money every time they place someone, they tend to work very hard for their employer- and employee-clients.

The drawbacks are that since it's so lucrative for them to place a client, they may have no qualms about sending you out for a job interview even if you aren't qualified. From their point of view, it couldn't hurt. From your point of view, it's a waste of time and effort. And employment agencies will sometimes misrepresent a job (or an employer) in hopes of making a match. I have also gotten a good job through a private employment agency—but they told me that the salary potential was much greater than it actually was, and for this reason I advise caution.

Before you sign a contract with any private employment agency or even go on one of their interviews, make sure you understand who is paying the fee. Some agencies collect only from employers—others only from job applicants. If you pay the fee, it will likely amount to one month's salary. Sometimes the fee can be split, or if an employer is really excited about you, he may agree to pay the fee that you would otherwise be liable for. But all this should be understood in advance.

In general terms, a person who has a hard-to-find skill will not be paying employment agency fees—the employer will pay. But if the applicants are a dime-a-dozen, and it's the jobs that are hard to find, the applicant will pay the fee.

Government jobs. City, county, state, and federal governments employ a huge portion of the labor force. The federal government is the largest employer in the country.

If you want to work for the city or county, call the city or county offices and ask what the application procedure is. With nearly every government job you will be required to take one or more qualifying tests, and to meet certain criteria for education and experience. These tests and these criteria are relied upon heavily when it comes to government employment.

For state jobs, check the phone book for the State Civil Service Commission. Or call the closest state office building and, again, request information on the procedure. If you write to the State Civil Service Commission, they will usually be glad to send a list of current job openings and the examinations required for them (as well as when the examinations will be administered).

Federal government—it's the same drill. Examinations and openings. You're not going to be able to talk any of these guys into hiring you on a whim, or on the strength of your personality. All they care about are your qualifications for the jobs that they have available. Call or write the nearest local office of the Federal Civil Service Commission. If you're having trouble figuring out where to go, mosey on down to the post office—they have all the information you need.

The library is full of books that will help you prepare for civil service exams, and learn the intricate workings of government jobs. Some people think a government job is a plum; others would rather starve than work for Uncle Sam. Are you enticed by the news that working for the federal government can mean working overseas? Check it out, anyway.

Temporary jobs. Nearly every town and city has one or more temporary service agencies (Manpower, Kelly Girls, etc.). They are in the business of matching skills with jobs on a short-term basis: a furniture store needs extra help for a clearance sale; an office needs a clerk to deal with an accounts receivable backlog; a supermarket needs extra people to take inventory.

Temporary work has many advantages: it's a way to make money while looking for a permanent position, and it's a way to familiarize yourself with the employment climate of a city. Some employers will hire a temporary to fill a job, and then like that person so well that they hire him or her permanently. I once spent three weeks working for a temporary service while I was waiting for a full-time position to open up. During that three weeks I worked for two different companies, and was offered a job by each of them. Temporary services are sorry to lose a good worker this way, but are consoled by the big fat fee they charge employer-clients who hire away their employee-clients.

Some temporary agencies are structuring their companies so as to be able to offer full-time temporary work. That is, one can make a career out of temping. The biggest news is that fringe benefits are available to temporary workers who stick with it—including health insurance and paid vacation. If you are easily bored in a job, like new experiences, and can handle the constant change of scenery, you may want to be a permanent temporary.

Targeted company. Perhaps you know what company you want to work for. Sometimes a corporation is such a strong presence in a community (like Caterpiller in Peoria, or 3M in Minneapolis) that it's natural to seek employment at that company. Or your job skill makes a certain company or institution a natural for you—as when the state university in your city is about the only place you can think of that would hire a degreed research librarian. Family connections can target a company for you: you may be a third-generation Ford. Some companies are famous for being generous to their employees, and they may be your target company.

"In a hierarchy every employee tends to rise to his level of incompetence."
Laurence J. Peter

Large companies have personnel departments that generate lists of positions available. That's a place to start. You can also just drop by and fill out an application, attach a copy of your resumé, and hope for the best. When a position becomes available for which you are qualified, you can pray that the personnel department sifts through the applications on file before advertising elsewhere. The problem with this is that your application and resumé may not make you appear qualified or interested in a position that you'd really like to be considered for.

Call and ask to speak to the head of the department where you would like to work. Ask about openings, now and in the future. Drop names of people you know already work for the company—this can be important. "You probably know my uncle—Bill Washington. Yes, he works in Research and Development. He's your boss? Well, that's interesting!"

"Work is achieved by those employees who have not yet reached their level of incompetence."
Laurence J. Peter

Out-of-the-blue offers. Sometimes a job will come looking for you. A man stops you on your way out of church, says he hears you've been doing a great job with the junior high youth group, and wonders if you'd like to work for him as a camp counselor for gifted children. Or a woman you used to work for years ago as a messenger calls and offers you a supervisory job with her company. Or a business colleague expresses an interest in hiring you away from your present position.

As long as your out-of-the-blue offer isn't off-the-wall, give it some serious consideration. You are probably being approached because you have talents or skills or capabilities that are highly sought-after by your potential employer. You are in a very good position to negotiate a higher-than-usual salary, extra benefits, and other perquisites. It may be your best and only chance to write your own ticket. When an employer comes to you, be aware that you have a lot of bargaining power.

Resumés

Resumé is a French word that means "summary." It is a brief summary of your life and your qualifications for a particular job. It advertises you. When you have not yet met an employer in person, it shows who you are and why you should (or should not) be hired.

Anyone who is serious about getting a job should have an up-to-date resumé printed and ready to distribute to any and all potential employers. I don't care if you're looking for employment along the lines of parking-lot sweeper at Pizza Hut. Apply for that job with a resumé in hand, and you might surprise everyone by being hired as a cook or management trainee. Your resumé is attached to every job application you complete, is given to everyone who is kind enough to grant you an interview (more on this later), goes to companies that you wish to work for, and is circulated amongst those in your personal network who might know someone who works with someone who heard of someone who might have a job.

When preparing a resumé:

DO include all important information about yourself. This means your name, address, and phone number; your educational background, even if isn't impressive; your work experience; your qualifications. In some cases it may be vitally important to include your hobbies, where you were born, or traveling you have done. You don't believe it? An applicant for a writing job with a newspaper who puts "photography" as a hobby has a leg up on someone who doesn't know how to work an Instamatic. How about a bank manager who's looking for tellers, a bank manager whose branch office is in an area with a 50 percent Mexican-American population? Do you think she'd be interested in an applicant whose father was in the foreign service in Spain, and who has a certain proficiency in Spanish? A mention of overseas travel will help some applicants—obviously, if the job is in a travel agency, or even if the job itself will entail some travel. At least you have some idea of what it's like to pack up and go.

DON'T lie. For one thing, many employers are now using services that check into the honesty of statements made on resumés. If you say you're a Phi Beta Kappa you sure had better speak Greek, because it's an easy thing for a resumé checker to verify. What do people lie about most on resumés? Their educational background (saying they graduated from college when they didn't, saying they got honors they didn't, saying they went to an Ivy League School when they actually went to a junior college); their previous employment (falsifying their job description and responsibilities, their previous salary, their length of service with the company); their personal history (lying about a divorce or separation, their health, their age). In short, people lie about everything on resumés.

And employers are sick and tired of it. Not only big corporations, but Ma and Pa operations have gotten serious about checking up on claims that job applicants make. So don't lie.

Are you overweight? Does it hurt to put your tonnage down in black-and-white? If you fudge about your weight on an application or resumé, you're going to embarrass yourself when it comes time for the interview. You don't have to be a weight-guesser at the county fair to know when a person has understated their weight by thirty, twenty, or even ten pounds. And although that may be the only thing you fibbed about, it will set you up as a liar on every other piece of information you provided. If you can't bear to tell the truth, then say nothing.

DON'T give uncalled-for information. It is illegal for employers to request information about certain things: race, religion, age, marital status, disabilities unrelated to job performance. Employers who request pictures of applicants may be doing so in order to screen on the basis of race or age or just looks. Unless you're wanting to work as a model or actor, be wary of employers who demand photos.

Don't give your spouse's name, your shoe size, your net worth, or your mother's maiden name. Don't tell what your previous salary was, or your current wage expectations. This is best discussed in person; it will do you no good on your resumé. Don't tell why you left your previous position. Don't put your references on your resumé. Instead, indicate that they are available upon request, and have them typed on a separate sheet that you can give to anyone who is interested. (Remember to check with all your references, making sure that they are willing to give you a recommendation and that what they say will, indeed, be a recommendation. If you've changed your name since they knew you, let them know.)

DO present material in such a way that it will make you look good. There are three basic approaches to your resumé:

(1) **The chronological resumé.** This is the traditional approach, where you list everything you've been up to in reverse chronological order—your most recent endeavor (be it school, work, or recreation) at the beginning, and

previous pursuits after that. Many employers prefer this type of resumé because it's easy to see what an applicant's history is, what he/she is doing right now, and what the employment trend has been.

(2) **The functional resum**é. If one's chronology is working against them, a functional resumé is the way to go. In it, emphasis is given to qualifications, not chronology. A blow-by-blow education and employment history is usually omitted; instead, there is a summary of talents, achievements, responsibilities, and skills.

(3) **The creative resum**é. Although the creative resumé includes all relevant data (name, address, etc.), it does so in a way that is designed to catch the imagination of the employer and isolate the applicant as a particularly creative and interesting person. Don't use this kind of resumé if you're seeking work in an analytical field, or one where employers might tend to be conservative. Which is just about everywhere, except: performing arts, graphic arts, advertising. Any resumé might be creative to the extent that it distinguishes itself from the others in a pile of resumés. On one end of the scale you might choose to have it printed on light gray paper instead of white, or to use an unusual typeface (never script; never gothic!) in its preparation. On the other end of the scale are resumés done poster-size, with cartoon illustrations, with photographic treatments, or humorous copy. Tread carefully where creative resumés are concerned. As soon as you get your foot in the door you can present your portfolio, or simply wow your prospective employer with your wit, charm, and humor in person.

DO be brief . . . as possible. A one-page resumé will delight an employer; a two-page resumé will be tolerated; a three-page resumé will be used to prop up the short leg of his desk. Especially at this stage of your life, you shouldn't have so much to relate that it can't be done on one page or, in special cases, two. Be as brief as possible, even if the whole business looks pretty scant when it's typed. Under no circumstances should you try to flesh it out by adding extraneous and unwelcome information. The shorter the better—every employer is agreed on this point.

DO have a neat resumé. Use the best quality paper you can, and have it reproduced professionally. Some photocopiers will do an adequate job; a trip to the nearest "quick-copy" establishment will be worth your while. They know how to do resumés well. It goes without saying that it should be typed on an office-quality machine by someone who knows what he's doing. If you have to hire this job out, that's okay. You've got a lot riding on your resumé. Make it look as good as possible.

Practical Application

You've gone to considerable work to get your resumé composed, typed, and printed. You go to apply for a job, and what do they do? They ask you the very same questions on their own question-naire. Rats!

If you are faced with a lengthy questionnaire that duplicates your resumé, ask the secretary, receptionist, or personnel officer if you can write "see resumé" where they are asking for information included on the resumé. Most will not object. Otherwise, it's just a case of copying what you already have onto their form—which may be required.

Applications are like resumés, only the employer isn't waiting for you to volunteer information—he's asking for it. Remember, if you are asked your age, sex, race, religion or creed, or national origin, that's illegal. Your disabilities are also your own business. Leave snoopy spaces blank.

You will be asked questions on an application that you wouldn't think of including on your resumé, such as whether or not you've had any indictments or convictions (does that Minor in Possession charge have to be confessed?); how many days of work you missed because of illness last year; salaries earned in your various jobs. If you don't want to answer a question, leave it blank—but be prepared to have your application disregarded, or to be questioned about it during an interview.

"Why did you leave this part blank about minimum starting salary?"

"Well, Ms. Van Dyke, I didn't put a figure down because much of it would depend on whether or not I'm being consid-ered for full-time or part-time work, what fringe benefits would be included, and if salary review would be scheduled in advance."

In completing an application, you will have to make some judgment calls. If you're really stymied by a question, you can write something like: "Please see me for clarification of this answer" or "Unable to give this information at this time" or a similar response.

And of course you use your very best handwriting (preferably printing) to complete the application; you bring a good pen that doesn't stick or glop; you don't lie; you know your Social Security number and the names, addresses, and phone numbers of your references; you submit a resumé with every application.

"Nobody Expects the Spanish Inquisition!"

If your resumé is impressive enough, if your application is inviting, you will get a chance to interview with your prospective employer.

A job interview works two ways. You know all about the first way it works: the hiring employer sizes you up to see if you have the qualifications needed for the position that must be filled. The interviewer will look at your application, read your resumé, check your personal appearance, notice your mannerisms and the way you speak, assess your personality, quiz you on anything and everything under the sun.

Since you want to make a good impression, you will dress up for the interview. This is crucial. The way you dress shows how serious you are about the job. If in doubt as to what you should wear, overdress rather than underdress. An employer will understand why an applicant for a job as a swimming coach would wear a three-piece suit much better than he will understand why someone who professes to want to work in insurance sales would show up for an interview in cut-offs and V-neck sweater.

You'll be on time; you'll offer a good, firm handshake; you won't chew gum or smoke during the interview; you won't interrupt; you'll be prepared to elaborate on information in your resumé and application. In short, you'll do everything you can to make a good impression.

As with applications, you don't have to answer any illegal questions during an interview. If you are sitting on the other side of the desk from a person who says, "Do you have any plans to start a family?" or "You're Jewish, aren't you?" or "Did you hurt your leg or do you always use crutches?" or "How come a handsome guy like you isn't married?" just smile and say, "If I'm not mistaken, that has very little to do with this job and my qualifications to fill it." Don't play ball with someone like this. Only rarely do such questions have justification.

The second purpose of an interview, with which you may not be so familiar, is to give you a chance to interview your prospective employer. Let's hope that you do not operate under the completely erroneous assumption that any job is better than no job. This is absolutely untrue. There are thousands of jobs that are worse than no job at all. Part of your job during an interview is to make sure that you don't get hired for one of them.

Let the interviewer do most of the talking at first. Then it's your turn. (If you like, you can bring along notes so you remember what you want to ask.) Make sure you understand as much as you can beforehand about the job opening—the exact title, what the responsibilities are, who you would answer to. Then find out about the company (or institution or employer) you'll be working for. Don't ask dumb questions: "Exactly what sort of thing is it that you do here at the Pentagon?" If you can, talk the interviewer into showing you around the office, factory, or plant where you would work. Get a feel for the job site—is it a relaxed, comfortable place, or is everybody uptight? What do the other workers look like? Potential friends? A bunch of losers?

You walk a fine line here—you want to find out as much as you can about the company, the job, and the work situation without appearing pushy as if you had already landed the job. Because you haven't. That comes later.

Sometimes you'll have several interviews. The first may be with someone in personnel who, if she likes you, will send you on up to the individual who is actually hiring. If that interview goes well, you could be invited back for yet another interview with other people in the department—possibly upper management. Don't get discouraged; as exasperating as it is, additional interviews are invariably a good sign—a sign that they like you and want to know more about you.

On rare occasions, you will be offered a job during your first interview. It doesn't happen often, but you should be prepared for that eventuality, even if you've only decided that if you *are* offered the job you'll say, "I'll think about it over the weekend and call you Monday."

Let the interviewer know, when it's all over, that you appreciated the chance to present yourself in person. The next day, write a businesslike letter thanking him/her for the interview and clearing up any ambiguous points. Skip the Holly Hobby note-paper—this is a business letter on your letterhead or plain white paper, typed. It could look like this:

January 6, 1986

1297 Richardson Circle, East
Memphis, Tennessee 38100

Mr. Walter Isaacs
Tate and Associates
Anderson Building
Suite 211
Dinsmore, Illinois 60100

Dear Mr. Isaacs:

I would like to thank you for taking time to visit with me about the accounting position that will be open next month. It was good to learn more about your company—I'm especially impressed with your recent computerization effort.

You asked what sort of system I worked on when I was in college, and I wasn't able to tell you. I remember now that it was an Aardvark 350. I believe it is similar to the system you are using now.

Again, thank you for your time. Having talked with you I am even more certain than before that I would enjoy working with Tate and Associates, and that you would be pleased with me as an employee.

I will look forward to hearing from you!

Sincerely,

[Signature]
Dee Sandborn

You don't want to pester a potential employer, but a follow-up letter to your interview is called for in almost every case.

The Job Offer

Don't discuss salary until you've got a job offer. Let the employer decide that you're the right person before talking about money;

that way, you'll be in a stronger bargaining position. If they already have you on board mentally, they'll be less likely to toss you over where wages are concerned.

Sometimes the salary is carved in granite and there isn't a thing you can do to change it. Government jobs, as we've already said, are especially inflexible. You have no room to haggle—they decide and you live with it. If you're with a union, pay scales will be predetermined. If you're working for a big company that has hundreds of people who do exactly what you do, it's unlikely that you'll be able to talk them into paying you more than they pay anyone else.

Otherwise, you have to use some savvy. Never, under any circumstances, be the first one to mention a salary figure. Always throw the ball back in the employer's court. Of course they'll try to get you to say a figure first, but don't do it!

"Nancy, I'm pleased to tell you that XYZ Company would like to hire you for the newly-created position of creative consultant."

"Thank you very much, Mrs. Roberts—I accept."

"Now, there's this business of salary. What did you have in mind? You didn't note your salary requirements on your resumé."

"I'd like to hear from you what you expected to pay for this position."

"Well, it's a new position. We've never had a creative consultant before. What did you make at your last job? We'll raise it $1,500."

"The salary at my last job doesn't have much to do with this Job, Mrs. Roberts. Why don't you tell me your salary range and we'll take it from there."

"Well, we just don't have a range."

"What did you budget for this position?"

"We were hoping that we could get someone for around . . ."

Whew! You won! Roberts had to say first. If you can, it's good to get them to quote a salary "range," such as, "Anywhere from $18,000 to $21,000."

Then you can say: "Since I have no experience, I'd be glad to accept the $18,000 amount. If you'll give me a salary review in six months, I'll hope to prove by then that I'm worth $21,000."

Or: "That's a little less than I was hoping to make. Even $21,000 would not be much more than I was making at my last job, but I'd be glad to accept it if we can make arrangements now for a salary review in three months."

It's natural for some people to shy away from talking about money with an employer. I'm embarrassed to admit that I once took a job without ever finding out how much it paid—and I didn't know until I got my first paycheck. This is a terrible thing to do. Don't take a job unless you know how much it pays. If you find that you've got a job but no salary figure, call your employer and confess that you neglected to get this very important piece of information and clear it up. Immediately!

Nearly as important as how much you're making are the benefits and perks being offered. They may include:

- paid vacation—how much you get; how long you have to be on the job to collect some of it.

- insurance benefits—how comprehensive it is (life? health? dental? accidental death and dismemberment? long- and short-term disability?); what percentage of the premiums are you expected to pay?

- profit-sharing and pension plans—how they work; how long you have to pay into it before you get anything out; what the employer contributes.

- bonuses and incentives—payment for extraordinary service.

- hours—do you get paid while taking lunch? How long is lunch?

You'll want to know when you're expected to be at work, and when the day is over; if you're getting paid by the hour or if you're on salary; how often you get paid (weekly, biweekly, monthly); what sick days you have; if you get personal leave.

Your employer will ask you when you can start. If both of you know that you're currently unemployed, don't be afraid to say, "Tomorrow!" Even if your new employer would rather you started at the beginning of next week, your enthusiasm will be noted.

If you are currently employed, tell your new employer that you have to give two weeks' notice, but that you'll start work immediately after that. Some employers balk at this, especially if they need you right away. But they'll respect you for your answer; it shows that you're not the kind of person to leave an employer in the lurch. And that's just the kind of employee they want.

If, after handing in your resignation with your present employer you realize that you could start work earlier, then call your new employer back and tell him so. "I gave my resignation today, and my supervisor said that I could just finish out the week with no hard feelings. So, if you like, I could start work for you next Monday."

"It is well for a man to respect his own vocation whatever it is and to think himself bound to uphold it and to claim for it the respect it deserves."
Charles Dickens

5.

BOSSES

Poor bosses are less likely to be intentional in their meanness than simply careless, unaware of their effect on their employees, preoccupied, untrained in management skills and techniques, busy and overworked or bored and unchallenged, scared about their own corporate climb, under pressure from their superiors, and vaguely threatened by their employees. Some bosses are going through a divorce, a midlife crisis, a battle with alcohol, or personal financial difficulties. The bosses who own their own businesses are dreadfully afraid of going under. Many hate their jobs, and their unhappiness spills over and infects those who work for them. Others are forced to supervise a group of workers that they had no say in hiring; they're stuck with a bunch of joy boys who won't get with the program.

Which is all very touching, but doesn't solve the problem of what to do about a bad boss, who probably resembles one of the following:

"One of the greatest failings of today's executive is his inability to do what he's supposed to do."
Malcolm Kent

Basic Boss Types

The Incompetent-But-Nice Boss: He's a real teddy bear, a guy who wouldn't hurt your feelings for anything in the world, is loyal to the company, always gives everyone the benefit of the doubt . . . but his elevator simply does not stop at every floor. Since nice guys are hard to find, a boss like this may stay on the job for decades without anyone ever dreaming of encouraging (or forcing) him to either perform or get off the stage.

The Stab-Em-in-the-Back Nice-Guy Boss: Just as amiable as her inept associate, the only difference is that Miss Congeniality is ferociously competitive and she uses the confidence and trust of others as a weapon against them. Always a smile, always a cheerful word, always a card at Christmas, always a knife in the back.

The Seat-of-the-Pants Boss: He thrives on disaster, and if no genuine ones exist, he will certainly create a few. Operating at a fever pitch, he can be seen pacing the halls, climbing the walls, and mopping his sweaty brow. He is so busy putting out fires that he has no time (or inclination) to prevent them by planning ahead. He barks orders at his employees and demands that they obey, but never gives a clue as to what's going on. Gives a whole new meaning to the term "crisis management."

The Fair-Haired Boy: The owner of the company met him at the country club, where they played tennis together. His top-spin was so impressive that he was hired as a special assistant to the vice-president (who didn't need one) and is on a fast-track to take over the company. He may or may not have the qualifications for the job—this is irrelevant. The important thing is that in the eyes of upper management he can do no wrong. There is no defense against him.

The Fascist: "Do it or die," she says. "I am not in this world to live up to your expectations," she says. "When I want your advice I'll ask for it," she says. This boss has no concept of teamwork and camaraderie. From her point of view, everything will be just dandy if each person understands her role: hers is to direct and yours is to follow. There is no discussion, no "why's" and "wherefore's," no listening. Committed to maintaining control, she is completely devoted to her own power and tends to surround herself with weak, submissive employees. Reads a chapter of Machiavelli's *The Prince* before dozing off to sleep each night.

The Prodigy: Tremendously talented, she is intent on making her first million by the age of thirty-five—and guess who's going to help her do it? She is a self-starter, a go-getter, and come-here-er. She can't understand why everyone else doesn't work sixty hours a week, and take work home on the weekends—the slackers! She exhausts everyone around her with her enthusiasm, her tenacity, and her expectations. The bright side of all this is that prodigies rarely stay in one place for very long, convinced that another company will always be able to offer them more in the way of career advancement.

The Bureaucrat: "We've never done it that way before," is no joke when uttered by this guy. He would rather sell his firstborn to the gypsies than change an accounting procedure or reduce paperwork. Triplicate is his middle name, and he apparently derives tremendous satisfaction from having his desk piled high with obscure forms and out-of-date memos. He jealously guards the little secrets of his job as though they were the key to Pandora's box. Heaven help you if you show any originality or creativity while working for a bureaucrat.

The Dead-End Kid: For some reason completely unknown (to her), she has been passed over for every promotion, every possible change in her position. She is a dim star, and there's a flag on her personnel folder: unpromotable. She sees her associates getting better jobs and more money and becomes bitter because life is passing her by. She is absent more than usual, sick a lot, takes long lunches, and has little good to say about the work she does.

The Skimmer: He operates on the verge of dishonesty. He's always got an angle, always figuring how he can get by without doing his work, always there to pick up any freebies that the job brings. In addition to paperclips, office furniture, and ashtrays, he steals the praise that should be distributed to his employees. He may delegate responsibility, but never credit. His job is a means to an end, and the end is whatever he can get for himself.

Tactical Moves

All rules of etiquette go double when you're dealing with your boss. Be as polite and cheerful as you know how, no matter what. You are expected to be loyal to your boss (and loyal to the company you work for, too). This means that you refuse to participate in backbiting and rumor spreading. Everything you hear about your boss stops with you; it goes without saying that you don't initiate rumors.

Be as agreeable as you can. There will be times when your boss will tell you to do something that you think is stupid, unproductive, or just plain wrong. If it's a little thing, let her have her way. Maybe she wants you to keep your desk neater, or answer the phone in a certain way, or implement an experimental procedure. These aren't so important that you can't compromise.

When you must disagree with your boss, do so in private. If you call her down in front of all her other employees, she'll be your enemy for life, and with good reason. Do whatever you must to speak with her privately—even if that means visiting with her at home or outside the office. Avoid these meetings when you are charged with emotion, likely to say something that you'll regret later on. Never attack her personally; confine your comments to actions, not character.

"I've met a few people in my time who were enthusiastic about hard work. And it was just my luck that all of them happened to be men I was working for at the time."
Bill Gold

When you go to your boss with a problem, be equipped with a possible solution to that problem. I had a boss who always used to say, "I don't have the time to come up with a solution myself, but I'll know a good one when I see it." He encouraged all his employees to recognize problems, formulate solutions, and then present both the problem and the solution to him. He was right —when shown two or three ways to handle a situation, he was invariably able to recognize the best plan.

Seek work and responsibility. Be constantly on the lookout for jobs that you can do and (this is very important) do well. Does she hate doing her expense account? Is there a customer she doesn't get along with? Don't get pushy, or give the impression that you're trying to get her job (even if you are), but rather convey your willingness to accept responsibility for those tasks she'd rather not handle.

Fess up to your own mistakes. Don't try to hide them from your boss. The consequences of ignoring this advice can be tragic. People hate to work around someone who never admits a mistake, who tries to shift blame to coworkers, or who avoids difficult situations. When you are wrong, say so.

Play to your boss's strengths, not her weaknesses. As an employee, you can help your boss be a better supervisor than she is right now by refusing to accommodate her shortcomings and encouraging her in her areas of proficiency. Here's an example: I once had a boss who used the lunch hour to meet with his employees, catch up on what had been happening in their department and get about five gin-and-tonics into his system. By the third drink, the business component of the lunch was pretty weak. The official purpose of these lunches was to do business, but the functional purpose was obviously to engage the company in funding his drinking problem.

Some business/social occasions are command performances—you must go. But I realized that these lunches were unproductive and getting me and him nowhere (not to mention the company). I began to decline the invitations, asking instead if I could meet him at such-and-such a time—making a formal appointment with him, always in the morning (when he was sober). Our A.M. meetings were always very good; in spite of his drinking problem he was an excellent manager who was a tremendous help to me.

Keep your sense of humor. Even more important than a smile on your face when you come to work is a lighthearted approach to your job. Some jobs are deathly serious—as an emergency room physician, police officer, or clergyman can tell you. If you can't laugh, you can't survive. Other jobs are inane, ridiculous, boring, or bizarre. What's the point in being overly serious about washing cars, mowing lawns, or restocking the bread shelves at the IGA?

In addition to keeping you sane, a sense of humor can effect a change in your boss. I once worked with a person who was struggling in his first management-level position. Although he was a bright enough guy and had obvious potential, he was unskilled as a manager. His biggest problem was that he was afraid to make a decision. Whenever asked a question, he hemmed and hawed and asked for another month or two to think it over, during which time he would consult his boss.

When Christmas came, his employees conspired to give him a joke present at the company party—an engraved plate for his desk that read, "THE BUCK PAUSES HERE." Everybody got a good laugh over it, and I think he got the message; he was about 14 percent more sure of himself from that point on.

If problems develop between you and your boss that you are unable to work out on your own, you may have to go over her head. This could mean skipping her rung in the corporate ladder and appealing to her boss, contacting the owner of the company, or meeting with the board of directors. Before you do this, be prepared to look for another job. It is strictly a last-resort move. If you go over your boss's head, the person to whom you address your appeal will automatically brand you disloyal, which is sin enough to discredit you. That person may even refuse to talk to you, in which case you have made an enemy for life. If you do get a hearing and you lose, both your immediate supervisor and her boss will be in league against you, and you won't have a chance against them. As soon as they can get rid of you, they will.

In some cases you already have nothing to lose, and appealing to a higher power is your only hope. For example, a publishing concern had hired a big shot executive to put their sleepy little company in the fast lane. Immediately he started finding fault with the existing employees, and fired several of them, replacing them with his hand-picked people. It was a disquieting time, to be sure, because nobody knew where the hatchet would fall next. Morale was understandably low. But everybody knew that he had the blessings of the president of the company, and that it would be futile to object.

Eventually he went too far—he fired the wrong person. When she got her pink slip, she marched into the president's office, and several of her coworkers marched with her. They told the president exactly what had happened, and threatened to re-sign en masse if the big shot wasn't fired. From their point of view, they had nothing to lose—the woman who got fired had already lost her job, and her coworkers were convinced that if she could be let go, they were next. The ending was happy—for everybody except the big shot. He got the axe.

Her Job and Your Job

If all this advice on how to deal with your boss sounds demeaning, remember that your job is to make your boss look good. That's what you're there for. Your boss's job is to represent you to the owner or management of the company you work for. If each person fulfills her role, everything will run smoothly. This does not imply that you have no rights, or that you can be mistreated or degraded by your boss. But the more you can serve your boss, the better off you'll be, since you serve your boss by doing your work well. An elementary schoolteacher makes her principal look good when she inspires her students to learn, because educating students is the principal's main concern, too. A salesperson makes her sales manager look good by selling well, since the sales manager, too, is judged by the overall performance of her sales force. A youth worker who develops a good rapport with the kids he works with and encourages them to act responsibly reflects on his boss, because their goals are the same.

When you make your boss look good, you will distinguish yourself as a valuable asset to the company or institution that you work for. You will be seen as promotable, as trustworthy, as an asset. Your boss will treat you better, and you will be happier in the work you do.

"Most people like hard work. Particularly when they are paying for it."
Franklin P. Jones

A GOOD BOSS:

1. Will train you. Expect her to explain the job responsibilities to you, and to show you the ropes around the company.

2. Demonstrates a personal interest in you (which is different from being personally interested in you). The good boss

remembers your name, is conversant with your background, and communicates a concern for you.

3. Demands your best. By maintaining high standards, she inspires, encourages, even forces you to be the best you can at your job.

4. Keeps you informed of events in higher levels of the company. She'll be the first to inform you of a relocation plan, a new chief executive officer, or a budget cutback.

5. Represents you to others in the company. She runs interference for you, and acts as a buffer between you and her superiors. She often takes the heat for your mistakes.

6. Gives you the credit you deserve. She praises you for a good job, and lets others—clients, her boss, your coworkers—know when you've done especially well.

7. Gives you space in which to do your work. Though she is always ready with helpful advice, she doesn't breathe down your neck while you're working. She lets you exercise your creativity as much as possible.

A BAD BOSS:

1. Doesn't know anything about your job. She couldn't take over for you if she had to, and consequently has little appreciation for your problems or achievements.

2. Refuses to delegate responsibility—or credit. She insists on doing everything herself, and hogs the credit that might be due others.

3. Gets personal. She fails to maintain a businesslike posture with you. This can be anything from demanding personal favors to attacking an employee's character to outright sexual harassment. She may expect to be respected because of some personal favor, or on the strength of her personality.

4. Over- or undersupervises. She either hounds you or ignores you. She may demand strict adherence to her pre-

ordained procedures, or neglect to provide any kind of framework in which her employees can operate.

5. Displays incompetence in her own job. You may be called upon to cover up for her inability to handle the responsibilities given to her.

6. Shows signs of being threatened by your competency. She knows that when her job performance is put in relief with that of her capable employees, she will be found wanting. For this reason she encourages mediocrity from those around her.

7. Avoids her employees. She doesn't want to communicate, and she sure doesn't want a confrontation. She slips into her office by the back door, won't look you in the eye, and refuses to get involved in any meaningful dialogue.

6.

COLLEAGUES

The people you work with are a lot like your family. You don't pick them, but are forced to work with them—and be productive and happy, by golly. Where you interviewed with your boss and have a pretty good idea what he's like, and where you understand what is expected of you where your boss is concerned (you're going to make him look good, remember?) the responsibility to your coworkers is much more ambiguous. You don't know exactly what you owe them, or how to act around them.

And if that weren't enough to grapple with, they possess personal traits, work habits, and career ambitions that can drive a person crazy.

Meet the Gang

Milchers, Pulers, and Lickspittlers. The number one complaint that employees lodge against their coworkers is that they don't carry their load. Since each person is paid a wage to do his or her assigned tasks, it seems especially unfair when one or two refuse to do their part. It's bad for morale—when one gets by doing so little, where's the incentive for others to work hard? In some cases, the slacking of one forces others to do their work.

These ten-toed sloths create a bad work environment for everybody. When the boss comes around, they are invariably the first to sit up, look busy, and bluff their way through so as to appear the only ones working hard. Who needs them?

Pincocks and Puckfists. Less common but equally irritating are the eager-beavers who hog all the work, responsibility, and praise. They come in early and stay late—every day. They take work home—every evening. When the gang is laughing over some funny show that was on television the night before, they pointedly remark that they were too busy going over the Dittman prospectus to watch any television. Their desks are piled high with work; they always take the most time-consuming and treacherous jobs. They are conspicuously busy at every turn.

Cuttles and Bamamas. Relatives of the Pincocks and Puckfists, the Cuttles and Bamamas look at every coworker not as a colleague but as competition. They dare not cooperate or invest themselves in a team effort, convinced that they must do all their own work and get all their own praise so as to be distinguished (promoted) out of the sea of contenders as soon as possible. Favorite retorts of this group are (to coworkers): "Sorry, I have my own work to do"; (to subordinates): "Naturally I took credit for that project—you work for me, remember?"; (to the boss): "Obviously, the rest of them are trying to make me look bad." This guy looks bad without help from anybody.

Gongoozlers and Paloodlers. They ingeniously create passive interferences for those they work with. They do their job in such a way that others find it difficult to do *theirs* properly. Many of this type congregate in the accounting departments of large corporations, insisting on elaborate expense reimbursement documentation or holding accounts payable checks so long that individual vendors start hounding specific departments for payment. They nearly always operate under a guise of bureaucratic efficiency, talk a lot about standard operating procedure, and continually ignore the schedules and needs of others.

Fundyguts and Fustilugs. Irritating personal habits can make a person impossible to work with, especially when they are piled on top of a number of other vocational inadequacies. Some Fundyguts and Fustilugs are grumpy and impolite, others maintain a slovenly appearance—they never bathe, brush their teeth only on religious holidays, and suck their knuckles. They wear Budweiser T-shirts and gold lamé toreador trousers. They may be messy or superneat (either way, they're disgusting). They smoke, and drop their ashes on your final drafts. They pick their noses and have belching and flatulence problems. They listen to the radio with earphones (no complaints there), but insist on humming, whistling, or singing loudly with the music. They borrow money that they don't repay. Every other week or so they ask you if you've gained more weight.

Blatherskites. This low-life is concerned with nothing so much as nuzzling up to the boss. Blatherskites take personal credit for team efforts. Tattling on fellow employees is a stock behavior ("I told Jim not to pull those plants up, Mr. Wallace, but he insisted on doing it anyway. Boy, I'll bet Mrs. Jenkins will be furious when she finds out that Jim destroyed her marigolds!"). He is likely to be seen taking the boss out to lunch, inviting him over for dinner, or mowing his lawn on Saturday morning. He compliments the boss on every aspect of appearance and behavior ("That's a beautiful suit, Jane," and "You handled yourself so *well* against their accusations, Bill."). Call him Uriah Heep—ever so 'umble, 'e is.

Nodges and Drilligates. We come now to a less offensive coworker-type who can nonetheless put an entire department on edge—the person who simply is committed to a work style so different from the others in the company that the harmony of the team is turned to discord. He's too slow or too quick; too methodical or too creative; too boisterous or too quiet; too demanding or too content. He's the salesman from New York City who takes a position with a small firm in Mobile, Alabama, and proceeds to drive himself at 90 mph when everyone else is doing a cool 55. She's the teacher who tries to incorporate Montessori methods into a strict parochial school classroom. He's the cement finisher who takes so long to do his job that the concrete has all but hardened by the time he gets around to the final finish.

There's nothing intrinsically wrong with these people, or the way they do their job, but they're misplaced—they need to be in a different environment. Until they find their niche, they upset the balance in the workplace.

Dizzards and Clodpates. Finally, there are those workers who are out of their depth. It's no fault of their own—the guy who hired them should take the blame. Intellectually, physically, temperamentally—they don't have what it takes to get the job done. Two bricks shy of a load. They may try hard, they may be lovely people, but the fact remains that their incompetence forces coworkers to cover for them. It's the off-key tenor in the church choir, the diminutive hospital worker who always needs help lifting heavy patients, the secretary who can't type. Since they mean well and would invariably like to do better, it's hard to go to the boss with a complaint about such a person.

Plans A, B, C, D, E . . .

Many of the survival tactics that you are using with your boss will work equally well on your colleagues. Show simple courtesy with them. This has been said several times now, because it's basic to working well with other people and enjoying your job. "Please" and "thank you," a morning greeting and evening blessing—the importance of these phrases can hardly be overstressed.

During the first few months on a job, keep a low profile. Don't come on too strong. You should concentrate on learning your job, and getting the feel of the place—what the company is like, what your coworkers are like, how your boss operates, what systems are in place, what the written and unwritten rules are. Initially, you should try to adapt yourself to others. Once you know the ropes, then you can break out and shine like the star you are.

"Promotion should not be more important than accomplishment, or avoiding instability more important than taking the right risk."
Peter Drucker

Remember that you are in this job to do your best. If you do it well, you will have few complaints from your coworkers. You'll hear people say things like, "He's slow as a snail, but when he does a job, it stays done," or "She drives me crazy with her gossiping during coffee breaks, but I've never seen anyone who was so good with the patients." An excellent performance on the job will mean a lot more to people than your personality flaws and irritating habits.

You are not being hired to be everybody's friend. It's nice to have good friends on the job, but that shouldn't be your main concern. If you're overly interested in getting your coworkers to love you, you'll probably turn into a poor worker—a doormat who gets stuck with everybody else's work, or who compromises her position in order to please others.

This isn't to say that you should throw your weight around, or give no thought at all to the feelings of others or how they feel about you. But it does mean that you put your job before your popularity. Sometimes you'll have to be unpopular with your colleagues. You'll have to refuse to help them because you're busy with your own projects; you'll have to turn a deaf ear to their incessant personal problems because it's taking time away from the jobs you must do; you'll have to disagree with them.

When you can, do help coworkers. You will be evaluated on your individual performance, to be sure, but the performances of your department, of your company, and of your coworkers will also reflect on you. Everybody likes a team player. The added benefit to you is that you will be able to get help later from those you help now.

Try to familiarize yourself with the responsibilities of your coworkers to the extent that it makes you better able to understand their pressures—so you don't become one more problem for them. Accounting departments, for example, have a notoriously bad reputation in most corporations for being nit-picky, tied up in red tape, and unresponsive to the needs of other employees. But most workers don't know enough about accounting procedures to understand why expense reports must be filed in duplicate, why paychecks don't reflect the overtime worked the day before they were issued, or what the limitations of the company's computer are.

Sometimes a secretary must handle work for several people—have you ever stopped to think how difficult this is? He or she must constantly prioritize the work on the desk and hope to get it all done in time. The person who says to the office secretary, "It must be frustrating to work for so many people. Everybody acts like their work is the most important. I'll admit I think this report is important—when do you think it'll be done?" has shown empathy for the plight of a secretary.

Be critical of your own irritating habits. Honestly, now, are you an inconsiderate smoker? Do you interrupt conversations? Is your desk so cluttered that it's spilling onto the floor? If even one of your coworkers has gotten up the nerve to criticize you on such a point, be assured that a dozen more have noticed it and are bothered by it.

On the other hand, when it comes to similar behaviors in others, do your best to ignore them. Your fellow teacher who never turns off the lights in her classroom; the salesman who always raps on your desk when he walks by; the janitor who invariably has a drip of something on the end of his nose—let it go. It's not important.

Include yourself in activities that will show your solidarity with your coworkers—even if you're not interested in the activity itself. I worked in an office that had a thousand little activities (all of which I thought were stupid) that the employees took part in and that showed their identification with the group. On payday, we each put up a dollar and played poker, using the number of our paychecks as a poker hand. I hate that sort of thing, but did it anyway, because if I hadn't, I would have been the only one on our floor who refused to participate. The women also established a "birthday club" which one could choose to join or not—although I never heard of anyone refusing to join. When someone had a birthday, everybody in the club pitched in another dollar, and a gift was purchased for the birthday girl. I thought it a bit contrived (as I did the gift exchange at Christmas, with its pre-scribed five-dollar limit), but participated anyway, because to refuse would have been to reject all the women in the office.

These are little things that take on great importance if handled incorrectly. If you want to get along, keep your eyes open, and learn about these command performances.

"Working with people is difficult, but not impossible."
Peter Drucker

If you have a disagreement, take it to the person involved, and do it in private. Sometimes it's good to do it over lunch, or during a coffee break, or simply to ask to use the conference room to settle your differences. As unemotionally as possible, state your concern. Be sure to avoid accusations; stick with statements of fact about the situation and your feelings. "I am aware that you disagree with my assessment of Jaime's learning disability, and feel that this is interfering with my teaching effectiveness."

Use humor to settle difficulties if you can. I once worked with a woman who was consistently late for work. She was a good worker, but until she arrived everyone who had shown up on time had to field her phone calls, and this was irritating. One morning she surprised us by showing up for work at 8:30 on the dot—starting time. As soon as she walked in the room, we all stood up and clapped and cheered her arrival. I think it was the first time she considered how her lateness affected her coworkers, and she tried to be more punctual after that.

Only as a Last Resort

If you are having serious problems with a coworker, you are entitled to go to your boss (who may also be your coworker's boss) and ask for help with the situation. Do this only when all other possibilities have been explored. It's humiliating for an adult (you) to admit to another adult (your boss) that you can't get along with others. It reflects as badly on you as on the person whom you believe to be at fault. You're going to look like a little kid who has to come running to Mama because little sister pulled her pigtails.

A good boss will be glad to mediate, or to talk to your problem's boss about the situation, but it's unlikely that matters will improve without someone losing face. You will identify yourself as someone who cannot manage her own disputes, and your coworker will be put on trial. Not much good will come of it, so go to your supervisor only in extreme cases.

7.

WHEN YOU'RE THE BOSS

Lucky you, if you're the boss. Maybe not *the* boss—not the big guy with the corner office and the bottle of Maalox on his desk—but you have people who answer to you. You supervise them; you don't have to do every stinking thing yourself. You can delegate. You make more money, get more perks, and have greater status. Your work is more interesting. You have higher ambitions, naturally, but still there is a sense of having arrived. You're here. This is what you've wanted, and now you have it.

Of course, it has its problems. You are likely to be younger than the people who answer to you, and that makes you uncomfortable. It makes your employees a bit jealous. Maybe you were promoted to this position and are now supervising the people who used to be your colleagues. That's no picnic.

Probably you lack management skills. Even if you took eight college courses on employee management, you don't have the experience under your belt that makes you confident and productive as a manager. Since you lack a history of achievement, your mistakes count against you to a greater extent than they do with bosses who have a proven track record.

That's not to say you don't like being a boss. But you are less starry-eyed than you were when you got this position, and you're considerably wiser about how difficult it is to motivate people and how frustrating it can be to be judged by the performance of others.

Improve, Improve

Chances are that you have been given the position you're in not so much on the basis of your past performance as on the basis of your potential. After all, you're somewhat of a rising star. You have caught the eye of higher-ups because of your education, your technical expertise, your personality, or your dedication. Everybody has high hopes for you.

So it would be foolish, once having been given a supervisory position, to lean back, put your feet up on the desk, and assume that you already possess the qualities necessary to succeed as a boss. Sit up straight and get your feet back on the floor; you've got work to do.

Seize every opportunity to improve your management skills; consider yourself a student of management for at least the next ten years. Go to the library and check out books on management theory, and practice; read the literature of your profession; subscribe to the trade and professional journals in your field. Learn as much as you can about supervising in general, and your job—and the jobs of those who work for you—in particular. Strive to be the most knowledgeable person you can in every aspect of your job.

"The executive exists to make sensible exceptions to general rules."
Elting E. Morison

Attend every seminar you can on management technique; if you work for a large company, advise personnel and your boss that you would like to know of any in-house opportunities to learn more about management. If nothing is available there, inquire with professional organizations—do they offer classes of any kind that will help you? Maybe you could attend extension classes at a community college.

Be open to the advice that your own boss can give you. In my first management position, I learned a lot from my boss. What I (and my employees) did on the job reflected directly on him, so he was anxious to help me succeed. Your boss should feel the same way. Accept his or her constructive criticism. For that matter, you should try to learn from any criticism you receive, whether it's from your boss, your colleagues, or your subordinates.

Make an effort to meet with others, either in your company or outside of it, who have a similar position and can offer encouragement and advice with the problems you face. Build a network of support.

Keep a journal of your experiences. Take notes. Learn from the bad and practice the good. You could make a note of the fact, for example, that the day you stomped out of your office and read the riot act to three employees who were playing cards at their desk preceded a week of substandard quality and quantity from those three.

You are expected to grow in this position. The folks who placed their confidence in you by making you "boss" are anxious to know if they did the right thing. Do whatever you can to improve, improve, improve.

Getting Along with the Help

While you are boning up on your management technique and refining your skills, you should remember that courtesy—the kind we've encouraged with your boss and your coworkers—should also be lavished on your subordinates. You are the boss; you don't have to prove it by barking orders, slamming doors, interrupting and insisting that your employees bow thrice before you. When it comes to matters of courtesy, act as though nobody will do anything for you unless you can woo them into compliance by your grace and charm. Because that's probably closer to the truth than it should be. Some people react so strongly against rudeness that they'd risk losing their job rather than cooperate with a boor—even if the boor is the boss.

Keep in mind at all times what your job is. Reread your job description every morning if you have to. It's easy to get caught up in giving dictation, conducting meetings, and issuing edicts— the trappings of management—and forget what you've been hired to do. A production-line supervisor can get so fascinated by signing timecards (an activity that gives him a feeling of power) that he forgets that he's responsible for what happens on the line. An assistant principal may spend so much time in meetings with the principal, the business manager, and the superintendent of schools that she fails to adequately communicate with her teachers, or to get to know her students. Don't let superficialities displace your true responsibilities.

Similarly, you should be absolutely certain that your employees understand their jobs. Part of this is training them, communicating their responsibilities to them, and encouraging them to perform well. But do you remember the biggest job your employees have? Yes, it's to make you look good. Since most employees are unlikely to think in these terms, you may have to sit down and have a chat about it. My first and best boss did, and I'm grateful to this day. He said, "Alice, your job is to make me look good. You do that by performing each and every task you are given to the best of your ability, by improving in your work, by making money for this company, and by helping create a pleasant atmosphere in this office. In return, my responsibility to you is to represent you to top management, and to go to bat for you whenever I can. But I will do that for you only if you make me look good—otherwise I have no reason to help you."

"By working faithfully eight hours a day, you may eventually get to be a boss and work twelve hours a day."
Robert Frost

In my case, it took a few weeks to sink in. You can give your employees at least that long. It will seem like bitter medicine to some people, but if they refuse to swallow it you're in big trouble, and so are they. It's nothing more than the law of the jungle. It doesn't mean that you think any less of them, only that you want them to succeed—and they can go places only if you're going places.

It's natural for employees to test their bosses—you should be prepared for this. They want to know what your style is, how much you'll put up with, what your standards are, what your expectations are. It will be easier to communicate all this to your employees if you have it figured out in your own mind. But whether you do or not, whether they like you or not, whether they agree that you should be their boss or not—they must respect your *position* as their boss. They owe you loyalty.

Now, maybe they don't think you ever should have gotten this job (which is likely to be the case if you got a promotion that they were eligible for). Your employees may not, in their heart of hearts, respect you or think it's fair for you to be supervising them. You don't have to explain to them why you're the boss and they're not. You may have striven for the job, but you didn't give yourself the job. It was awarded to you by someone else higher up, so you have no need—indeed, no right—to get into a lengthy argument about why you deserve to be the boss. If there are questions, direct them to the person who made the decision.

Remember, above all, that you'll get farther with flowers than with a whip. This is not to say that problems should be ignored, that confrontations should be avoided, or that incompetence and insubordination can be overlooked. But it does mean that if you praise every good effort on the part of each employee, you will be an easier person to work for. YOU ARE THE BOSS. You don't have to prove it each day. Concentrate on your own responsibilities and foster a work environment in which your employees can do the same. Strive for personal improvement, and encourage your subordinates to do the same.

8.

OCCUPATIONAL FINESSE

There's a big difference between working at a job and going to school, and even kids who hated school with a vengeance have a hard time adjusting to the work grind.

On a job, you'll have two weeks' vacation a year—if you're lucky. No free summers, Christmas vacation, or Easter break. The sheer length of the working day is daunting, not to mention the employer's demand that you show up for work day after day and week after week, months—really, *years*—at a time.

When you were in school, you took a break after taking exams. Now you finish a mega-project, and still must show up for work the next day as though nothing happened.

You will also miss the grading system. Sure, you griped about it—it was unfair. But at least you knew where you stood. It's much more difficult, on a job, to tell if you're passing or flunking. Feedback is scarce, and ambiguous. The cues of failure are less obvious than they once were. It could be that one day you'll be told that you're fired (you flunked) and you won't have had the slightest idea that you were doing so poorly.

In school you had a teacher or professor who told you exactly what to do; when term papers were due, how long they should be, how many questions on the test, what lab work to complete, etc. Your teacher told you how often you had to come to class, how many "skips" you could have, renegotiated deadlines, and granted incompletes when you were unable to finish the job. Nobody's going to do that for you now. Employers don't baby-sit workers. Your supervisor is typically less available, less helpful, and less understanding than most of the teachers and professors you have encountered.

In school you made steady progress, were promoted from one grade to the next on a yearly basis, and had the assurance of achievement. But this job you have—a promotion is years down the road, and even pay reviews only come once in a blue moon, when they come at all.

There's almost nothing you can do about all of this except get over your disappointment and adapt. Sooner or later, you will. If you're otherwise satisfied, resist the urge to quit every May; don't confuse spring fever with job dissatisfaction. If it makes you feel better to buy school supplies the last week in August, go ahead—that's harmless. You may find yourself taking a night course when fall rolls around—that's fine, too.

Business Etiquette

Etiquette in business is like etiquette in everyday life: it's a tool for getting along with other people and showing consideration. In that sense, your regular good manners will be just fine on the job.*

Some key principles:

(1) Greet your coworkers with a smile every morning. Nobody likes to work with someone who grumbles into work, taking no notice of the people around him. All of the people around you, including your boss, deserve a "Good morning" and a smile.

(2) Keep your workspace clean—and silent. It is rarely acceptable to have a Bo Derek poster tacked up next to your work table, or to let your radio blare. Other people do it, but that doesn't mean you're going to.

(3) If you smoke, make sure it isn't bothering anybody. Any complaints about your habit should be taken seriously. Smoke on your break so as not to alienate your fellow workers. If you are a

---

*Recommended reading: *The New Office Etiquette* by George Mazzei (New York: Poseidon Press, 1983).

nonsmoker, you have every right to insist on simple consideration: no smoke in your face, and as little near you as possible. You would be well within your rights to ask your supervisor for a work area that is free from smoke.

(4) Keep your colds to yourself; stay home if you're sick. If a coworker shows up sick, you may (tactfully) ask him to go home. You'll miss work yourself if the bug bites you.

(5) Show consideration in personal habits; brush your teeth before coming to work; bathe regularly; no overpowering perfume; dress modestly.

(6) Tell no dirty jokes; use no bad language; refrain from put-downs.

(7) Discuss your salary only with your boss, your spouse, and the Internal Revenue Service.

(8) The people you deal with on the job are people—not to be distinguished on the basis of sex where business is concerned. A woman shouldn't get a compliment that a man wouldn't get ("Boy, you look stunning in that suit") and vice versa ("You have beautiful handwriting, Bill"). Should a man open a door for a woman, or help her with her chair? Only if he'd do the same for another man (which he probably should!).

Women working in predominantly male-dominated fields, and men working in predominantly women-dominated fields, have special problems. Just keep in mind the idea that fair's fair: if a woman, for example, lets it be known that she expects male coworkers to open her doors, compliment her looks, and pay for her lunches (when they don't do the same for other men) she will have no reason to complain when she's perceived as being weak or less competent than the men in the office.

(9) Pursue romantic interests on your own time. Here's a good example: a couple I knew met at work, and were attracted to each other. He got his nerve up and asked her out—by calling her at home after hours. They dated, fell in love, decided to get married. The first their coworkers even knew of all this was when the engagement was announced. To my mind, that's probably the best possible way to conduct an office romance. Keep it private, because it is.

(10) Conflicts with coworkers, superiors, and subordinates are inevitable. Fight fair. Don't yell. Throwing a fit is sometimes effective, but only if it's absolutely justified and you don't make a habit of it. Otherwise, keep your disagreements as low-key as

possible. If you decide to make your point by storming out of your supervisor's office, or hanging up on a client, you may lose your job. Tantrums don't make it in the world of adult work.

(11) If you are participating in a business lunch, you must merge business etiquette and personal etiquette. It goes without saying that you use good table manners. Whoever initiated the lunch picks the restaurant and pays for the meal, regardless of sex.

(12) If you wish to terminate employment, give at least two weeks' notice. It's only polite.

The Business Trip

Many jobs carry with them the duty of travel. If you are ever asked to travel on business, you know that it's because your boss thinks you can be trusted and you will do a good job of representing the company. That thought should inspire you to handle yourself in the most professional way you can.

Before you start any job, you should ask if travel is involved. The amount of travel, if slight, is expressed in number of trips per year, thus: "The person in this position generally makes two trips a year—one to the national convention, and one to the regional sales conference. Beyond that, there may be one or two calls on corporate clients, but that's rare." When there's a lot of travel it's given as a percentage figure: 20 percent travel, 50 percent travel, 100 percent travel.

It's important to know ahead of time how much you'll be gone, if possible. Even though the travel opportunities may excite you, workers who travel should be compensated for their inconvenience. When you travel you're working longer days, you're away from your home, you may incur personal expenses that you wouldn't otherwise, and you're doing the company an extra service by acting as its spokesperson.

Sometimes employers will over- or underestimate the amount of travel a job requires, in order to trap a job applicant into a hard-to-fill job. You may be promised several exciting trips that never materialize, or be assured that you'll spend no more than one week a month on the road when in reality you're traveling almost constantly. If an employer is less than honest with you, have a talk about it.

Remember, on all business trips, that you're there for business and are expected to remain businesslike for the occasion.

This is not a vacation. I know this only too well: I spent a week in Honolulu on business. All my friends were jealous—an expense-paid week at a luxury hotel in Hawaii seemed like a gas. I'll admit it had its moments, but there was hard work, too: setting up a booth in a big convention hall, manning the booth, talking to clients, strategy sessions with my boss. I could have lived without it.

Business is your main concern. If you can have a great time, go for it. But make sure that your business is taken care of first. Your boss is counting on you to get the job done. Travel is expensive, and you'll be called on the carpet if you waste the trip.

Find out as much as you can about your destination before you go. Ask coworkers who have made the trip, your boss, your friends, the contacts you'll be seeing while on your trip. You need to know the climate so you can pack the right clothes. If you will have free time, you'll want to know what's worth doing and seeing. If you can get leads on good restaurants and hotels, you'll appreciate it.

If you are driving to your destination, get a city map so you don't waste a lot of time wandering around once you arrive. If you are flying, make sure you understand the situation at the airport—what's the best way to get to your hotel? Does the hotel provide a limo at the airport? What about buses and cabs? Some airports are so small that there isn't even a cab stand to accommodate incoming passengers. If you can get someone to meet you at the airport, that's nice. Will you be renting a car? Arrange this ahead of time.

Make your hotel reservations in advance. If you do a lot of traveling, you may have a chain that you like to use. Some give incentives to regular customers, like free meals, rebates, or free nights. There will be enough surprises along the way—don't invite trouble. Make as many arrangements in advance as possible.

Travel light. What you normally wear to work will usually be appropriate for a business trip, although you may want to take into consideration the fact that in big cities (especially on the East Coast) dress will be more formal and conservative than in the South, Midwest, or on the West Coast. If you can manage your trip with just carry-on baggage, do it. It's murder to lose your luggage on a business trip.

Keep track of your expenses daily. It is almost impossible to remember what was spent a week afterwards. Keep a notebook in which to note expenditures, and an envelope that can hold receipts.

Your expenses will be reimbursed, but don't go throwing the company's money around. It makes you look like a rookie, for one thing, and when the day of reckoning comes (when your boss sees your expense report) you'll have a lot of explaining to do. Before you leave, ask your boss if this is a "Days Inn" or a "Hyatt Regency" trip.

Most employers will give a traveling employee an advance for the trip, so that you aren't out-of-pocket on expenses. If you do a lot of traveling, or business entertaining, ask for a company credit card—all expenses charged will be billed directly to the company. I wouldn't go on any business trip without about $100 more cash than I planned on spending, and a credit card to handle contingencies.

If you get sick on a trip, you can go to a hospital emergency room, ask the hotel for a doctor, or pick one out of the phone book. If necessary, have your out-of-town doctor call your regular physician to discuss your case. Don't get talked into any serious medical treatment while away from home. It's much better to get patched up sufficiently to get back home where your own physician can treat you.

"Airline travel is hours of boredom interrupted by moments of stark terror."
Al Boliska

Finally, remember who you are when you travel. There's something about airports, jumbo jets, big hotels, and expense accounts that make people space out. Corporate presidents act like naughty schoolboys; conventioneers act like celebrities, and salesmen act like fools. I've done more than my share of business traveling and have seen a lot of craziness along the way. In my experience, business trips seem to have the effect of causing people to do things that they wouldn't think of doing at home. Try to maintain your composure when traveling. If those who are traveling with you cannot do the same, keep what is said and what happens in confidence. Try not to hold it against them; if you've done any traveling, you know the temptations.

Mentors

Before Ulysses went on his ten-year odyssey, he entrusted his son Telemachus to the care of Mentor, a wise man who served as the boy's guide, tutor, and counselor. (Actually, Mentor turned out to be Minerva in disguise, but that's another story. . . .)

In recent years, observers of the business scene have noted that when newcomers to any work situation have a "mentor" to encourage them, guide them through the intricacies of the company, and tutor them in the ways of their profession, these protégés excel.

So all over we have entry-level managers, budding entrepreneurs, and professional workers desperately seeking mentors. The trades have had this sort of "guidance from above" for years—an apprentice cabinet maker learned from a master cabinet maker, and so forth. It is this sort of supervision and encouragement that newcomers into other occupations are looking for.

What qualities should a good mentor possess?

(1) A good mentor is higher up on the oganizational ladder than her protégé. The mentor is, in a sense, a scout or trailblazer who can only show the way if she's already been there once already. Having one's own boss as a mentor is generally considered a bad idea. Even having a mentor who operates within the same chain of command is not desirable, because she may secretly view her protégé as a threat to her own position and, consequently, sabotage his career. A schoolteacher who is mentored by a principal in another school; a research chemist who is mentored by the vice-president of sales; or a community worker who is mentored by the mayor of the city have all found mentors who are well-placed organizationally but outside their own chain of command.

(2) A good mentor is an authority in his field. Why hitch your star to an incompetent? If the protégé will be learning from the mentor, he might as well learn from someone who has something to teach. In the medical profession, doctors will often establish a mentoring relationship with physicians who are experts in esoteric medical specialties—organ transplants, reconstructive

surgery, or neonatology, for example. Many times the only way to develop one's own skills in a highly specialized area is to study—independently—under a recognized authority.

(3) A good mentor is influential. Since it is part of the mentor's role to represent and promote the advancement of her protégé, it stands to reason that the mentor must wield some degree of influence within the organization. She must be a respected voice, so that when she speaks well of her protégé others will listen. If she is often ignored by her peers and superiors, she can do little for her protégé.

(4) A good mentor is genuinely interested in her protégé's growth and development. She must care enough to help, which is why it is important that there be no competitive element between the mentor and the protégé. In most cases, the mentor's interest will extend beyond mere matters of business and profession, and include the protégé's personal life. The pitfalls are obvious (keep reading), but it is vital that the mentor have a true concern for her pupil.

Mentoring brings two people into a reciprocal relationship. The advantages to the protégé are obvious: she gets to sit under the wing of a colleague who will help her learn the ropes in the company, give her an insider's view, encourage her to learn more about her job, and present her in a favorable light to the upper echelons of management.

What does the mentor get out of all this? The mentor gets the status of having a rising star in his orbit, gains a loyal disciple who will present him in a favorable light to the *lower* echelons of management, and the satisfaction of being able to pass along his years of experience and mountains of expertise to an individual who is part of a new generation of leadership.

While many mentoring relationships work to the mutual benefit of the mentor, the protégé, and the company, they can sometimes deteriorate and leave everybody worse off than they started, too. There is the ever-present danger that a newcomer will pick an inappropriate mentor, for one thing. Many times the would-be protégé is not in a position to judge who can best help him, and he'll latch onto anyone who shows an interest in him, only to find out later that the mentor is incompetent in any number of ways. The protégé may pick up the bad habits of the

HOW TO ASK FOR A RAISE

1. Document why you deserve a raise. Devise arguments and collect exhibits that show:
- increased productivity on your part;
- added responsibilities that you have assumed;
- experience, expertise, and education you have garnered which has made you a more valuable employee;
- a rise in the cost of living;
- a significant change (increase) in the going rate for your skills (make sure to arrive at this without raising suspicion that you have been comparing salaries with coworkers).

2. Rehearse your plea for a higher salary. Recruit a friend who will act as your boss in a role-playing exercise. Anticipate your boss's objections, and be ready with your counter-arguments.

3. Make an appointment to talk with your boss. Do *not* plan to talk about salaries when in the midst of a work- or budgetary-crunch, or when you've been doing a poor job. *Do* make it a point to discuss salaries when you have completed a big project, when your boss is writing her budget (or revising it), when the company is making a profit, or when your boss is feeling optimistic about business in general and you in particular.

It is often a good idea to write a memo to your boss letting her know your intentions: "I'd like to meet with you at the beginning of next week to discuss my salary. . . . "

4. Present your case to your boss. Explain why you deserve a raise (back this up with the documentation you accumulated); be prepared to answer objections; have a specific figure in mind. You will be asked how much more you wish to earn, and you should never say "More" or "You decide."

5. If you are refused, ask your boss when you may approach her again, and what evidence will be required at that time to justify an increase.

mentor, follow him too closely, and be perceived by others in the company as the same sort of nincompoop.

Mentoring relationships may turn sour. A disagreement between mentor and protégé can be devasting for the protégé. The mentor, because he is powerful, can make or break the newcomer, and if there is a serious difference of opinion between the two it will be the young cub who suffers, not the king of the jungle.

When the relationship gets too personal—especially if it gets sexual, or is perceived to be sexual by others in the company— both parties lose credibility. This is especially the case when young career women are mentored by older men. Women are still easy targets for gossip centering around possible intimacy with their male coworkers. When women are perceived as sleeping their way to the top (whether they are or are not is, at this point, irrelevant), they become the objects of ridicule, gossip, and (who can figure it?) envy. Alas the day! No legitimate achievements will be recognized in light of the supposed love affair. The same is true when the mentor is an older woman, the protégé a younger man, and when the mentor and protégé are same-sexed.

The lesson? Mentor with caution. Don't rush into such a relationship simply because you've heard it's the thing to do. It can definitely be worse than nothing if mishandled. You may be one who should determine to make it on your own, avoiding the mentor entanglement altogether.

9.

YOU'RE FIRED

It's a memo from the boss—the legendary "pink slip." Or a Friday-afternoon interview in which the employee is told to clean off his desk—for good. Or a series of warnings that culminate in the final blow, "You have been dismissed of your duties." Or rumors of bankruptcy, a corporate takeover, or loss of funding. The rumors become more specific, more credible, and one day all suspicions are confirmed: the party's over.

The sacked employee begins to feel numb in his fingers and toes. He can't see too well; maybe it's tears in his eyes that he can barely contain for the duration of the exit interview. His heart is beating loudly, and irregularly. His voice is changed slightly—a little higher, a little louder, a little more shrill. His pupils are dilated, and his face is red. That childhood rash on his forearms is starting to itch again. He's somewhat uncoordinated, and has trouble concentrating on matters at hand. He clenches his fists. He may have urges to violence, or simply cry uncontrollably. Or he's in the "ozone," and hasn't heard a thing that his boss said after, "It is the decision of management that your employment here be terminated. . . ."

No matter how it happens, no matter what the reasons and regardless of forewarnings, getting fired is more like being hit by a gravel truck than anything else. The shock is disabling—for a short or long period of time—and the person who has gotten sacked must now reorganize his life and figure out what he's going to do. Immediate reactions are to cry, yell, plot revenge, hibernate, leave town, and kick the cat.

One personnel manager offers this advice for newly fired employees:

What to Do the Day You're Fired

(1) Don't call your old girlfriend or boyfriend. Ex-lovers never understand.

(2) Don't try to write a resumé. You're in no condition to do anything that skillful.

(3) If you decide to write a long letter to someone, don't mail it.

(4) Don't tell yourself that you don't care. You do.

(5) Don't say the word "fired" or any synonym for it. If you do, you'll choke on it. Say you're temporarily unemployed or freelancing. Everyone will understand.

(6) Don't make any long distance calls or send any telegrams at your own expense.

(7) Don't tear up your files.

(8) Don't buy a ticket to Tahiti unless you're sure it is refundable.

(9) Don't contemplate suicide, a heart attack, or a nervous breakdown. The first you can put off till later. The other two will come if they come whether you contemplate them or not. (Quoted by Barbara Howell in *Don't Bother to Come in on Monday*, p. 28.)

If you follow that advice, you won't go far wrong. Here's my advice for those who have been fired:

Understand why you have been sacked. And don't settle for lame excuses and naive explanations. When you are sitting on the far side of the office, across the desk from some hatchet man who has just given you your walking papers, you have a right to know exactly what is going on. Why, exactly, are you being dismissed? Poor job performance? Demand that your boss be specific about that, even though it could hurt. He might be bluffing, and it is entirely possible that you are being wrongly accused of some offense you didn't commit. If you are able to defend yourself against spurious accusations, you may be able to retain your position.

If the firing is inevitable, find out the exact date of termination, what severance pay you have coming, what you will get from your profit-sharing or vested pension plan, if you can retain health insurance benefits, and if you can count on your superior for a good recommendation. Sometimes the personnel department of your company is prepared to assist you in your "outplacement" and rehiring, with services such as use of their switchboard, assistance in resumé writing, free resumé printing, or classes in conducting a job search and interviewing.

Severance pay is very much a negotiable item. Don't settle for such statements as, "We have no policy for disbursing severance pay," or "You will get the standard severance pay, equal to two weeks' salary." You can get more.

Since you're stunned, it's likely that you won't have the presence of mind to think of all this at the time. Request a second exit interview for the next day—even if it's not a work day or you are being asked to leave the office immediately. If you give yourself twenty-four hours to think about all your questions, you'll have plenty to ask during this second interview.

Get the files from your desk that you are entitled to. This does *not* include company secrets, product formulas, marketing strategies, five-year plans, and advertising surveys. Nor does it include a gross of Pentel pencils from the supply cabinet, or an armload of clothes that you pull off the retail rack. It does mean that you should get your personal files, your Rolodex or address book with the names of your business contacts and clients, lesson plans that you have generated, reports and projects that you have worked on, documentation of your job responsibilities and achievements, and anything else that is going to be helpful as you search for another job.

Tell your employer that you intend to do this. Invite him to watch while you gather your belongings, and encourage him to inspect what you take out with you. This protects you from any future allegations that you stole secret documents or took away anything to which you were not entitled.

Immediately engage at least one confidant who is willing to listen, sympathetically, to your tale of woe. It could go on all night, and for the next few days, so it should be someone who is truly on your side: your best friend, your parents, your spouse.

You don't have to share your shame with everyone, but it's absolutely vital that you have at least one person to talk to. You can't keep something like this inside.

If you, or your friend, think you're not coping well, you should seek the help of a professional counselor. You are in a critical period, and it is important that you get your head straight about what's happened to you. If you have to lay on a couch to do it, so be it.

Call the Job Service Office and make inquiries about your eligibility for unemployment benefits. Some nonprofit agencies are not required to pay unemployment insurance premiums, and consequently their former employees are not entitled to benefits. But you should call anyway. Since unemployment is payable only to those who have been fired, as opposed to those who have quit their jobs, think carefully before you get into a "You're fired" —"No, I'm not, I quit!" situation with your employer.

Applying for unemployment benefits isn't fun. You have to go to the Job Service Office and stand in a huge line and admit to a petty clerk that you were fired, and talk to a counselor about it, and document the fact that you're looking for a job, and for this you get a measly weekly allowance that won't begin to make up for your loss of income.

But it's worth it. Money is tight for you, even with severance pay, and you should remember that unemployment benefits are no handout; you're not on the dole. Your company has been paying this money in, and you're entitled to receive your share if your company fires you. Did you ask for unemployment? No! Your company decided that you would be jobless. So let them do their small part in providing some relief until you can be reemployed.

Begin your job search as soon as you are emotionally able. When you are preparing your resumé, don't feel guilty about dancing around the fact that you've been fired (this is where a functional resumé is so useful). When it comes time to interview, you may be forced to admit that you were canned at your last job. I wouldn't volunteer that, but if you find yourself unable to avoid it, don't worry. It will likely be better received by your potential employer than it was by you. If you can explain why you were fired (on the basis of the information you extracted from your boss during your exit interview), you may come through relatively unscathed. Especially if your termination can be blamed on a slump in the economy, an arbitrary cutback in the number of employees at your company, or even a change in management, you needn't be ashamed.

The Up-Side of Failure

Being fired is terrible—devastating—but it's not the end of the world, especially at this stage of the game. You'll definitely live through it.

You might even emerge from it better off than you started. Firing is sometimes the only practical way out of a safe but boring or dead-end job. Many people have been fired from mediocre jobs in which they gave mediocre performance, and gone on to more challenging jobs in which they were able to exercise previously untapped creativity and display their exceptional abilities.

When you're fired, you learn a lot about yourself that you didn't know before. Sometimes this learning process starts during the exit interview, when your boss rattles off your shortcomings—"You talk too much, you don't work well with others, you consistently underwhelm me, you are a lazy bum, etc." Many ex-employees, after they are over the hurt and embarrassment, come to the point where they agree with what the boss said, and go on to either improve themselves or change fields of endeavor so that they are doing something they like more and are better suited to.

"How far high failure overleaps the bounds of low success."
Lewis Moris

The learning process may commence with the first few days of unemployment, where each day brings a string of revelations about your personality and coping capabilities, all brought to the forefront because you are stripped of the job title and salary that have previously defined your existence. When a person can no longer identify himself to others by his accustomed handle—chemical engineer, schoolteacher, dance instructor—he must find new and more valid means by which to understand himself.

The out-of-job period can be enriching. It is a forced escape from the day-to-day pressures of the previous job. It provides time to relax, to get some sleep, to be with friends, to work around the house, to write in a journal, to take long walks, to contemplate the moon. These are all the kinds of activities that can rejuvenate the person who has devoted all his energy—physical and emotional—to the demands of an occupation.

And, finally, the person who has been fired will ideally learn how to deal with failure. "But if I hadn't gotten fired, I wouldn't *need* to learn how to deal with failure," whines the guy who instantly recognized the catch-22 of this statement. Nevertheless, there is a strength that comes from rejection and failure, and this strength is applicable to more than occupational situations. The person who knows what it means to be out on the streets without a job is better able to empathize with the needs of others, and more able to draw strength for life's other disappointments. And there will be disappointments.

"Clean Out Your Desk, Alice."

This is not book learning I'm sharing with you, because I have had the blessing of being fired from a job—an important job. Considered a very promotable person in a large company where I worked, the inevitable finally happened: I was promoted into a position for which I was completely unqualified and totally unprepared. I wanted the job, and I can honestly say I did my best, but I wasn't up to it; after six months I got the word from my boss: "Clean out your desk, Alice. The vice-president has asked for your resignation."

There are a number of things I might have done at that point that could have worked in my favor. I could have demanded a more specific delineation of my inabilities, and I certainly should have at least pointed out that the job was one I never asked for, and that it was mostly the fault of upper management that I had failed. But I was too stunned to do anything like this. My jaw tightened, my voice shook, and my knees began to have fellowship, one with the other. Despite my physical instability, I did have the presence of mind to demand a substantial severance settlement, and I made my boss fire me (as opposed to "accepting my resignation"), which cost me face but gained me thousands of dollars in unemployment benefits.

It was my first failure. I had never been anything but successful. I couldn't quite take it in, the fact that what I had attempted had not been done to the satisfaction of that bunch of bozos I worked with and for. Since my self-esteem had, up until that point, been tied in heavily with the glowing evaluation of others (since kindergarten), I had to determine—in the wake of being fired—if I was worth anything.

After a couple of weeks I decided that I deserved to live. So I got busy looking for jobs. While I was looking I helped my husband and his friend set up a little photographic agency they were working on. When the job offers failed to materialize, I devoted more and more time to the photo agency. Finally we all decided, what the heck, and had some business cards printed that christened me "Alice Lawhead—General Manager" of the partnership. I got good use out of all my dress-for-success business suits, called on my clients faithfully, ran the office to the best of my ability, and built the business up to a respectable level, making a good salary for myself while in business, and selling it after fourteen months for $8,000. Which everybody thought was pretty good, considering that it started with a $300 investment.

But that didn't take all my time. I had hours each day to pursue my true love in life—reading. No longer forced to grab a page or two of my current novel while eating breakfast or flying to Detroit, I was able to spend hours at a time tackling the big fat books that had beckoned me for years: *Anna Karenina, War and Peace, The Covenant,* and *Garfield Goes on a Diet.* Although at the time I perceived it as the indulging of an obsession, I see now that it was really vocational training for my present job of writing.

As I look back on the experience of getting fired, I cannot honestly say I'm glad it happened; there was too much pain. But I can say that I survived, and that I put my life back together better than it was before. I might have stayed with that crummy company all my life, commuting forty-five minutes a day to work, traveling out of town 80 percent of the time, and looking forward to a Christmas turkey as the highlight of the work year.

Dr. Ernest Dichter, the father of motivational research in marketing, says this about getting fired:

"Most men and women see life in static terms. They think 'making it'—having a big house and a membership in the country club—is their life goal. They want paradise on earth.

"But that isn't the reason we are alive. Life's purpose is not to experience a South Pacific type of fulfillment or to be in the Garden of Eden any more than it's to become chairman of the board and stop right there. It's the opposite.

"We should never be quite happy. We should always want something new and different. Life's purpose is what I call 'constructive discontent.' That's not a terribly new thought. Goethe talks about it in *Faust* and other writings. The answer to life is continuous striving. That's the purpose: never to find. Shall I put it another way? Getting there is not half the fun. It's *all* the fun. Therefore firing is an episode that's good for you because it pushed you further." (Quoted in *Don't Bother to Come in on Monday*, by Barbara Howell, pp. 104, 105.)

Most of that is true, I think. It's the journey, not the destination, that's important in life. In the Bible, this principle is represented by what some call "the upside-down kingdom," in which the meek inherit the earth, and the last become the first. Few of us understand the meaning of success.

Bill Vaughan said, "In the game of life it's a good idea to have a few early losses, which relieves you of the pressure of trying to maintain an undefeated season." My own early failure freed me to take chances, with the full knowledge that I might fail again. So what? It's easier to face the possibility of failure having already done so and lived through it. Before I had failed, I feared it, but after I had failed . . . the worst was over.

Part III:
The Basics: Food, Shelter, Clothing and Mobility

10.

LIVING OPTIONS

Where you live is obviously of great importance. No matter what it is—a twenty-eight-room mansion along the lines of Southfork, a warehouse loft on the waterfront in San Diego, a log cabin in North Dakota, or a fourth-floor walk-up in St. Louis—it will be your home. You will leave it in the morning, and return to it in the evening. Your friends will be entertained in your home; your parents will come to visit you in your home; you will turn to your home for comfort in hard times, for warmth in the winter, for rest when weary. You will spend many hours of each day between the walls of your home; you will sleep there at night and eat most of your meals there. It's important to have a nice home.

Nice does not mean extravagant. A good rule of thumb is that not more than 25 percent (30 percent tops) of your take-home pay should go toward housing, including rent, utilities, parking, and upkeep.* Already you know it's not going to be plush. But you should do the best you can to get the best you can. Your search for a place to live deserves your most careful attention, your most dogged research, your most inquiring attitude, and your most discerning eye.

---

*This good rule of thumb is brought to you by the same folks who say that every person should have the equivalent of 6 months' salary in accessible savings. Ha!

You may think that your only living space choices are "rent" and "own." You can't afford to own your own home, so you're going to rent something.

It's true that home ownership is a burden that probably should not be carried by someone who is new at living on her own. The first and biggest problem is that a significant down payment is usually required (less so in the case of veterans who qualify for VA loans), and large monthly mortgage payments must be paid —either of which could break the budget of someone just starting out.

"A hick town is one where there is no place to go where you shouldn't go."
Alexander Woollcott

I have known people who literally dropped out of life when they bought their first home: a great little "fixer-upper" for the first-time buyer that left them with hardly a minute of free time. They were so busy with their handyman's delight—shoring up the porch, painting the trim, reseeding the lawn, wallpapering the bathroom, rewiring the basement, and patching the roof— that the rest of their life had to be put on hold while they tackled their housing difficulties.

So let us put home ownership on the back burner for a while. It's not for most people who are starting out. It will be enough for now to address the challenges of independent living without having to move to the advanced lessons of domicile management.

Still, "renting" is not your only remaining option. The accompanying chart shows that renting an apartment in a large building is different than renting one in an old house, or renting an entire house, or living with a family, or in a co-op or commune, getting room and board in exchange for work, housesitting, or finding a live-in job. Before you start your search, consider the "Housing Options" chart which follows.

Neighborhoods

Nearly as important as the amenities of the dwelling you choose are the amenities of the neighborhood in which it is located. Not everyone looks for the same thing. Richard may want to rent a tract house in a suburban area, appreciating the spacious lawns, the friendliness of the many young families, and the peace and quiet he gets on the outskirts of town. Doug wants to live close in; he likes the feel of an older home, thrives on the pace of the city, and wants a neighborhood that is ethnically, culturally, and socially diverse. Kathi insists on being within walking distance of everything she needs; she looks for an apartment close to her office, close to grocery, drug, and hardware stores, and accessible to public transportation—but she doesn't care if it's inner city or out in the country.

"I'd rather wake up in the middle of nowhere than in any city on earth."
Steve McQueen

Neighborhoods are a personal thing. The neighborhood I live in is considered "undesirable" by many of my friends. They wouldn't think of buying property within three miles of it. But I like the fact that it's close to the center of the city, that property values make large, older homes affordable, that we have an active neighborhood association working to improve the character of our community, and that my neighbors include retirees, young families, single adults, and residents of a group home. To me, my neighborhood is just right.

Since your apartment rental rates reflect the condition of the neighborhood, you might as well appreciate what you're paying for.

Is this you? You like to drive; a long commute doesn't bother you. You like peace and quiet when you get home at night. You like a home that is neat and clean, easy to maintain, and equipped with modern kitchen and bath. You enjoy a well-kept yard. You want to live around other people like yourself who take care of their property and create a lovely neighborhood. You lean toward suburban living.

Or is this you? You like to drive, too. You want to see wide open spaces when you look out the window. If you can see your neighbor, he's too close. You like having the freedom to raise a ruckus and make a lot of noise without having some nosy neighbors call in a complaint. You like to smell fresh-cut grass and share your living space with the rabbits, squirrels, and field mice that live in the country. You need a place where your dogs can run; you like country living.

"A neighborhood is where, when you go out of it, you get beat up."
Murray Kempton

Maybe you're like this: You like being around other people. You are not bothered by the sounds of traffic, nor by the congestion of a city. You want to be close to theatres, shopping areas, and restaurants. Your life is enriched by your encounters with other people—all kinds of people. You appreciate eccentricity. You like to live in the city.

These are stereotypes. And it's possible that, because of the size of your town, your financial limitations, or the location of your place of work, you can't live where you'd really like to. If you live in Smallville, population 2,345, you won't be able to find "urban living" no matter how hard you try. And if you work in New York City suburban living will come at a very high price—financially and time-wise.

But it is good to get in touch with your preferences. Why rent a suburban house only to find that the long commute and pressure from the neighbors to get the clover out of the lawn are driving you crazy?

Assessing a Neighborhood

Once you've found a place where you'd like to live, you should interview the neighborhood. Drive though the area. Then park

LIVING OPTIONS □ *111*

your car and walk a while. If you are a bicyclist, ride your bike through. This is the best way to get a feel for the character of the neighborhood. Obtain additional information by talking to merchants in the area, people you meet on the street, the tenants in your building, or the real estate agent who is handling the property. These are the things to look for:

(1) Is it attractive? Are the houses painted? Lawns mowed? Is it nicely landscaped? Are there trees, or promise of trees? Does it please the eye?

(2) How does it smell and sound? Like it's downwind of the city landfill? Like it's on the flight path of three hundred jumbo jets a day? Like it's near a busy highway?

(3) Where is the nearest grocery store? The nearest drugstore? The nearest dry cleaner, hardware store, service station, Dairy Queen?

(4) How far is it from work? From church? From friends' homes?

(5) Is access to public transportation nearby? How far to the train, bus, subway?

(6) Where's the nearest park? Is there public greenspace? How about swimming pools, tennis courts, and other recreational areas?

(7) Are the streets well-lit at night? Does this look like the kind of place you could enjoy in the evenings?

(8) Do the neighbors seem to be out and about, or are they holed-up inside their houses and apartments? Does the street have a good "feel"? Does it *look* neighborly?

(9) Is there an active neighborhood association or citizens' organization? Is there a Neighborhood Watch or similar community crime prevention program in operation? Do the neighbors socialize? Do they have block parties? Do they cooperate?

(10) Have property values in the neighborhood been going down or up in recent years? If it's an older neighborhood, has it been well-maintained through the years? Are there any revitalization efforts?

Not all of these will be important to you. You may not care if there is public transportation, for example, because you never use it. Determine what's important to you and then do your best to locate in an area that meets your needs.

HOUSING OPTIONS

Option	Example	Availability	Range of Amenities	Price
Apartment Building	You rent a unit in a building especially built to accommodate tenants. Each unit is self-contained with kitchen, bathroom, living and sleeping space.	Usually good; may be hard to find in large metropolitan areas, boomtowns, or very small towns.	Can be anything from an efficiency unit in a flea-bag hotel to a penthouse suite with swimming pool, tennis courts, and maid service.	Super-cheap to skyhigh
Conversion House	A large older home, no longer practical for single-family use, is partitioned off into rental units. (Remember "The Mary Tyler Moore Show"? Mary Richards lived in a conversion house.)	Usually good; hard to find in built-up urban areas, and newer parts of town.	Varies. Each unit will have kitchen and bath. Due to architectural limitations, some amenities may be difficult to find, such as a swimming pool, laundry room, security, appropriately-sized rooms.	Moderate
House	You rent a two-room bungalow and have the run of the place, including basement, attic, driveway, and yard.	Can be scarce. Non-existent in urban areas; likely in rural areas and small towns.	Might be a shack, might be a mansion. Runs the full gamut of single-family homes, though luxury rental homes are not common in most areas.	Moderate to expensive
Living with a Family	A single person pays rent to a family and becomes a "member" of that family.	Hard to gauge; many families have barely enough room for themselves, much	Same as the family possesses. Depending on the situation, the boarder's "space" may be anything from his own	Cheap

continues on page after next

Advantages	Disadvantages
1. Property is purpose-built. 2. Tenants get privacy. 3. Variety of leases available. 4. Building superintendent or land-lord is (or should be) prepared to help tenants with maintenance matters.	1. Often located in high-density urban areas. 2. Leases may be restrictive. 3. Upkeep of building may be poor, and out of the control of tenant.
1. Often available in good, established neighborhoods. 2. May get more square footage for the money than with a conventional apartment. 3. House may possess pleasing archi-tectural features. 4. Opportunity for camaraderie with other tenants and neighbors (Mary and Phyllis and Rhoda, remember?). 5. Property owner may live on prem-ises, which almost always insures proper maintenance.	1. May be located in deteriorating neighborhood. 2. Rental units are often oddly-shaped and sized due to conversion. 3. Integrity of the building—not to mention stability of the structure—may have been sacrificed in the con-version. 4. Resident-landlord may infringe on privacy.
1. High degree of privacy. 2. Simulates satisfaction of home ownership. 3. Generally provides greater space and flexibility, especially with access to greenspace. 4. Renter is perceived as a member of the neighborhood; opportunities for neighborhood involvement.	1. Renter may be expected to do rou-tine maintenance and repairs, includ-ing lawn care. 2. Cost may force renter to have sev-eral roommates. 3. Utilities are often high. 4. Owner may be renting until he finds a buyer for the house, making the renter's situation tenuous.
1. Renter is accepted into the bosom of the family; a good hedge against loneliness and isolation.	1. The family may have tensions that are bothersome to the nonfamily boarder.

continues on page after next

HOUSING OPTIONS (Continued)

Option	Example	Availability	Range of Amenities	Price
Living with a Family (Continued)		less a "boarder." In some towns this is common practice, though.	room only to the use of a basement and full run of the house.	
Co-op or Commune	A group of people who are friends or who share some other affiliation (agriculture students at a university, for example) pool resources and live together in a big house or apartment building.	A few co-ops and communes are already in existence and will take new members; interested people can form their own. This arrangement was very popular after World War II, and again in the '60s and '70s.	Entirely depends on the resources and wishes of the members. Can be rural or urban, bare-bone or extravagant.	Cheap to expensive
Room and Board in Exchange for Work	A young family offers a basement apartment and kitchen privileges in exchange for child care and household help.	Varies. In some areas, it's nearly unheard of; in others, live-in arrangements of this kind are highly sought after.	Those who can offer this arrangement are often wealthy, and the "help" shares the employer's standard of living to a certain extent.	Obviously, cheap. Often carries a small salary in addition to room and board.
Housesitting	A college professor taking sabbatical in England needs someone to live in her house for four and a half months.	Usually good; the biggest problem is matching absent homeowners with willing housesitters, but most people who are going to be gone from	As good as the homeowner's. Most people who seek out housesitters live in a house worth protecting, ergo: nice.	Housesitter pays nothing and usually receives nothing.

continues on page after next

Advantages	Disadvantages
2. Meals nearly always included. 3. Living arrangements are simpler, logistically. Less time, effort, and money is invested in day-to-day housing and food concerns.	2. Family may be unamicable, leaving the boarder to feel left out. 3. Food may be bad or of insufficient quantity. 4. Lacks privacy. 5. Boarder is expected to adapt to the family's schedule and lifestyle, which may be confining.
1. Group buying—or renting—power can get members a property that would otherwise be unobtainable. 2. Provides a built-in support group, often of like-minded people. 3. May be used as a means of working toward a common goal, or developing an experimental lifestyle. 4. Members can share cost and work of upkeep.	1. Co-ops and communes often go sour; the original purpose can be lost in the day-to-day hassles of living in community. 2. Privacy is often sacrificed. 3. Dissolution can be financially disadvantageous and personally devastating.
1. Good accommodations in exchange for the kind of work you did for nothing when you were living at home. 2. See "Living with a Family" above; all advantages apply.	1. Work is sometimes very demanding and can restrict freedom of movement in regard to hours away from the house, etc. 2. See "Living with a Family" above; all disadvantages apply.
1. Absolutely free living accommodations in a place much nicer than you could afford. 2. Privacy.	1. Difficult to find consecutive positions; gaps between jobs may leave one homeless. 2. Living space is not your own; can grow tiresome living in and around another person's house and chattel. 3. Housesitter may be legally liable for damage to property while it is in his care.

HOUSING OPTIONS (Continued)

Option	Example	Availability	Range of Amenities	Price
Housesitting (Continued)		nice homes for any period of time want someone to watch their property for them.		
Live-in Job	A job as a counselor at a group home requires the employee to live in the home; wrangler at a dude ranch is provided living quarters near stables; elderly man hires a live-in caregiver; motel or apartment building needs on-site manager or superintendent.	Some professions provide many opportunities (social work, counseling, recreation, youth ministry, health care, motel management, apartment management, teaching).	Limitless. Anything from a basement studio apartment in a fifty-three-unit rental building to the top bunk in a log cabin at a church camp in the Rockies.	No cost for living space; lower wages may reflect the value of accommodation.

THE TEN HEALTHIEST PLACES TO LIVE IN THE U.S.

1. Anywhere, Hawaii
2. Eugene, Oregon
3. San Francisco, California
4. St. Cloud, Minnesota
5. Austin, Texas
6. LaJunta, Colorado
7. Utica, New York
8. Kenab, Utah
9. Ketchikan, Alaska
10. Middletown, Connecticut

(From *Science Digest*. Reprinted by permission. Copyright 1977, The Hearst Corporation. All rights reserved.)

Advantages	Disadvantages
Live-in Job 1. Proximity to work place and job responsibilites. 2. Noncash compensation often escapes taxation.	1. Lack of privacy is inevitable. 2. Working so close to job can result in burnout. 3. Accommodations may be substandard.

"Nothing makes you more tolerant of a neighbor's noisy party than being there."
Franklin P. Jones

11.

AND THE SEARCH IS ON

In some areas finding an apartment is harder than finding a husband or wife. Manhattan comes to mind: prices are exorbitant, and availability is extremely limited. A person who is known to be vacating an apartment will be deluged by friends and acquaintances who wish to take over after that person has moved out. The occupancy rate is almost 100 percent on decent rental property. A similar problem may exist in very small towns. If the population is stable, the housing market may not be able to accommodate you—the new field representative or special education teacher—who wants a modest apartment or house to call home. Everything's taken. And boom cities, like Austin, Phoenix, Dallas, and Atlanta, may experience periodic housing shortages as developers struggle to stay on top of housing needs.

In cities with depressed economies, exceptional housing may be available for modest prices. Detroit and its outlying suburbs are an example. Because of slowdowns in the auto industry, many auto workers have left the area. This caused a glut of houses on the market. Consequently, many people who want to sell their homes are very happy just to rent them, often giving the tenant a beautiful home for the price of a modest apartment.

The majority of renters though, are faced with a rental housing market that offers a variety of possibilities at a variety of prices. Bargains may be found in such a market; a property owner who is more interested in a responsible tenant than a windfall profit may lease a unit at a very favorable rate. Another landlord whose property is located in a desirable area might rent dilapidated apartments to a needy public at preposterous rates—which are paid.

Here are possible resources for finding a place to live:

Classified advertisements. These may be in the local newspaper (Sunday edition will have the most), real estate tabloid, or neighborhood advertiser.

Bulletin board notices. Check grocery stores, student unions, laundromats, etc.

Real estate agents. An agent will often charge a fee equal to one month's rent for finding an apartment for you. Since you get help deciphering the lease, and valuable information about the neighborhood and landlord from a knowledgable professional, an agent's fee is often money well-spent.

Word of mouth. If an acquaintance lives in a building and is happy with the size and price of the apartment, the maintenance of the building, the landlord and the superintendent, it would be well worth your while to get an apartment in that building, or to rent from that landlord. Friends also have friends who have friends who are going to move out of a great little duplex on Tenth Street, and if you can get to the property before the landlord has to advertise it—which costs money and may necessitate a vacancy of the property—you might even get a break on the rent, in addition to getting a nice home.

Drive-bys. In perusing your desired neighborhood, you should look for "For Rent" signs, or buildings that appeal to you. If you have your heart set on a certain property, call the landlord and let him/her know that you are interested. Even if it's currently occupied, you may ask to be advised of vacancies as they occur.

The Premises

Having found a vacant apartment, you may be tempted to do a cursory tour of the unit and sign a lease right away. This would be a big mistake. Since you're going to be living there for a year or more, you should perform a careful site inspection of the property.

In large apartment complexes, the management often maintains a couple of "model" apartments that they show to prospective renters. Not wishing to disturb their tenants, and faced with scores of people each day who want to see what the apartments look like, they have furnished an apartment or two that are allegedly representative of the other apartments.

My own experience has been that these model apartments are decorated to the max, are filled with expensive furniture, and give a generally false impression of what you are being asked to rent. There will be a mirrored wall in the living room to make it look bigger; a dinky bed in the "large master bedroom suite" surrounded by built-in bookshelves; fancy wallpaper in the kitchen, and a microwave oven on the counter; nonstandard Tiffany-style light fixtures; a big-screen television . . . it seems that there is no limit to what will be done to make the apartment look like it's the answer to your dreams.

Enjoy looking through the model apartment. But before you sign anything, insist on looking at the unit that *you* will be renting. The model faces onto a courtyard; your unit has a view of the K-Mart parking lot. The model has plush beige carpeting; yours has matted-down olive drab shag. The model has miniblinds and pleated valances on all windows; yours doesn't even have curtain rods.

There is no substitute for seeing the actual unit that you propose to rent. Once inside it, check the following:

(1) Adequate lighting. Are there overhead fixtures in all the rooms, or will you need to provide your own lamps?

(2) Security. Is there a security guard? Security locks with intercoms? A deadbolt lock on your door? Locking windows?

(3) Windows. Are they airtight? Are they letting in drafts? Are they equipped with storm windows and good screens?

(4) Check for signs of water damage on the walls, floors, and ceilings.

(5) Kitchen appliances. Are they clean and in good working order? Does the refrigerator shake, rattle, and roll? The kitchen should have an exhaust fan in most cases. How about electrical outlets—are they sufficient?

(6) If there is a fireplace, ask if it works. Smoke stains on the wall over the fireplace are a very bad sign. Don't pay for it if you won't be able to use it.

(7) Phone jacks. There should be enough for your needs. You

will have to pay to have them installed or install them yourself if there aren't.

(8) Is there a television antenna? Are you wired for cable? Can you get a good picture on your TV if you decide *not* to have cable?

(9) Look out the window(s) and decide if you like the view. Is there adequate daylight?

(10) Check to see if you can control your own heat and air conditioning, especially if you are paying your own utilities. Same thing for hot water.

(11) Are window treatments included?

(12) Fire safety. Look for fire extinguishers, fire escapes, and obvious fire hazards.

(13) Open drawers and bottom cupboards in the kitchen and check for evidence of mice and bugs.

(14) What additional storage is available? Bins in the basement? Use of the attic or garage?

(15) Where is the mail delivered? Is it a secure situation? Do the mailboxes lock, or is your mail set out for all the neighbors (and possibly thieves) to see?

(16) Turn on every faucet and flush every toilet to check for leaks and adequate water pressure. Run the hot tap; how long does it take for the water to get good and hot?

(17) When was the last time the unit was painted? Will the landlord paint before you move in? Clean the carpets? Wash the windows?

If it's possible to do so, find the opportunity to visit with one of your prospective neighbors, without the owner or building manager present. "Hello, I'm Alice Lawhead. I'm thinking of renting the unit next door. Can I ask you a few questions about what it's like to live here?" Ask about the landlord or building superintendent. Are repairs made quickly? Is maintenance good? Have there been any thefts, burglaries, or assaults in the building? Fires?

I once lived in a lovely apartment in a beautifully landscaped apartment complex for which I paid a handsome rent. In the three years I lived there the fire alarm in our building went off about twelve times; twice there actually was a fire, complete with firefighters, axes, hoses, and water in the hallway. A woman was raped in the laundry room on my floor. The locked storage bin provided by the management was broken into and all my sporting equipment was stolen. Obviously, there is no direct correlation between the appearance of a place and the reality of living there.

Special Concerns

You may have special concerns about your housing. If you are disabled, or have disabled friends who will visit you, you must check for barrier-free design and accessibility. Is the landlord amenable to a ramp in the back? (You'll have to pay for it, of course.) Can you install a trapeze over your bed? Are the elevators reliable? If they are your only access to your apartment, they must be foolproof. Any necessary alteration of the unit must be discussed in detail with your landlord.

Some apartments bar children. That's fine, you don't have children. But do you have nieces and nephews, or a younger brother or sister, or a Y-Pal who would visit? Even visits by these youngsters may be barred, especially if you contemplate an overnighter. And what if you and your spouse decide to start a family? Believe it or not, your bundle of joy may be grounds for eviction at a time when you really don't need the hassles of moving.

Pets are another problem. Ask about them if you own or anticipate getting a pet. Don't think you can hide your Doberman, parakeet, or hamster from your landlord or neighbors. If it's a no-pet situation, make sure that you ask about your goldfish, too.

A bike can be a special concern. Is there garage space for it? Can you keep it in the hallway? Many landlords and other tenants will object to having your bike chained to the staircase. If you have a porch or patio or balcony, that may be acceptable, but you should check first.

Think about your furniture and how it will fit into the rooms. The ceilings in some apartments will not accommodate large antique secretaries and cabinets and bookcases. If you have a conversation pit living room suite or a king-sized waterbed with overhanging padded rails and bookcase headboard, it could possibly be larger than the room it's intended to furnish. The same goes for a full-sized car or passenger van. If you're paying extra for use of a garage, make sure you can get your wheels inside it.

Speaking of waterbeds, make sure they're allowed. If your landlord balks (although he shouldn't—waterbeds have gained respectability), go to a waterbed store and ask them for information about the weight and safety of waterbeds. Most likely they will be glad to arm you with the information you need to answer your landlord's objections; they have to do it all the time.

The time to discuss special needs or potentially problematic situations is before you sign a lease. If you hide something from your landlord that is prohibited and which later causes damage to the property or problems with other tenants, you could be liable for a lot in the way of repairs or punitive damages.

ENTRY FROM "THE DIARY OF A NEW YORK APARTMENT HUNTER"

Saturday:

Uptown to look at co-op in venerable midtown building. Met real estate broker in lobby. A Caucasian version of Tokyo Rose. She immediately launched into a description of all the respectably employed people who were waiting in line for this apartment. Showed me living room first. Large, airy terrific view of a well-known discount drugstore. Two bedrooms, sure enough. Kitchen, sort of. When I asked why the present occupant had seen fit to cut three five-foot-high arches out of the inside wall of the master bedroom, she muttered something about cross ventilation. When I pointed out that there were no windows on the opposite wall, she ostentatiously extracted a sheaf of papers from her briefcase and studied them closely. Presumably these contained the names of all the Supreme Court Justices who were waiting for this apartment. Nevertheless I pressed on and asked her what one might do with three five-foot-high arches in one's bedroom wall. She suggested stained glass. I suggested pews in the living room and services every Sunday. She showed me a room she referred to as the master bath. I asked her where the slaves bathed. She rustled her papers ominously and showed me the living room again. I looked disgruntled. She brightened and showed me something called a fun bathroom. It had been covered in fabric from floor to ceiling by someone who obviously was not afraid to mix patterns. I informed her unceremoniously that

I never again wanted to be shown a fun bathroom. I don't want to have fun in the bathroom; I just want to bathe my slaves.

She showed me the living room again. Either she just couldn't get enough of that discount drugstore or she was trying to trick me into thinking there were three living rooms. Impudently I asked her where one ate, seeing as I had not been shown a dining room and the kitchen was approximately the size of a brandy snifter.

"Well," she said, "some people use the second bedroom as a dining room." I replied that I needed the second bedroom to write in. This was a mistake because it reminded her of all the ambassadors to the U.N. on her list of prospective tenants.

"Well," she said, "the master bedroom is rather large."

"Listen," I said, "I already eat on my bed. In a one-room rent-controlled slum apartment, I'll eat on the bed. In an ornately priced, high maintenance co-op, I want to eat at a table. Call me silly, call me foolish, but that's the kind of girl I am." She escorted me out of the apartment and left me standing in the lobby as she hurried off—anxious, no doubt, to call Cardinal Cooke and tell him okay, the apartment was his.

(From *Social Studies* by Fran Lebowitz.)

"*K-e-e-l* de Lan-lor"

Killing the landlord won't get you nearly as far as nuzzling up to him. Some of these guys are genuinely beyond hope: slumlords who buy up rental property, extract the highest possible rent, refuse to make necessary repairs and needed improvements, ignore tenant concerns, threaten and terrorize their renters, and sell the building at the first opportunity, for a tremendous profit.

The only way to deal with these bozos is to fight. Rent strikes, reporting code violations, and legal action may all be appropriate in dealing with blood-sucking landlords. If you are involved in dealing with an unscrupulous owner or manager, call the American Civil Liberties Union or your own lawyer and get tough.

Talk to your landlord before you get too serious about signing a lease. Sometimes the landlord doesn't manage the property; that is left to a management company or a building superintendent. The owner may be a real estate syndicate or large corporation. You should, at the very least, find out who owns the property. If you have problems in the future, you're going to need to know who is ultimately responsible, or else you'll get a big runaround. Know who owns, who manages, who supervises, who handles rent collections, and who will be fielding your complaints.

In the case of a resident landlord, or a landlord who takes particular pride in his property, you are wise to make a good impression right from the start. Wear a shirt. Really: think what it would be like to hold property worth thousands of dollars, and then have a bunch of strangers living in it—strangers who might abuse it, neglect it, even destroy it. If you can present yourself as a person who cares for the property, you will put yourself in position to get extra-good service from your landlord. You may even be able to negotiate a lower rent.

Let the landlord know what you like about the property as well as what is troubling you. "I like the fact that I'm in the back of the building, because that reduces the noise level from the street. But the view onto the alley isn't great." Or, "That self-cleaning oven will be a timesaver, I suppose, but those jobs really suck up electricity." Or, "The carpet is in good shape, but the color is going to make my furniture look terrible." The landlord may be able to suggest alternatives; a different unit, a break on the utilities, or some other redress.

Once you have inspected the property, make a list of everything that is wrong with it. Everything. The purpose of your list is twofold: it will advise your landlord of repairs that need to be made, and it will protect you when you move out. You shouldn't have to move into a rental unit with dirty carpets, dirty, smudged, or chipped paint, dilapidated stairs, peeling wallpaper, broken appliances, falling bathroom tile, or other major defects. By noting these on your list, your landlord will be advised that you expect repairs before signing a lease.

Some problems with the apartment will *not* be fixed by your landlord. He just won't do it. But even if you can't get him to fix it, you can make darn sure that you don't get charged for it when you move out. For example, maybe the broiler pan is a mess—

baked-on food, chips in the enamel, whatever. Your landlord won't fix it. Fine. You can live with it. But you cannot live with the possibility that when it comes time to move out, you will have the cost of a new broiler pan charged against you and deducted from your security/damage deposit.

So make a list of everything that is wrong. Try to get broken things fixed before you move in. If you can't get them fixed, have the landlord sign the list, acknowledging the conditions. Keep it for yourself so that when it comes time to leave you can defend yourself against any false accusations.

Normal wear-and-tear on the apartment is a part of what you're paying for. You should not be made to account for the natural and inevitable depreciation on the apartment or its furnishings. Nothing lasts forever. In this sense, the apartment will not be left by you exactly as you found it. It will be older, and it will be more worn.

A MANUAL: TRAINING FOR LANDLORDS

Lesson Four: Heat

The arrival of winter seems invariably to infect the tenant with an almost fanatical lust for warmth. Sweaters and socks he may have galore; yet he refuses to perceive their usefulness and stubbornly and selfishly insists upon obtaining his warmth through your heat. There are any number of ploys available to the resourceful landlord, but the most effective requires an actual cash outlay. No mind, it's well worth it—fun, too. Purchase a tape recorder. Bring the tape recorder to your suburban home and place it in the vicinity of your heater. Here its sensitive mechanism will pick up the sounds of impending warmth. This recording played at high volume in the basement of the building has been known to stymie tenants for days on end.

(From *Metropolitan Life* by Fran Lebowitz.)

Make every effort to present yourself as a responsible, desirable tenant in your landlord's estimation. You may be required to furnish references. This is a good sign, because it indicates that the owner takes pride in his property and cares about who inhabits it. Welcome the opportunity to impress the landlord with your better qualities.

But don't get soft when it comes to protecting your own rights. Your landlord will be making a profit off your rent. You are a customer; you have rights as well as responsibilities. Your monthly rent is probably your biggest expense; your home is important. Stand up for yourself when dealing with your landlord.

Lease

The rubber meets the road when it comes time to sign the lease. You've found an apartment, you're pleased with the neighborhood, the landlord (or property manager or building superintendent) seems like a responsible person, and you're ready to commit yourself.

A lease is a formal, legal commitment between the property owner and you, the renter. Such a commitment should always be in writing. Never move into an apartment without a written agreement. It might be a handwritten document that spells out a few specifics, it might be a lease form that your landlord picked up at the stationery store for a few cents, or it might be a complex document that goes into explicit detail on every conceivable point. But it must be written—always.

"A verbal contract isn't worth the paper it's written on."
Samuel Goldwyn

Your landlord will present you with a lease. Read it! Take it home with you and go over every word of it. If you have a friend with a lot of experience with contracts (say, a lawyer or real estate broker) ask for help understanding what you'll be asked to sign. Flag every item that you question or wish to delete. Then make a list of anything that should be added, especially verbal agreements between you and your landlord. ("Sure, pets are no problem!" and "I'll paint all the rooms before you move in if you like.") Obviously, this takes more time and thought than you can give it while your potential landlord is looking over your shoulder and waiting for you to sign your name. Make sure that you don't get pressured. Take it home and work with it there. If you have questions that you believe warrant it, talk to a lawyer.

The unavoidable disadvantage to you is that the lease always originates with the property owner. Consequently, it protects the owner to the hilt, and gives the renter only a few rights. There's no way around this; it's the way leases are. The best you can do is to make sure you understand what you are signing, and ask for the deletions and additions to the lease that will make it workable for you.

Then take the lease back to your landlord. If there are portions of it that don't apply to you, or that have been superseded by a verbal agreement between the two of you, make sure the lease reflects that. Delete incorrect and inapplicable paragraphs and add verbiage that reflects your agreed-upon conditions. Each party to the contract (you and your landlord) must initial the change.

A lease will contain the following:

- the date that you'll be moving in, and how long you will be staying.

- a description (usually the address) of the property you are renting.

- the amount of rent you'll be paying, when it's due, and in what form it is to be paid.

- the amount of security deposit, what it is meant to cover, and under what circumstances it will be repaid or forfeited.

- clarification as to who pays for utilities, repairs, decorating, etc.

- a provision for renewing the lease, and for raising the rent.

Added to the above may be instructions about decorating, alterations, subleasing, pets, roommates, insurance liability, etc.

Beware of leases that: give your landlord unlimited access to your apartment when prospective renters or buyers wish to view

it; don't protect you from capricious evictions; release your landlord from any responsibility for injuries or damages that befall
you while on the property (called "waiver of tort liability"
clauses); let your landlord cancel your lease if the house or apartment building is sold; make you liable for property taxes; do not
stipulate a means by which the lease can be broken. These are
leases that can make it dangerous to live in the apartment.

---

*"The minute you read something you can't understand,
you can almost be sure it was drawn up by a lawyer."
Will Rogers*

The lease may be an impressive document, and you may feel
in awe of its legalese, but that's no excuse for failing to read and
understand what you are signing. The point is that if everything
goes well, no one will ever look at the lease again. You'll stay as
long as you like, move out when you please, and both you and the
landlord will have been glad to do business together. But if the
landlord decides that she wants you out, that lease you signed will
become The Law of the Medes and the Persians and there won't
be a thing you can do about it. Your landlord will be perfectly
within her rights to cite chapter and verse of some obscure condition of the lease and have it her way—even if she's been overlook-
ing that obscure condition for the past eight months.

Your lease will never really reflect your rights as a tenant.
That's too bad. But at least you can avoid giving your landlord
the equivalent of a loaded rifle with which you can be shot at any
moment. Do the best you can with your lease. Protect yourself
from unfair responsibility. Retain your rights to legal action.

12.

MOVING

If you're lucky, you're a highly sought-after Harvard Business School graduate who is accepting a position with Hewlett-Packard at a starting salary of $42,000—and they're going to move you to the district office. If you're average, you're going to borrow a friend's pickup truck, toss your few earthly possessions into some battered Miracle Whip boxes, and transport yourself to a little one-bedroom place on the other side of town.

Both kinds of move, different as they may seem, are essentially the same. They involve making decisions about what will be moved and what will not; they require work and planning; they are traumatic; they necessitate a myriad of change-of-address notices and updated identifications; they raise questions about decorating, settling into a new neighborhood, and acclimating to a different environment.*

The Company Move

Knowing that your moving and relocation costs will be paid by your employer goes a long way toward making moving less horrible. Obviously, you get such a move only if you're being hired for

---

*A recommended book on this subject is *Do-It-Yourself Moving* by George Sullivan, which—interestingly enough—covers professional moves as well. Publishing information in the Bibliography.

or transferred to a job that's beyond normal commuting distance from where you currently live (usually considered to be fifty miles in an urban area). In such a case, your employer can be expected to pay for a professional move, including packing and unpacking, boxes, the full cost of transporting and, if necessary, storing your household furnishings. Be fair: they're not going to be thrilled to move a cord of wood, old scrap lumber, or the cinder blocks supporting your waterbed (old bricks that are an integral part of your rustic-look bookshelves are okay, though).

Beyond that, company policies vary. They may pay for your personal transportation to the new locale; living expenses that you incur while your goods are in transit; househunting expense (which includes a premoving trip to the new town to line up accommodations); help selling your old house and buying a new one (if that's an option); a "settling-in" allowance to cover the cost of installing utilities, telephone lines, new drapes, etc.; professional cleaning of the old and new places; extra charges for shipping pets, plants, and bulky hobby equipment (your twenty-two-foot sailboat); the cost of breaking your lease; and extra insurance for your possessions.

Obviously, it's great to be moved by your company. But don't count on making money on the deal. It will nearly always cost you quite a bit out-of-pocket, no matter how liberal the company reimbursement policy is.

It probably doesn't need saying, but I'll say it anyway: if your company is moving you, you can impress your boss by appearing to approach the whole thing with an eye for thrift, but you'd be crazy to overdo it. If they say a professional move is okay, don't go volunteering to rent a U-Haul. If packing and unpacking are included, don't pass it up. It's all their way of saying that they like having you on board. Don't deny them their expression of affection.

However, unscrupulous professional movers (of which there are many) know a yahoo when they see one. Pay attention to what the packers do; in no case should you leave a packer unattended in your apartment. They'll carefully wrap and fastidiously box full garbage cans, plates with moldy watermelon rinds on them, used styrofoam cups. This is ridiculous, and you'll feel ridiculous for putting up with it.

When you've made an appointment for the mover to come, tell the agent that you wish to be present when the truck is weighed. A time will be set when you can meet the van foreman and the truck that he'll be using at a certified weigh station. Watch what happens. The truck should be weighed as-is (usually someone else's stuff will already be aboard), with the driver in the truck along with all the dollies, moving pads, and other paraphernalia that they'll be using for your move. After your belongings are packed up, then go to the weigh station again, and supervise *that* weighing. If you didn't know it yet, your move is being charged according to weight. They'll figure it by taking the difference between the truck before loading and then after loading. During this second weigh, make sure they don't have a bunch of husky mover types sitting on the front end or hiding in the van. This is called "weight-bumping." They're going to bump the weight up and charge more than they should. But not with you, they aren't. You weren't born yesterday. You know what's what.

It would be hard to overstress the importance of supervising your move. Be there when the movers are packing, weighing, loading, unloading, and unpacking. Professional movers employ a lot of amateurs—college kids working on summer jobs, ex-cons who need work, short-term labor of all kinds. Don't assume that they know anything about *anything*. Where your belongings are concerned, *you're* the boss.

An Adventure in Moving

You're tooling down the highway in your self-rent truck. You feel pretty good. You've packed your own goods, loaded them in this dandy stick-shift truck, and now you're on your way to the land of milk and honey. What's that ahead? A bridge? No sweat. Oh, oh, there's a sign. *Low Clearance. 14'8"*. How high is this truck? Darn! Where's the book? The book? You reach over to open the glove compartment, at the same time down-shifting and applying light pressure to the brake. Wow, this incline is steeper than it looks. The bridge approaches. Your hand is so sweaty you can hardly keep it on the wheel. WHERE DOES IT GIVE THE HEIGHT OF THIS MONSTER?!? Oh well, here goes . . . You're through the bridge, you didn't feel anything, no drag while going under it. Disaster averted. Hey, this is fun!

When you're moving yourself you want to keep things as simple as possible. Start by divesting yourself of as many of your material possessions as you can possibly bear. Everything that you can't throw away, give away, or sell will have to be packed, loaded, transported, unloaded, unpacked, and baby-sat during the course of the move.

If you can pare down, you will save money by renting a smaller truck—or not renting a truck at all, getting by with a station wagon or pickup. Look at that piece of junk, now. When was the last time you used/wore it? Seriously? If it's been longer than a year, you probably don't need it. Maybe you use it here, but will you use it there? Do you know someone who needs it more than you do? Is the color all wrong for the new place? Would it sell well? Would it ship poorly? These are all questions to ask yourself as you contemplate moving your belongings.

If you have a lot of stuff to get rid of, you can have a garage sale, or call a junk dealer who might offer to haul the whole mess away for a sum. Or you can invite your friends to make an offer on a few of your better treasures. This is often a good approach, since you know what your friends like, and what they've been coveting of yours. Sell it to them, or give it to them. Either way, you'll be dollars ahead, since you'll save the cost of moving it.

Then call Goodwill or the Salvation Army or Disabled American Veterans or some other thrift organization and ask for a pickup of what's left. Yes, they'll pick them up. They won't? Call someone else.

Good. Now you're down to the important things in your life. Since you've gotten rid of all superfluous items, we'll proceed with the assumption that what you're moving is worth moving well, and that you want to take all reasonable precautions when packing, loading, and transporting.

First step: commence your search for boxes. Boxes are vitally important to a good move, but tremendously difficult to find in sufficient quantity when the time comes to pack and go. Try these sources:

(1) Liquor stores. Liquor boxes are of a manageable size and very sturdy. Supermarkets have good boxes, too, but most stores won't save them for you. They flatten them in big machines, bundle them up and sell them to scavenger services. Liquor stores are the place to go.

(2) Friends who have recently moved. You must get to your friends before they have begun to unpack, since used boxes are generally discarded as soon as they are empty.

(3) Your employer. Ask the janitor to keep an eye open for

suitable boxes. The boxes that photocopier paper comes in are good.

(4) A commercial mover. This is a last resort. They're nice boxes, but expensive. You needn't be a moving customer to buy boxes—Joe's Transworld Movers will make a profit either way.

Begin your box search as soon as you know you're moving. Carry a utility knife with you at all times so that you are prepared to seize promising containers, flatten them, and transport them to your home. Be eternally vigilant.

Once you've got your boxes, you're ready to pack: second step. This can begin weeks, even months, before the actual move. Out-of-season clothes, most of your books, seldom-used kitchen furnishings, old records, and your junior high school files can all be packed up well in advance.

Get good strong strapping or cellophane packaging tape and reconstitute your flattened boxes with that, making them as strong as possible. Don't skimp on the tape, or you'll regret it. Wrap breakable items in crumpled newspaper. Use soft towels, blankets, throw pillows, and clothing to cushion items that might get crushed. Fill boxes to the top so they don't get scrunched down in loading. Seal them well with your tape, and mark the top of the box with contents and what room it should be placed in. Examples: "Bedding, Green Bedroom," "Bakeware, Kitchen," "Medicines, Bathroom," "Lampshades, Living Room." If it's fragile, mark it as such.

Keep a few boxes open and designate these as "Pack Last, Open First" boxes. They will contain a few eating and cooking utensils, bedding and towels, clothes, and toilet articles that you need right up until you leave and immediately when you arrive.

Recruiting Help

The most important component in moving is friends who will help you. You need willing hands and strong backs when it comes to loading boxes and vacuuming the rugs.

Plan to do the packing yourself. I have never in my life had a friend close enough to help me do my own packing. There are too many decisions to be made and too many personal effects to be dealt with. Do your own packing at your own pace. A box or six every day will have the job done in no time. Don't involve your friends in this highly personal task unless you're willing to lose them.

This is what friends are good for:

(1) Loading boxes into a truck.
(2) Driving said truck.
(3) Unloading boxes at the new place.
(4) Cleaning out the old apartment.
(5) Painting the new apartment.
(6) Running out to the liquor store for more boxes.
(7) Throwing a *bon voyage* party for you the night before you depart.
(8) Eating pizza and drinking Cokes the day of the move.
(9) Hanging around the house waiting for the guy from Sears to come and connect the stove.

Recruiting helpful friends is a problem. Few people are willing to spend a hot, sweaty Saturday exerting themselves for someone they don't like a lot. So only solicit the help of your best friends. Call in all your markers. If you have to, remind them of the time that you lent them your twenty-foot ladder, or helped them paint their kitchen, or took care of their dog while they were in Dallas. Come on, think back! Surely you did one small favor that can be repaid in this, your time of need!

Let your recruits know when the big event will be. Get specific: "1800 South Lake, Saturday, October 7. 8:00 A.M. sharp. Be there. Aloha." If the people you need most think that they might not be able to make it, give serious thought to changing your moving date. Let the strongest person you know suggest a date of his/her own! The statistics run like this: 47 percent of the people you ask to help will actually show up; of these, 60 percent will leave three hours before the job is done. You take it from there and decide what kind of commitments you want before you begin loading.

Treat your help as you would like to be treated. Have a refrigerator full of cold drinks, a freezer full of ice, the phone number of Domino's Pizza ready, and money to pay for all the food. No one's going to show up if you tell them to bring five dollars for eats. You may think that feeding this crew will be expensive, but you can't afford not to.

MOVING CHECKLIST

ONE MONTH BEFORE THE MOVE:

- break the news to your family and friends—you're moving
- start collecting boxes
- sell, give away, or throw away all items you would rather not move
- get change-of-address kit from post office; notify all correspondents, periodicals, and junk mail clearing houses of your new address
- call all your doctors and ask what their procedure is for transferring your medical records to your new physician (for out-of-town moves)
- begin eating up the food in your pantry and refrigerator
- approach friends with their opportunity for service (i.e., heavy lifting the day of the move)
- call truck rental agencies and get rates for comparison; reserve a vehicle

TWO WEEKS BEFORE THE MOVE:

- contact utilities and telephone company; arrange to have current service disconnected and new service hooked up
- stock up on any medications you take regularly now so you won't have to worry about it while in transition
- get a firm commitment from your friends who will help you move

ONE WEEK BEFORE THE MOVE:

- start packing in earnest
- call your new landlord and confirm that your new quarters are now or will soon be vacated and ready for your arrival
- arrange with your current landlord to inspect the premises for check-out on moving day
- accept all dinner invitations; you've got no time to cook

THREE DAYS BEFORE THE MOVE:

- packing should be almost all done, with the exception of "Pack Last, Open First" boxes
- stock up on food and drink for helpers
- if it's an in-town move, inspect your new place and make sure it's ready for you. Raise a ruckus if it's not
- do the major cleaning of your stove, oven, refrigerator, cupboards, and closets

THE DAY BEFORE THE MOVE:

- all packing should be complete
- call your friends–remind them of tomorrow's adventure
- pick up your truck from the rental agency—or friend
- wrap blankets or other padding around furniture that might be scratched or dented in the move
- go to a movie, play some Putt-Putt, try to relax

Don't work them too hard. At appropriate moments, it may be in your interest to say something like, "Hey, Dick, don't lift that heavy thing—I'll do it!" or "You guys are terrific, but you're working too hard. Let's take a break." Spend at least as much time doing the grunt work as you do supervising. Troop morale is your responsibility; don't let it wane. The last thing you need is a mutiny while en route to your new abode.

Arrival

Having made the best of preparations, moving day went like a charm. Of course it did! Plenty of cold drinks, deli sandwiches for lunch, a sumptuous pizza with everything for those who stayed on into the evening. All the boxes that were once sitting in the living room of your old place are now sitting in the living room of your new place. It's Sunday morning. You ache, you wish you didn't have so much unpacking to do, you'd like to find your speaker wire so you can hook up your stereo and have some music. But all in all, it went pretty well.

Approach the business of unpacking and settling in at your own pace. Some people like to tackle it like a full-time job until every box is empty, every picture is hung, and every cup is sitting quietly in the shelf-papered kitchen cabinet where it belongs. Others drag out the unpacking over a long period of time. This has obvious merits, since if you delay long enough your lease will be up and you'll be moving to another apartment before all the boxes are unpacked—a terrific timesaver in the long run.

Aside from getting clothes in the closet and books on the shelf, there are a number of other necessary tasks to be taken care of before you can consider yourself *really* moved in. Depending on whether your move was intra-city or inter-state, you will do one or more of the following:

Utility hookups. "So that's why the refrigerator isn't getting cool," you lament. Yes, you need to check with the utilities in the area and make sure everything is copacetic. It is possible that you will have electricity and gas when you get to your new place, but be prepared for a 12:00 midnight shut-off on the night you get there unless you've made arrangements. Call the utility companies—electric and gas, water and sewer—and make sure you've got an understanding. (More about utilities later.)

Telephone hookups. In some areas it can take a week or more to get a phone hookup, especially since you have to agree on a time when you (or a friend or neighbor) can be there to greet the serviceperson who will activate your service. When you call the phone company, be prepared to tell them if you will be using your own equipment or renting from them, how many lines you want, and what kind of a calling package you'll be buying (more about telephones later, too). Until you get all this worked out, plan on keeping a pocketful of dimes for pay phones.

Mail delivery. It's a good idea to call the local post office, just to say, "Hi, guys. It's me, Richard Longton. I'm going to be staying here at 123 Easy Street for the next year or so." Although the post office is prepared to take the initiative and deliver your mail without a formal introduction, it's important to do it anyway. Make sure that the previous occupant of your place is having their mail forwarded to *their* new address. You have already, of course, made similar arrangements for your mail. Tell the P.O. clerk if you have any aliases—like "Bubba Longton," "Richie Longton," or "Occupant." They would also like the names of others at your address who will be getting mail—family members, roommates, etc.—and if business mail will come to your home: R.L. Enterprises, Inc. If you have a spouse with a surname different from your own, let 'em know.

Refuse service. Trash pickup arrangements may be made for you already by your landlord; in some cases, it's your responsibility. It may be a service of the local city or county government, or the domain of private contractors. In the case of the latter, the city is usually divided up and each area is serviced by a different contractor. Ask your landlord or neighbor how it's handled.

Driver's license. If you are living in the same state as before, you should go to the licensing station and have a new license issued that reflects your current address. Not to worry; you won't have to take a driving test or anything. It's simply a clerical function to have the important data updated. It will cost a few bucks in most cases, and should be done within thirty days of moving.

If you're in a different state, you may be required to take the written test and do a driving test for that state. Before you go out and stand in line for an hour and a half, call and make sure you understand what you'll need and what you'll have to do when you get there.

Auto registration. In most cases, you don't need to worry about this if you're living in the same state as before. If you're in a different state now, it must be changed, usually within thirty days of taking residence. People are sometimes hesitant to get their license plates changed, especially when the current plates won't expire for several months. But don't worry. You'll get a refund for the unused time on your old plates when you get your new ones.

Voter registration. This is a simple matter that takes only a few minutes—and every good citizen should be registered to vote. Look in the phone book to find out where you can have this matter taken care of—usually at the city offices building or county courthouse. Regulations vary from place to place, but in most cases you must be registered to vote thirty days prior to any election. Remember that this includes primary elections, local referendums, bond issues, etc.

Library card. To get your card, show up at the local library with identification that includes proof of address. Sometimes, just a letter addressed to you will suffice. Libraries frown on nonresident patrons; some will charge outrageous fees to out-of-towners who wish to borrow books.

Check-cashing cards. Now that you have a wallet full of current identifications (driver's license, voter registration card, etc.) you can begin the process of obtaining check-cashing cards. If you have always lived in a small town or city you don't even know what I'm talking about. You can write a check at the A & P, the Esso Station, or the McDonald's and no one asks for anything more than your signature on the bottom line. But most grocery chains in urban areas now require that patrons be in possession of a check-cashing card, issued by the store, in order to pay for merchandise with a check, or have a personal check cashed.

You should have cards at all the stores you will patronize frequently, but don't get overloaded; it's a waste of time and energy to apply for more than you could ever use. Two or three wouldn't be too many. When you apply at the customer service window, be prepared to show accurate identification (which you now have), a bank reference (more about choosing a bank on pages 245 to 247), and a business and/or personal reference.

Optional: store credit. You may wish to establish charge accounts at one or more local stores; it depends on you. I have charging privileges at a florist I use occasionally, the biggest downtown department store, a pharmacy that delivers, and an office supply store.

In some cases, obtaining credit is as easy as saying, "Could you bill me for that? Here's my address . . ." Other stores will require you to complete a credit form that looks like a mortgage application. There's a lot more about getting, using, and keeping credit on pages 251 to 261.

The sooner you can get all these things taken care of, the sooner you'll feel like a real member of your community. If you put it off, you'll just inconvenience yourself. Get everything as current as you can as soon as you can.

13.

HOOKUPS

You were promised more on the thrilling subject of utilities, so here we go:

The logistics of obtaining and using public utilities vary from locality to locality. Even the utilities available may differ: some buildings and housing developments are all electric; in rural areas it is not uncommon to heat with propane gas that is contained in tanks; some heat with oil, some with natural gas; there are homes that are entirely warmed by a wood-burning stove or solar power. A common combination is gas for heat (including water) and electricity for everything else—lights, appliances, and air conditioning.

You may be living in an apartment where all utilities are paid by the landlord. Of course, the utilities are paid by you, but their cost is included in your rent. This is a common situation where a single-family house has been converted to a multiplex residence; individual metering of the rental units in such a case is impractical. Usually, the landlord estimates the monthly utility bills for the building, and prorates it between tenants.

This is very convenient: you don't have the initial hassle of calling electric and gas companies, arranging hookups, and paying deposits; nor do you have the monthly aggravation of utility bills.

From a conservation point of view, though, you are less likely to be concerned about energy-saving practices since you don't actually see what the energy waste costs. You know that you're going to pay the same amount of rent even if you do leave the air conditioner running while you're at work.

It is also possible that you are being overcharged for your utilities. How are you to know what you're using? You generally must rely on the owner's honesty to assure that your rent isn't being unfairly loaded with imaginary costs. And unless your landlord volunteers you access to his utility bills for the last year, it's virtually impossible to know if you are being cheated or not.

The Meter Is Running

It is more common for apartment renters to pay for their own utilities. Most buildings have meters for each rental unit, and tenants are charged individually for what they use, and are billed directly by the utility company.

Before moving into a new apartment or house, call the utility service, notify them of the date you will be moving in, and ask them to set up an account for you and to commence service the day before you plan to move. In some cases you will be required to put down a deposit on your utilities, which is a nuisance. It can often be avoided if you have paid for utility service in the past (a utility in another city can provide a letter of credit) or if you can get a friend or relative to cosign for you—in which case they obligate themselves for any charges that you fail to pay. If you do pay a deposit, you are usually entitled to get it back, with interest, after you have proven that you pay your bills on time (usually a year or two).

It may be that you will be required to be present when your utilities are turned on. (I've never really understood this: if they decide to disconnect your service, they don't necessarily need you there—why when you're getting hooked up?) This is another nuisance, since it often means that you have to miss work, sitting in your empty apartment while the serviceperson is having coffee at Dunkin' Donuts. These folks are notoriously late. Or early, in which case you'll arrive for the appointment only to be greeted by a note on the door saying that they're gosh-awful sorry they missed you, please call the office to make another appointment.

Once you're plugged into the utilities, you're ready to address yourself to the task of making those bills as low as they can be. Some energy-saving measures are already second nature to you—you don't stand in front of the open refrigerator for extended periods of time trying to decide what to fix for supper; you turn off the lights when you leave a room; you make sure the windows are closed if the heat is on.

"The only means of conservation is innovation."
Peter Drucker

But the art of low utility bills is much more sophisticated than that. If you own your home, you are in nearly complete control where energy is concerned. You may choose to insulate, to install solar collectors, to put awnings on the south side, or to weatherstrip all the doors. But when you're renting, you find that the energy bills *you* pay are largely dependent on how well your landlord has addressed himself to energy costs. The hazard of paying a utilities-inclusive rent is that *you* become unconcerned about energy conservation; the danger of paying your own utilities in a rental unit is that your *landlord* loses interest.

If you are paying your own utilities, you should get this minimum cooperation from your landlord:

(1) All obvious windgaps should be repaired in the appropriate way; there should be no cold air coming in under doors, around windows, or through cracks in the walls.

(2) During the winter, windows should be fitted with storm windows; or if storm windows are out of the question, clear plastic film should be tightly taped to the inside of each window.

(3) The furnace should be serviced once a year, and filters should be changed every month. Same goes for the air-conditioner, whether it's a window unit or central system.

(4) The hot-water heater should be insulated if it is in a basement, uninsulated utility room, or crawlspace.

(5) The refrigerator should be airtight; if you notice cold air escaping from the door, your landlord should fix it.

(6) If you have a gas range, the flame should be blue. If the flame is yellow, it should be adjusted.

(7) The oven door should be tight, not leaking heat.
(8) All dripping faucets should be fixed.

That's the minimum. If you can talk your landlord into insulating, caulking, weatherstripping, and installing energy-saving appliances, so much the better.

These things are your responsibility:

(1) Vacuum or dust your radiator surfaces frequently.
(2) Turn down the heat when you're at work, and when you're sleeping. If you're having a party, set the register a degree or two below its normal level, since people generate heat. Use an electric (or just an extra) blanket at night instead of heating your entire apartment.
(3) Make or purchase energy-saving draperies and curtains. In the winter, open the drapes to let the sunlight heat the house during the day, and then close them at sunset to keep the cold air out. In the summer, do the opposite: curtains drawn during the day, open at night.
(4) Defrost your freezer whenever there's a quarter-inch of frost on the inside.
(5) Use small appliances—slow cooker, pressure cooker, electric skillet, etc.—instead of your range whenever possible.
(6) Don't let the water run. Take short showers, turn off the tap while brushing your teeth or shaving, and use cold water instead of hot for anything you can.
(7) Set your water heater (or have your landlord set it) at 120° F, which is adequate for most needs.

Telephone Q & A

And now, incisive answers to your most troubling questions about the matter of telephones and telephone service:

Q: Should I buy a phone, or rent from the telephone company?
A: By all means, you should buy your own phone. Renting a phone makes about as much sense as renting a toaster or clock radio.

Q: Where should I get my phone?
A: Wherever you like. You can go to the AT & T phone store, order through the mail, or find phones at catalog showrooms, discount stores, hardware stores, drugstores, department stores, electronics stores—even the supermarket sells phones.

Q: Do all those places sell good phones?
A: No, some of those places sell cheapo, good-for-nothing phones. Beware of sets that are suspiciously inexpensive—I wouldn't waste my time or money on anything under twenty dollars, for example. You'll always sound like you're standing in the shower if you get a cheap phone. Don't buy *any* phone from *anyone* unless it is expressly understood that you can bring it back for a full refund if it fails to perform adequately once it's installed.

Q: Won't the phone company be mad if I don't use their telephones?
A: The telephone company has no personality; consequently, it cannot get mad. Besides that, they aren't a monopoly any more, so they have to let you do what you like. Don't worry about offending the telephone company—it's a waste of timidity.

Q: What kind of equipment should I get?
A: No more and no less than you will use. Watch out for fancy add-ons like music-on-hold, look ma—no cord units, two-line adaptors, and that sort of thing. They tend to be expensive and/or unreliable. On the other hand, you may need a modem to hook up to your home computer, a battery backup to prevent loss of memory in your automatic redial feature, or a privacy code if you are bothered by crank calls.

Shop for your telephones at a store where knowledgeable salespeople can help you make a decision. Electronics nuts like to work in phone and computer stores; take advantage of their enthusiasm and expertise. But remember that they're working on commission, and don't overbuy.

Q: How do I get my phones installed?
A: You do it yourself. Your house or apartment is already wired and jacked. The type of jack may be inappropriate for your

equipment, so it's possible that you will have to make some adjustments. It's very easy. All you do is go to an electronics, telephone, or computer store that sells adaptor plugs and jacks. Before you go, take a good look at the kind of jack you currently have; take an instant picture of it if you don't think you'll be able to describe it. Then tell the clerk what kind of jack you have, and what kind of equipment you want to plug into it. You'll be given (actually, sold) the right kit for your need. It's unlikely that the kit will cost more than five dollars.

Some people worry about getting electrocuted. Nonsense! There isn't enough juice in the phone lines to give you more than a tingle. You get a tingle "plus" when the phone is ringing, however; if you don't want the experience, take another extension off the hook, so no calls will come through while you're working. You can also wear rubber gloves. Of course, if you have a pacemaker (you do?!?) you should avoid this kind of work altogether.

The only tools you'll need are a screwdriver, scissors, a few insulated staples, and a little hammer for tapping the staples in place. If you doubt any of this, defer to the helpful clerk at the phone store.

Q: **The jacks in my apartment aren't where I want them. Are you sure I should be doing this myself?**

A: Of course. If your jacks aren't where you want them, buy some telephone wire and run it along the baseboards or under the rug, or around the door frame, or alongside the ceiling molding until you're where you want to have your phone, and then install an extension outlet there.

They're your phones, and you can put them wherever you like. Be sure to tack down your extension wires, though, so you aren't tripping over them.

Q: **This is a lot of work. I'd rather just call up the phone company and have them install the phones, and I'll rent the equipment from them, and if anything goes wrong they'll come out and fix it.**

A: No one is stopping you. Maybe it is easier to have the phone company take care of it, but increasingly they are charging for service calls and encouraging you to do your own installations anyway. If you're made of money, you can have them do it, of course. But on the average, two years' rental of phone equipment could buy the equipment you're renting. After two years have gone by, you own it outright, and you're saving a lot of money. You can also take your phones with you whenever you move—no hassle.

Q: I'm still going to have to pay a monthly fee to the phone company.
A: That's true. Once you're all hooked up with your own phones, call the phone company and ask them to commence service, telling them you own your own equipment. They'll take it from there, making a monthly charge for use of their lines.

Q: Does it make a difference how many extensions I have?
A: Not if you own your own equipment—one price, no matter how many phones you have.

Q: What about call packages, and unlimited dialing, and all that?
A: Most phone companies offer a selection of calling packages. Usage-sensitive options base your monthly charge on one or more of the following: number of calls made, duration of the calls, distance, time of day. Your basic monthly fee entitles you to a specified number of calls or specified dollar credit; when you have exceeded the allotment, additional charges are made.

Q: Wouldn't it be cheaper to get a flat-rate option, and then not worry about having to pay for every call?
A: If you make a lot of calls, you'll be better off with the flat-rate option. But most people lose when they pay for unlimited calls, because they just don't make as many as they think they do.

  If you are currently on a flat-rate plan, try keeping track of the calls you make in a month's time—where you are calling, how long you stay on the phone, and what time of day you call. Then call the phone company and ask them to give you an estimate of what those calls would have cost you with a usage-sensitive plan. (Perhaps it will be obvious to you without consulting the phone company.)

  If you are currently on a usage-sensitive plan, pay attention to your bill. If you didn't use up all your credits, maybe you could do with a cheaper plan. If you consistently overuse, maybe you need a more comprehensive plan.

In general, your local telephone company will be happy to help you figure out the best plan for you, especially if you give them some data to work with.

Q: What about these discount long-distance services?
A: It used to be that long-distance phone calls had to be carried through cables. There are cables all over and under this country, and under the Atlantic Ocean, and over and under the rest of the world. Then we started sending up satellites and setting up microwave towers—these can transmit phone calls, too, and they are accessible to entities other than the phone company. When you use a discount phone service, you are making a local call to a microwave tower which transmits your call to another microwave tower, which then makes another local call to your destination. It sounds more complicated, but it's far cheaper than using cables. Discount services like MCI and Sprint use AT & T lines for the local calls, and their own microwave equipment to cover the big distances.

Q: I don't make a lot of long-distance calls, but I'd like to save money if I can. Should I check into one of these?
A: Sure, check into it. Page 151 has a list of questions that you should get answers to when considering a long-distance service. If you think you can save, by all means, go for it.

SAVING MONEY ON LONG-DISTANCE CALLS

1. Investigate long-distance services.

2. Call people at times of the day when they're unlikely to be available; leave a call-back message and let them use their nickels.

3. Always call station-to-station. Operator assisted calls are extravagant. You can afford to call a few times without reaching your party before you pay for an operator-assisted

call. Use the operator only if you're absolutely sure the party you wish to reach is unavailable. If they don't take the call, you've let them know you want to talk—and it costs nothing.

4. If you dial a wrong number, call the phone company immediately. Tell them the number you dialed, and they'll make sure you don't get charged for it.

5. Keep track of all the calls you make. Sometimes the phone company gets confused and charges you for calls you didn't make. Also keep track of wrong numbers, making sure you don't pay for those.

6. The phone company is starting to charge for directory assistance. Keep track of numbers you use. If you do need directory assistance, ask for two numbers each time—you'll only be charged for one.

7. Use 800 (toll-free) numbers whenever you can. If you want to call a company, but don't know if they have an 800 number or not, dial 800-555-1212. It's a no-charge call, and the operator will let you know if an 800 number is available for your use.

8. Call when it's cheap. It's cheapest to make long-distance calls from 11:00 at night to 8:00 in the morning; also all day Saturday and Sunday (except from 5:00 P.M. to 11:00 P.M. on Sunday). If you're calling another time zone, it's possible to call at a time that's cheap for you, but still very convenient for the person you're calling. For example, if you live in California, you can call a friend in New York at 7:00 A.M. your time (cheap) which is 10:00 A.M. her time (convenient).

9. Get off the phone before the call gets too long. "Sorry, Aunt Darlene . . . There's been an auto accident outside and the police need to use the phone . . ." is useful.

10. Write a letter. Postage is outrageous, but it's still cheaper than calling.

LONG-DISTANCE SERVICE CHECKLIST

1. Is there a start-up fee? A monthly service charge in addition to "per-call" charges? If so, how much?

2. Will I get charged for a local call in addition to the long-distance call whenever I use the service? Will this have an impact on the usage-sensitive calling package I have?

3. Is there a minimum usage requirement? How much?

4. Is there a high-usage discount? How much?

5. In figuring the billing for calls, does this company always round the time up to the nearest minute? The nearest six seconds, half minute, or what?

6. Does it cover most of the areas I'm likely to call?

7. Does it operate twenty-four hours a day? Does it operate when I'm likely to be using it?

8. Can I use the service only from my own phone? Can I use it from a pay phone? When I'm out of town?

FASCINATING FONE FACTS

Texas has the greatest number of miles of overhead telephone wire; Pennsylvania is twelfth.

More long-distance telephone calls are placed on Mother's Day than any other day of the year; Christmas Day is a close second.

The first female telephone operator was Emma M. Nutt. She began in September of 1878, working for the Telephone Dispatch Company in Boston. Before that time, all telephone operators were men. Way to go, Emma!

The first commercial transatlantic telephone service was begun on January 7, 1927, between London and NYC. The charge for a three-minute call was a modest seventy-five dollars.

Almon B. Strowger, a Kansas City undertaker, invented the first practical telephone switch in 1889; this replaced the need for operators to connect calls. He was motivated by the belief that phone operators were diverting his calls to competitors—other undertakers who were getting business that was rightly his.

There are 14,667 coin-operated phones in the state of Mississippi.

In Washington, D.C., there are 1.6733 phones for every resident, a worldwide high. Bombay is lowest at 4.6 phones per 100 people.

From *The Phone Book*, by Larry Kahaner and Alan Green.

14.

HABITAT MISCELLANY

Furnishings

Moving into new digs creates a need for household furnishings. We're talking chairs, tables, beds, and rugs. The television commercial that shows a beautiful young couple in a bare room sharing champagne and caviar laid out on the top of an old orange crate . . . well, it looks better than it really is. Sooner or later you want someplace comfortable to sit, a real bed for sleeping, and a table to eat on. There are many sources of household furnishings. . . .

Parents and relatives. As you leave the family home you may receive offers of the raggedy bedspread-covered hide-a-bed in the family room, the old kitchen table your dad has been using in the workshop, and your late Aunt Sylvia's most prized possession: daVinci's Lord's Supper beautifully rendered in black plush, with gold satin fringe.

Garage sales and auctions. Most garage sales are long on clothing and short on truly useful furniture, but it doesn't hurt to check the ads to see who's trying to get rid of what you're trying to acquire. When an elderly person breaks up housekeeping, there is often an auction of household furnishings. You can get some very nice old pieces of furniture at an auction; be prepared to pay what it's worth, since an auctioneer knows the value of antiques.

Thrift stores. The Salvation Army, Goodwill, and other thrift stores usually handle furniture. Most items will be in fairly good shape, since teams of recovering alcoholics, runaways, and disabled folks are employed to refurbish old sofas, tables, bookcases, etc.

Improvisation. This is when an old mattress is doubled over to become an easy chair, an old door serves as a desktop, and a cardtable becomes the dining room table.

Kits. You can get a kit to make anything from a breadbox to a log home. Many magazines advertise kits that may be purchased by mail order.

Furniture stores. They run all the way from used junk to Ethan Allen; from unfinished pieces to French antiques. You probably know of several accessible furniture stores; they all have their own type of wares, and vary in the quality of goods they carry.

No matter how you plan to or are acquiring your household furnishings, there are some simple rules to keep in mind. The first is to give some thought to a motif that will carry you through the next few years. Even if you're picking up odds and ends from your parents or the dumpster outside your apartment building, you can do it with a view toward collecting items that harmonize and work toward a common goal. Your criteria may be very broad, such as "wood or wood-looking," "high-tech-ish," or "functional." Or you might think of a color scheme—"anything that goes with that maroon carpeting" or "brown, rust, and beige." If you don't exercise some kind of discernment, you'll end up with a hopeless room full of junk that you can't stand to look at. Naturally, if you are colorblind or have no taste whatsoever, this advice doesn't apply. But don't invite me over and expect compliments.

The second rule is to buy only those pieces that you are able and willing to move, or that you won't mind trashing when the time comes. If you're anything like the average guy, you'll live in your first place for a year or less; you'll move several more times before you "settle down." You already know that moving is expensive, back-breaking, and frustrating. Look at each potential furnishing and ask yourself, "Will it be impossible to get up/down the stairs? Will it fall apart if it's moved? Does it break down into smaller, more transportable pieces?" If it fails the movability test, then it should pass the "I'll just throw it out the window when I leave" test. For sure. (Keep packing cartons when you can, especially the ones that a stereo, VCR, or TV come in. They make moving these delicate pieces much easier later.)

Rule number three is this: if you can't have a houseful of gorgeous furniture, try for one stunning piece. A beautiful sofa, a nice antique oak table, or a beautiful area rug arranged to its best advantage, can overpower, aesthetically, the faded drapes, frayed upholstery on the side chairs, or lack of coffee- and end-tables. A baby grand piano, a bentwood rocker, or a huge tapestry wall-hanging can make an otherwise scuzzy room look great.

Observe rule number four now and evermore: if you're going to buy real furniture, get real quality. These places that advertise a nine-piece living room suite (which includes sofa, loveseat, armchair, coffee table, end-tables, lamps, and 24-by-36-inch framed print for the wall) at the unbelievably low price of $299.99 should be avoided like the plague. You may be anxious to outfit your living room, tired of sitting on old cushions, and chomping at the bit to have enough furniture to entertain, but this is *not* the way to go about it. It will be $299.99 (plus sales tax, delivery charge, and possibly interest if you're buying on time) down a large rat hole. The junk will begin falling apart in a matter of weeks, maybe even days. It's better to invest in a single piece of quality—even if it's from a kit, it's used, or it's unfinished—and have something that will last.

Finally, as a fifth rule, look for versatility in what you buy. A sofa bed is better than a couch; a flip-flop chair that turns into a bed is better than a chair that doesn't; a bookshelf with movable shelves is better than one that can't adjust; and a bed with storage possibilities underneath is a real find.

If you go to your public library and look up "furniture" in the card catalog, you'll find that there are a number of good books on how to procure furniture—and many of these creatively address the problems of little money to spend, small apartments, the probability of moving, and your desire to express yourself in your environment. Some of the better books I found are:

Nomadic Furniture 1 by James Hennessey and Victor Papanek. This book concentrates on furniture that can be easily folded, collapsed, stacked, knocked down, deflated, recycled, or simply thrown away in the event of moving. Although its hippy-dippy approach is hard to access, and many of their fantastic ideas suggest absolutely horrific furnishings, the authors give good theory on how to choose furniture that will move with you—or can be left behind.

Low Tech by Rick Ball and Paul Cox. If you're wondering how to fashion an attractive hanging lamp out of a vegetable steamer or cheese grater; if you'd like to make a wall-mounted storage unit out of the pockets of old jeans; or have rolls of carpet tubing sitting around that might make an excellent easy chair, you can get detailed directions in this fine book. The low tech creed: If it serves a purpose, anything goes. Nothing is inappropriate if you like it and can get some use out of it.

The Kit Furniture Book by Lynda Graham-Barber. Using the many kits available, anyone with a hammer, screwdriver, and few hours to spend can create top-quality furniture in a variety of styles—Queen Anne, Modern, Shaker, or Colonial. This helpful book introduces the reader to what's available, and provides addresses of suppliers. This isn't cheap furniture, but good quality stuff that can be assembled by you, cutting the cost in half.

(Publishing information for these books is found in the Bibliography.)

Safety

Here's some good news to brighten up your day: YOU ARE SAFER THAN YOU THINK.

"Are you serious? Just yesterday I was reading in the papers about this gang of kids that has been stealing Social Security money from old folks. And how about that guy in Illinois who killed all those young boys? Last year a paperboy was abducted—never found again. And there was that TV movie a couple of weeks ago based on the true story of a woman who had been mugged *eight* times in the New York subway! Anyone who thinks he's safe is crazy!"

Obviously, we all live with the prospect of having a crime

committed against us, or against someone we know and care about. But we also live with vivid media coverage of crime, television programming whose dramas, sitcoms, and documentaries are based on crime (sometimes real, but most often fabricated), heightened public awareness of crime and the victims of crime, and consequently a growing sense of doom. We fear that the next victim will be us.

It's apparently the case that those who watch a lot of television perceive the world as a perilous place to be, whereas those who watch little or no television generally have less fear overall. It's not hard to figure out why: three hours in front of television on a given weeknight will net a viewer three hours of murder, robbery, arson, burglary, and basic violence. By 11:00 the average vidiot is convinced beyond a shadow of a doubt that it's only a matter of time—probably minutes or hours—before he too is gunned down by dope-crazed thugs while driving through East L.A.

The fact is that crime is down in many areas. Is yours one of them? Could be. Some reports of crimes are up (rape is the best example of this), but experts suspect that actual *incidence* is holding steady.

How nervous are you about your personal safety and the safety of your possessions? This will, in a large part, determine what measures you take to protect yourself. Where do you live? If you live on the West Side of Chicago, you should conduct yourself differently from someone who lives in a town of 4,650 sterling inhabitants. What are your personal limitations and lifestyle? A ninety-eight-pound woman has a challenge to her safety that doesn't exist for a 210-pound ex-linebacker. A disabled or elderly person is more vulnerable than a person who can run the 100-meter in ten seconds. Do you live alone or with roommates? Are you by nature passive or aggressive?

Law enforcement officers point out that a triangle of components make up a criminal act. It looks like this:

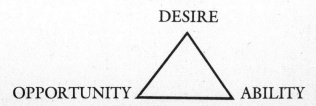

DESIRE

OPPORTUNITY · ABILITY

First a criminal must want to commit a crime: that's DE-SIRE. Then he or she must be capable of following through on that desire: ABILITY. Finally, the criminal must perceive a chance to carry out his or her plans: OPPORTUNITY. Any community that is concerned about crime will try to thwart it on all three levels, working to reduce the desire that people have to commit crimes, keep them from obtaining the ability to do so, and taking away opportunities. It is on the level of OPPORTU-NITY that you can do something about becoming a crime victim.

You cannot be 100 percent safe. No one can promise you that. If you're looking for 100 percent safety, you will find your-self absolutely obsessed with your personal protection and the guarding of your property. You won't have time for anything else. You won't leave the house, and you'll always be afraid.

But there are some basics. There's no reason to ignore the obvious.

At-Home Security

(1) Be generous with lighting. Whether you're away or at home, have plenty of lights on. When you're out, use multiple lighting timers in all rooms to make it look as though you're still there. Have a trusted friend or neighbor reset the timers every few days. Or get photoelectric devices that will turn on automati-cally when it gets dark. If your neighborhood is spooky, call the city agency in charge and request additional street lighting.

(2) Keep your lawn mowed in the summer and your walks shoveled in the winter. Bring in newspapers, flyers, and mail as soon as they appear. Have a mailbox big enough to hold all mail you're likely to receive. A record mailer or oversized magazine sticking out of your mailbox is a sign that you're not home.

(3) Lock your doors and windows. Use all the security that is provided in your building. If you have an entry security system that allows you to screen your visitors, use it always. No excep-tions. Secure your patio or balcony door.

(4) When you move into your apartment, arrange with your landlord to have the lock changed. Pay for it yourself if you have to, remembering that every person who ever lived in your apart-ment may have a key to what is now your home.

(5) Keep your curtains or shades drawn. Don't let anyone see into your apartment. Do not place valuable possessions, like your stereo, in front of a window for passersby to see.

(6) Be careful what you say on the phone. Never let it be known that you're alone. As proud as you may be of your trip to St. Thomas, don't advertise the fact in any way, including on the answering machine that's taking calls in your absence. Don't give callers a taped message saying that you're not at home. Better try this: "You have reached 555-4325. Please leave a message at the sound of the tone so that your call can be returned." If you give your name or a clue to your whereabouts on the tape, you're giving valuable information to a burglar who wants to know if you're home or not. If you travel a lot, having an unlisted number isn't a bad idea.

(7) Don't put your name on your mailbox. All it needs is your address and/or apartment number. Your mail carrier knows who you are and where you live.

(8) Don't open the door to strangers—*ever*! Ask for identification from service people and the like. Don't be embarrassed about yelling to your would-be visitor through a shut, locked, and bolted door.

(9) Call the police if you'll be out of town for a week or more. They can keep an eye on your place while you're gone. Leave your itinerary with a trusted neighbor; tell the police who that neighbor is in case you need to be notified.

(10) Make friends with your neighbors. Give them permission to be nosy. Ask them to feel free to report anything that looks amiss, on your behalf, assuring them ahead of time that you will appreciate their intervention.

Away-from-Home Security

(1) Stay away from unfamiliar places. You're at a disadvantage if you don't know where you are, or where you're going.

(2) Carry a flashlight to help you navigate dark areas at night.

(3) Go out with a companion whenever you can. You're more vulnerable when alone.

(4) Elevators are safest when they're empty (except for you) or filled with a crowd of people. If the person in the elevator looks suspicious to you, don't get in—another lift will be available shortly.

(5) Lock your car, when you've parked it and when you are driving it. Always check your backseat for uninvited passengers *before* entering your car.

(6) Know your neighborhood—that way you can detect suspicious activity.

(7) When talking to strangers, never give them information that could be used against you. Don't say things like, "Yeah, I just moved into that yellow place on the corner of Twentieth and Vine. No, no roommate yet, but I'm hoping!"

(8) Change your schedule from time to time. If you're a jogger or walker, avoid running or walking the same route every time you go out. Mix it up.

(9) Carry deterrents if you're so inclined. A whistle around your neck, a can of mace, or a siren in your purse are all excellent ways of scaring off a mugger.

This is the basic kind of stuff that we all can do. It doesn't take a lot of time, money, or effort to protect ourselves —just a little thought. An excellent book on the subject is *Crime Stoppers* by Wesley Cox (New York: Crown Publishing, 1982). It contains hundreds of low-cost ways to effectively protect yourself. The cheapest, easiest deterrents are also the most effective. Elaborate alarm systems can be quickly disengaged by an expert, and we all know what kind of trouble handguns can cause; these dramatic efforts at protection turn out, in the long run, to do the least good. Cox's sensible and sane approach is to do what is easiest and smartest first.

SOME CRIME STATISTICS

1. Most probable months for burglaries are December, January, and February.

2. Most probable night for burglaries is Saturday night.

3. Most burglaries occur between 6:00 P.M. and 2:00 A.M.

4. Most assaults, rapes, and murders take place in July and August.

5. Most murders happen on a weekend.

6. Most murders occur between 6:00 P.M. and 6:00 A.M.

Won't You Please, Won't You Please, Please Won't You Be My Neighbor . . .

. . . sings the lovable Mister Rogers. Anyone who has recently moved can attest to the fact that the guy next door is not in the habit of welcoming folks to the block, or the building, extending a hand of friendship to newcomers. Even my mother, to whom baking a cake for every new family on the block was once something of a religious rite, has long since abandoned the practice.

Why? Probably because people move so much nowadays that it's hard to stay on top of the situation. Just as soon as you make friends with the Simmonsons and welcome them to town, they've left and the Kerreys have moved in. In apartment buildings, it's as if people are saying, "I have to share this hallway with you, and this wall, and I can hear your toilet every time it flushes . . . but I'll be hanged if I'm going to be your friend, too." Psychological isolation substitutes for physical privacy.

The rules have changed. If you're the new kid in town, it's up to you to introduce yourself to your neighbors on either side. If you wait for someone else to do it, you could wait years. If you work a different shift from the others in your building or on your block, you may never even see them. So don't be afraid to knock on a couple of doors, introduce yourself as the newcomer, and hope that it takes off from there.

What are the other ways of meeting people? Every year the March of Dimes, Cancer Society, Heart Fund, and other charities solicit funds by asking one person on a street or in an apartment building to walk around with an envelope and collect donations. Call the local office and volunteer for the job when the time comes. This gives you a chance to introduce yourself, and find out who's who.

Make friends with the doorman, building superintendent, or janitor. Listen to a little gossip about the other tenants; present yourself as a friendly person. You might get an introduction out of the thing.

Plan on doing outside work on Saturdays if you live in a conventional neighborhood. This gives you the opportunity to strike up a conversation with other neighbors who are doing the same thing. Ask questions to break the ice: "Are you having trouble with clover, too?" or "How long has that streetlight been out?" Compliments are welcome: "That's a great paint job on your Porsche" or "Your little girl is really sharp!"

Large apartment complexes often have social activities that are organized by the management. There may be parties in the club house, craft classes, or Friday-afternoon mixers. A swimming pool, tennis court, or weight room in your complex is a good place to meet people. Afraid you'll end up standing around with no one to talk to? Bring a big fat book with a provocative title with you to the swimming pool, or a magazine that will provoke a response. (Examples: *101 Things to do with a Broken Computer*, or *Hang Gliders' Monthly*, or a map of Australia may elicit a response from a soulmate who hates computers, loves hang gliding, or is also dreaming of a trip to the Outback.)

Watch for signs indicating that a tenants' organization or residents' group is in operation. What about a neighborhood association? The one to which I belong has a yearly ice cream social and sponsors a number of improvement projects—from alley graveling to tree-planting to sidewalk replacement—that provide excellent opportunities to meet neighbors.

Call your city's police department or crime prevention unit to see if there is a program like Neighborhood Watch in place. Is your block or building organized? If so, get the name of the block coordinator and contact that person, indicating your desire to participate. Or start a program on your own. Remember, the protocol is different. It's going to be *your* responsibility to take the initiative in meeting your neighbors.

Finding a Church

A local church or place of worship may be your best way to meet people who are on your wavelength.

You can make your church-hunt more efficient if you can get leads from your previous minister, or friends who know the area and have conducted their own search. If the denomination you have always been associated with has no churches in your new locale (many are regional), ask someone in the know to recommend a group with a similar creed.

The Yellow Pages are a good place to start. They list churches by denomination, which is helpful. If you see one that looks good to you, give the church office a call and ask to talk to the minister. Explain that you're new in town and are investigating churches. Ask the minister about aspects of church life that will have a bearing on your decision. What's the membership size? How many people attend worship? Sunday school? Are there programs for single people? Young married people? Be honest about doctrinal issues: what creed or confession has this church adopted? Go ahead—ask what this minister thinks about predestination and foreordination (if you can spit it out); eternal salvation; women in ministry; political issues . . . anything that's important to you. Remember, you're trying to save some time here. You could go to a church for weeks before realizing you cannot buy into most of what's being taught and practiced.

Once you've got a church in mind, attend the morning worship *and* the Sunday school class designed for you *and* any midweek services that are appropriate. Don't judge a church on the basis of just one activity. Some wonderful churches have less than scintillating preachers; when judged solely on the basis of the morning message they always lose. But the teaching is good, the fellowship is good, the caring is good. Another church may have a Billy Graham-caliber preacher and, unfortunately, not much else.

If you think you're onto a hot prospect, find some time to visit with the minister or other staff person. Invite him/her to your home, or make an appointment for the church office. Talk about the church, and where you might fit in. What opportunities are open to you for service? Ask for an explanation of anything you're unsure about, whether it be a matter of faith, doctrine, practice, or church organization. Get a brief history of the church, and an assessment of where it's going.

Finding a good church is hard work. And then, of course, one must contend with the fact that a logical assessment of a church's strengths and weaknesses is only a part of the process; God works in the decision of matching seekers and believers with others who will support them on their journey, and join with them for the purpose of worship.

Into the Community

Community involvement deals with service and leadership; for the most part, leadership is available only to those who have served, so that's the place to start.

Many cities have a volunteer bureau that matches givable skills with the agencies that need them. You could call and offer to do something worthwhile, which could be as enjoyable as coaching Little League, delivering hot meals to the elderly on weekends, or helping plant flowers in the city's parks.

The League of Women Voters is a good place to meet people (if you're a woman); so are the local Democratic and Republican committees. If there's a campaign or cause that interests you, volunteer to help promote it. If it's the social aspect you enjoy, let someone else do leafleting while you do clerical work in the office, or telephone polling, which will put you in contact with other people.

Aside from the obviously worthwhile pursuits, you can get to know people in your town by accepting invitations to home demonstrations (for Discovery Toys, Mary Kay, etc.); by joining a bowling league (you don't have to know anybody to get on a team—just sign up at the bowling alley); by joining a racket or health club, or the YMCA; by attending Newcomers Club (let the Welcome Wagon lady call on you—she'll explain how it works); or by taking an extension class at the high school, junior college, or university. While you learn quilting, auto repair, or tax return preparation, you have an opportunity to meet people with a similar interest.

It takes a lot of work to feel at home in your community. But old-timers are usually thrilled to death to meet a nice young person who is so willing to become a contributing member of the community. Your willingness to be a good neighbor and to involve yourself in your church and community will put you in contact with others of like mind.

15.

HOUSE PROUD

Home Maintenance

Since you are renting, the maintenance of your apartment or duplex or house is generally the responsibility of your landlord, or the building superintendent. And unless he's a slumlord, the owner of your property will probably appreciate being notified of problems as soon as they occur. If the handle falls off the refrigerator through no fault of your own, if the newly-painted windows are stuck shut, if the tile is coming off in the bathroom, tell the owner or super.

The trouble comes when you're the cause of the problem: you were careless, you used the chair for something that a chair shouldn't be used for, and now you've got a situation you'd rather not bring to the attention of your landlord. What to do?

The best advice this book can give is to read a book: *Reader's Digest, Better Homes and Gardens,* and a lot of other people have published really good, fat, comprehensive tomes on how to handle home maintenance—everything from repairing that chair, fixing a lamp, sanding wood floors, or caulking windows. A book like this is a good investment. *To wit . . .*

I had a nice spot lamp, the kind you can put behind a chair, shine onto the wall, and create "mood" lighting with. I had had it for years, and then it must have gotten rattled, because after the

Chicago move it didn't work. Then for Christmas I got one of these books on how to do anything, and one day I decided that I'd give that lamp a try, since I was doing a lot of groping in the dark. So I sat down with the lamp and the book. I opened to the chapter on fixing light fixtures. I located the instructions for table lamps. It read:

(1) Begin with a new light bulb.

So I went and got a new light bulb. I took out the old (perfectly good) bulb and replaced it with a good one. I tried the switch. Miraculously, the lamp was fixed. Sixty watts of brilliant white light gave testimony to the fact that, after four years, it was once again on the job.

This is why I recommend these fix-it books. If you are solely responsible for the maintenance of your house or apartment, or if you're faced with a repair that you'd rather handle yourself, the books help. They are somewhat expensive—upwards of twenty dollars in most cases—so check out the assortment at your local public library and review the possibilities before making your investment.

THE MINIMUM-REQUIREMENT TOOLBOX

- Hammer—claw-type so you can pull out all the nails you hammer in crooked

- Small assortment of nails

- Small assortment of picture hangers—the kind with little guides that help you pound them in right

- Pliers

- Screwdriver—one regular and one Phillips, or a screwdriver with interchangeable heads that will handle both

- Small assortment of screws and bolts

- Duct tape—not a tape so much as a tool. Duct tape will do the trick hundreds of times in the course of your lifetime

- Utility knife—the kind with a razor edge

- Glue: Elmer's—for wood, especially, and almost everything generally

    Super Glue—for repairing broken dishes, smashed
    vases and, of course, gluing your hardhat to a steel
    beam so you can hang from it

    Goop—a relatively new product, it's a lot like rub-
    ber cement with true grit, and will bond anything (in-
    cluding the sole of your running shoe to the nylon up-
    per, the chrome trim back onto your car door, and your
    fingers to one another)

- Crescent wrench—get a conventional one, or go for the
  specialized "vise grips" variety

- Tape measure—anything that can measure up to ten feet
  or so

Cleaning

This is not your mother telling you to pick up your socks. This is
a friend telling a friend that there are certain minimum standards
of cleanliness that must be applied to one's domicile, just as there
are certain standards of personal cleanliness that are expected of
any civilized person.

A Philosophy of Filth

Filth falls into three main categories: dangerous filth, disgusting
filth, and simple debris.

Dangerous filth threatens your quality of life—and sometimes life itself. It encompasses oily rags and open cans of paint
thinner under the sink; spilled foodstuff in the kitchen that attracts rodents and other pests; a bottle of Thousand Island dressing that has been sitting on the counter for two days and is just
about to be glupped onto a chunk of iceberg lettuce; or a stairway
that has become unnavigable due to a conglomeration of books,
clothes, roller skates, and tennis balls that have collected themselves on the steps.

Obviously, such dangerous filth must be dealt with quickly

and decisively. If you are moving into a house or apartment that is already dangerously filthy, do everything in your power to clean it out before you move in—for safety's and sanity's sake, since it's easier to accomplish when you don't have to work around boxes and dishes. Remember all those bacterial cultures you grew in Biology 101, and keep an eye out for anything that resembles them. Think safety; imagine the worst possible scenarios. If you think there's a possibility that your place is seriously dangerous, call your local fire or codes administration department and ask to have a free inspection of your property. They'll alert you to the hazards. And then you can set about fixing them. Or getting your landlord to fix them.

15 PIECES OF TRASH AND WHEN THEY WILL DISINTEGRATE

1. Paper traffic ticket	2–4 weeks
2. Cotton rag	1–5 months
3. Degradable polyethylene bag	2–3 months
4. Piece of rope	3–14 months
5. Wool stocking	1 year
6. Bamboo pole	1–3 years
7. Unpainted wooden stake	1–4 years
8. Painted wooden stake	13 years
9. Wooden light pole	15–36 years
10. Railroad crosstie	30 years
11., 12. Tin or steel can	100 years
13. Aluminum can	200–500 years
14. Plastic six-pack cover	450 years
15. Glass cola bottle	disintegration period unknown

(John Eastman in *The Book of Lists #2*)

The problem with cleaning up dangerous filth is that it's often unpleasant and hard to deal with, has little cosmetic value when completed, and can cost a lot of time and money before the project is over. But remember, it's *dangerous,* and because it's malignant it's deserving of your immediate attention.

Disgusting filth is less urgent. It includes the stains left by your Newfoundland retriever on the shag carpet; the dust that has built up drifts on the windowsills; the icky yellow discoloration in the toilet bowl; the lime deposits where the faucet has been dripping into the tub; the waxy build-up on the kitchen floor; long black hairs in the sink; and the accumulated frost glacier on the inside of the freezer that has grown so large that it is now almost impossible to get anything more than a single ice cube tray into the compartment.

Oh yes, it's disgusting all right, even if it's not dangerous (unless you have allergies, asthma, or some other condition that mandates antiseptic cleanliness in your indoor environment). It makes you dread going home at night. It prompts you to use the restroom at the Sunoco instead of your own bathroom. It keeps you from inviting friends to come and visit. It haunts your Saturday mornings, and keeps your mother in a perpetual state of anxiety.

You can hire someone to clean out the unwanted filth, and that might not be a bad idea. For a price, a cleaning service will send over a crack team of trained experts who have all the equipment and supplies needed to tackle the filth in your home. These professionals have the necessary blow torches, sand blasters, and industrial strength room deodorizers. You could have them do it before you move into an especially filthy place, on an infrequent but regular basis, or for a special occasion—your birthday, perhaps. And don't believe what you may have heard about, "I don't do windows." For a price, anyone will do windows. (Shucks, *I'll* do your windows if the money's right. . . .)

Once the big stuff has been done, you're in a better condition to *maintain* a reasonable level of cleanliness. You don't want to do that? Then you can get someone to come in and clean every month, every other week, or every week. Again it's going to cost, but it could be worth it to you.

And finally we have simple debris. It's piles of magazines on the coffee table, a desktop made invisible by the spreading

mound of papers, or a similarly hidden chair that has been oblit-
erated by out-of-season clothes. It's dirty dishes in the sink and
cracker crumbs between the sheets. Basic clutter. Since you're the
only person who knows where it goes, or even cares that it exists,
you have to take care of it. But be encouraged: it's not dangerous.
It's not even disgusting. It's just there.

Attack Mode

The first thing you have to do is arm yourself to fight. You need
tools. Here are the basic sorts of things you should have in order
to keep a reasonably clean home:

Absolute necessities:

- broom and/or vacuum cleaner (you might be able to do
  without one or the other if your place is completely car-
  peted or completely uncarpeted)
- bucket—plastic or tin
- sponge, some rags, and paper towels
- toilet-bowl brush
- all-purpose cleaning liquid or powder (à la Mr. Clean or
  Spic and Span)
- scouring powder (Comet, Ajax, etc.)
- chlorine bleach
- ammonia
- furniture polish—liquid or spray
- dishwashing liquid

To make the job easier and better:

- dust mop (for wood floors)
- dustpan and whiskbroom
- sponge mop (so you don't have to scrub floors on your
  hands and knees)

- window cleaner (this can replace the ammonia—more expensive but less caustic)
- toilet bowl cleaner (either an in-tank contraption, a canister of crystals, or a liquid cleaner)
- floor wax or squirt-on polish (for the kitchen and bathroom floors—makes them shiny)
- rubber gloves (to protect your manicure and/or skin)

If you are something of a housekeeping gourmet, or if you need gimmicks to get you interested in cleaning at all, you can treat your broom closet to such delicacies as little disposable dustcloths that have the polish built right into them, spray wax for your kitchen appliances, supposedly nonabrasive liquid scouring cleanser, bathroom cleaners, room deodorizers and fresheners, soaped-up scouring pads, and sophisticated pots-and-pans scrapers . . . whatever your heart desires. But you can do a decent job with the basics.

Some things have to be done every day—sorry, but civilized people do a few things every day, no matter what. Others have to be done weekly or else they'll get out of hand. Most things that take any kind of time can be done even less frequently than that. This handy-dandy chart gives you a clue as to what needs to be done and when. You've got absolute minimums here, so don't be tempted to do any of these tasks *less* frequently than recommended.

DAILY

- Make your bed.
- Pick up dirty clothes and put them in a hamper, or wherever you collect them.
- Wash the accumulated dishes and put away food that might get funky.

WEEKLY

- Wipe off bathroom surfaces—a glass cleaner like Windex or an all-purpose cleaner like Fantastik and a few paper towels ought to do the trick. Just spray and wipe, as they say. Wipe off the sink, the stool, and the tub. Put out clean towels.

- Vacuum high-traffic areas—hallways, doorways, under the dining room table, etc.

- Wipe off kitchen surfaces—countertops, stove, whatever looks grungy.

BIWEEKLY

- (Oscar Madison types may opt for monthly, but that's the absolute limit!)

- Thoroughly wash down the bathroom. Scour out the tub, washbasin, and shower with cleanser; scrub the toilet inside and out with cleanser or chlorine bleach (not both at once—you'll get a "Bubble, bubble, toil, and trouble" scene happening in the bowl if you do); clean off all the surfaces; wipe the toothpaste off the mirror with an ammonia solution or glass cleaner; sweep the floor (or wipe it with a paper towel, which is good for picking up hair) and wash it with an all-purpose cleaner; put the caps back on the tubes, put the bottles back in the medicine chest; put clean towels on the racks.

- Sweep and mop the kitchen floor, in that order. Wipe off the kitchen surfaces, and give some attention to spaghetti splatters on the wall, grease spots on the stovetop, or spilled bottles of salad dressing in the refrigerator—whatever's obvious.

- Vacuum well. Go over high-traffic areas several times to get the dirt out.

- Sweep all the floors.

- Dust. Hit the high spots, concentrating on horizontal surfaces, and those that you look at all the time. Don't forget the telephone, stereo, and TV. Dust the TV screen with a fabric softener sheet or a cloth with fabric softener on it to cut down on static, which attracts dust.

- Change your bedsheets—please!

AS NEEDED (frequent)

- Pick up clutter and put it in its proper place.

- Take out the trash.

- Remove moldy, sour, and spoiled food from the refrigerator.

- Wipe up spills that may have occurred in the kitchen cupboards.

AS NEEDED (usually infrequent)

- Wax the kitchen and/or bathroom floors.

- Take a towel to the inside of the windows, and also to the windowsills. Use spray window cleaner or an ammonia solution (proportions will be on the bottle). You can use diluted vinegar, too, or strong tea.

- Dust thoroughly—baseboards, exposed beams, knick-knacks, bookshelves and books, vertical surfaces, woodwork, etc.

- Defrost the freezing compartment. If you have a self-defrosting unit, wipe up any spills and throw out any overkept food. Don't get too carried away with hacking off chunks of frost—you could break something. Wrap up your frozen food in a rug or beach towel, turn off the cold, put an absorbent towel in the freezer, prop the door open, and go to a movie. Wipe it out with a soapy cloth when you get back, and the job is done.

- Clean out the refrigerator. When there's mold growing in the fruit and vegetable compartment, when there isn't room for another quart of milk, when the food begins to look like a science project, when there are so many spills on the shelves that you can't pry the bottles off any more, it's time to clean it out.

- Tackle the kitchen cupboards. Throw out everything that's gone bad, rediscover foods you forgot you had, wipe surfaces so they're no longer sticky and gritty.

- Clean out the medicine cabinet. Throw away outdated medications, and anything that looks like it's changed color, consistency, or overall character. Restock the kinds of things you're likely to need on a moment's notice: Band-Aids, aspirin, Alka Seltzer.

- Throw the plastic or fabric shower curtain (and rubber tub mat) into a load of clothes—preferably terrycloth towels—to remove mildew. Do not put them in the dryer—hang wet.

ONCE IN A BLUE MOON

- Sweep out and organize the attic and/or basement and/or garage, if you have one (we can only hope you don't).

- Wash the outsides of the windows (actually, this is a job for landlords and rappellers).

- Invade your closet. Give away the clothes you don't wear; mend those that are broken; iron those that need it. Change the mothballs. Give the local dry cleaner some business.

- Clean the carpets. You can do this by yourself with a simple shampooer or a more complicated (and more effective) steam cleaning system. Or you can hire it out, which has always seemed to me a prudent and cost-effective thing to do. In any case, vacuum well before any cleaning so that your efforts don't just turn carpet dirt into carpet mud.

- Clean furniture upholstery. You can use spray can preparations for small problems, steam clean your upholstery with the same machine you're cleaning your carpet with (different attachment), have it done professionally, buy/make a slipcover, or trash the whole thing if it's very dirty and nearly worthless.

- Wash venetian blinds (or better yet, throw them in the trash), wash curtains, have draperies professionally cleaned, dust shutters—basically, put your window treatments back into shape.

- Clean the oven. If you keep a big piece of heavy duty aluminum foil on the bottom, it'll be easier. Shop for a good oven cleaner, protect your hands with rubber gloves, and have at it. It won't be pretty.

Getting Started

Well, it's all rather daunting, I know. How are you going to get started? It is obvious at this point that obtaining even the most rudimentary supplies and equipment will involve an outlay of funds that could set you back months on your entertainment allotment.

The best advice I can give is to contact the one person in the world who (other than yourself) seems to have the greatest interest in knowing that you live not in squalor—and that person is your mother (maybe your dad). I believe that a simple statement/request such as, "Mom (Dad), I need some cleaning things so that I can keep the new place shipshape. Do you happen to have an extra bucket, a few rags?" should do the trick. Most parents, communicated with on this level, will respond with not only the requested items but a fairly good carpet sweeper, a long crocheted deeleybob for dusting the high places, full or nearly-full bottles of household chemicals, brooms, dustpans, and other assorted convenience items. For, as hard as it is to gather together everything you need initially, over the years cleaning equipment and supplies accumulate in a home, and most parents will be more than happy to pass them on as a legacy to their child who is now out on his own and trying to make a go of housekeeping.

Failing that, confine your purchases to the "Absolute Necessities" listed on page 170. Brooms cost a few bucks; vacuum cleaners are more expensive, so don't go out and buy one until you're sure you can't get the use of one from your apartment superintendent, your next-door neighbor, or some other friend— perhaps in exchange for keeping the machine in bags and belts. Stay away from exotic cleaning supplies if your budget is tight. Chlorine bleach and ammonia are the active ingredients in many of those high-priced, fancy packaged cleaners. Save your old cotton underwear and T-shirts; even sponges aren't absolutely necessary if you have some terrycloth rags that can be used for scouring and mopping. If having your hand in the toilet is something you can manage, a toilet brush is superfluous. And don't neglect to watch for sales on the items you need, or to make use of manufacturer's coupons. Generic and house brands are often as good as name brands, and larger sizes mean greater savings in most cases.

And Now a Word About Creepy Crawling Things

We have already stressed the importance of keeping your home clean so as to discourage pests. But what should you do if, despite your efforts, you find yourself living with a couple hundred cockroaches, a few mice, or a thousand ants?

First of all, the pests may be your aggravation (or terror), but ultimately they're your landlord's problem. If you're your own landlord, skip this paragraph; but if you're renting and you've got critters, you have every right in the world to raise an unholy fuss until your landlord does something about it. This could include, but is not limited to: spraying for pests, setting *and emptying* mouse traps, cutting shrubbery away from the building, making structural repairs (plugging up holes, replacing rotting wood), caulking around water pipes, filling in cracks with steel wood, etc. If your landlord seems a little slow on the uptake, call the Health Department and see if they'd like to get involved. These crawly things are a hazard to the community as well as a deterrent to a happy life for you.

If spraying is going to happen, do it or have it done when you're going to be out of the house for a long time—before a weekend trip or while you're at work. Clear the counters of all food; put it in the refrigerator or freezer. Anything that's in the cupboards whose packaging might be penetrated should also be put away. Hide dishes in the oven or dishwasher. Get your pets out; put plastic sheeting over the fish aquarium. Your plants probably won't mind the spray, but check the insecticide label to make sure. Put your toothbrush in the medicine cabinet.

If you're going to do your own spraying, make sure you have the right chemical for your pest(s). Decide the dangers of what you're using. Know beforehand exactly where you will spray. Do it as quickly as you can, as accurately as you can, and then get the heck out of the apartment. Go outside and wash your hands and face with good strong soap. Have a change of clothes at the neighbor's house. Don't go back until you absolutely have to.

Nobody likes to think about the creatures that are running around in their walls or raiding the breadbox. But ignoring the problem won't make it go away. As soon as you think something's amiss, kick and scream and holler until someone (even if that someone is you) does something about it.

16.

KEEPING BODY AND SOUL TOGETHER

Grocery Shopping

The point of grocery shopping is (1) to obtain the staple foods you need to stock your kitchen for day-to-day eating, and (2) to procure specific items needed to prepare specially planned dishes. This is, basically, the dynamic that exists between Velveeta cheese and Jarlsberg Swiss. And just as an amateur handyman's skill can be assessed on the basis of how many trips he makes to the hardware store while installing a garage door opener, so too any chef who has to make more than three runs to the grocery store while preparing *coq au vin* must come under suspicion.

Of course, there are still some people who get a kick out of a daily trip to the supermarket (European-style shopping). They seem oblivious to the fact that they have refrigerator/freezer units in their kitchens, that the shelf life of canned goods is measured in years, and that bags of half-eaten potato chips can indeed be resealed with a largish paperclip and finished some other day.

If you're trying to get a date with the produce manager at The Food Barn or if long walks to the market are an integral part of your fitness program, then make as many trips a week as you like. But if you're interested in more genteel pursuits—singing, dancing, and roller derby—then plan your grocery trips to be as few and as far between as possible.

Fishmongers, Greengrocers, and Other Specialists

Most of us like to shop at a supermarket. These can be expected to have—at minimum—meat, dairy, frozen food, and produce departments in addition to canned and boxed foods. Depending upon their sophistication, they may also incorporate health and beauty items, an in-store bakery, pharmacy, dry goods, fresh fish and seafood, hardware and automotive supplies, delicatessen, house plants, fresh flowers, yard and garden supplies, books, magazines, cards, and who knows what else.

You may be presented with the option of a local meat market, a fruit and vegetable market, neighborhood bakery, drugs and sundry store, fish market, and other specialty stores. The bad thing about shopping at such stores is that you are forced to make a number of stops in order to find everything on your shopping list. The good thing is that when a person's entire life is devoted to the cause of fresh fish, those fish are likely to be of exceptional quality and wide variety. Supermarket fare, then, tends to be more mediocre, though more accessible, than that found in specialty stores.

There has also been, in recent years, a proliferation of warehouse markets. These are huge stores that sell mainly staple foods in mostly large sizes at usually low prices. Most warehouse markets are long on foods with a long shelf life and short on meats and produce. Customers are expected to take an active part in such activities as marking and bagging their own groceries.

So where do you shop?* Here's a possible solution: Go to a warehouse market once a month or once every two months and get canned goods, flour and sugar, coffee, spices, baking mixes, soft drinks, and medicine cabinet stuff. Then every week you could make a trip to the supermarket to get the items you need to fulfill your menu plans for the week. And frequent the specialty markets as needed (it's great if the meat market is right on the

---

*If you said, "At the local convenience store," you lose. Don't *ever* do any kind of serious buying at a neighborhood convenience store. The prices are high, and selection is limited. They're okay for Slurpees and emergencies, but that's all.

way home from work, or if the greengrocer is on your jogging circuit), keeping your eye open for weekly specials that will save you money.

All this assumes a working familiarity with your community. If that's something you don't have, then ask your neighbors, coworkers, and service station attendant where they shop, and start from there. The local paper will also have grocery store advertisements that are helpful. Even if you don't subscribe to the paper on a daily basis, it's worth buying the issue that advertises the weekly sales. In my town it's the Wednesday paper; new promotions start on Thursday.

Clip, Clip, Clip

Now that you've gotten hold of a copy of the local Wednesday (or whatever) newspaper, you've probably noticed that the pages are full of cents-off coupons. Oh, oh, they're in the Sunday paper, too. And in magazines. Now they're coming in the mail! Argh!

Manufacturers offer cents-off coupons to promote their products—especially new items, luxury items, and products that need a boost in sales, or for which there is an especially high level of competition between brands. So you're likely to see coupons for new and improved laundry detergents, soft drinks, coffee, and pain relievers.

The bad thing about coupons is that they rarely exist for the items you buy most (milk, butter, bread, tuna, hamburger, and frozen peas), and seldom make the high-ticket items they are intended to promote cost significantly less. A coupon for fifteen cents off a $2.69 frozen diet entrée is hardly enough to make me call my stockbroker.

"Wait just a minute," you say. "I saw this woman on *Donahue* who was sitting on stage with $187.48 worth of groceries that she got for $16.03, and that's not counting rebates . . ." to which I say, "Oh yeah? She may have been surrounded by boxes, but could she make a meal out of any of it?" Because she probably had a lot of Zip-Loc bags, Tide detergent, Pampers diapers, and Old El Paso diced green chilis. Nice, but what's for supper?

Okay, if you spend forty-three hours a week devoted exclusively to the pursuit of coupons and rebates you can do some impressive things. But what if you've already got a full time job?

As a modest proposal, I would suggest that you keep your

eyes open for new products that interest you, interest you enough that you would buy them even without the coupon. Don't waste too much time chasing the seven cents off on baby gherkins coupons; look for the forty cent, sixty cent, and even one dollar off coupons for things you have to buy anyway: coffee, laundry detergent, and dog chow.

"Let advertisers spend the same amount of money improving their products that they do on advertising and they wouldn't have to advertise."
Will Rogers

In areas where the grocery business is supercompetitive, some supermarkets have initiated days when they will double the value of any cents-off coupon. That's worth looking into. And if you use a cents-off coupon on an item that's already on sale at the supermarket, you're that much better off.

The List

When making a grocery shopping list, you need to look behind and look ahead.

In looking behind, you note everything that you have run out of, or that looks like it's about to go. The best way to keep track of them is to have a piece of paper or a shopping list pad (long, skinny-lined paper especially for this purpose) in a convenient place in your kitchen. When you finish off the last of the peanut butter, write it on the list. When the milk starts clinging to the side of the carton, put "milk" on your list. When you use the last tissue (this, of course, always happens when you are in the middle of a gruesome summer cold), put it on the list.

When it's clear that you need to go to the store (trust me, you'll "know" when it happens—kind of like falling in love), then take a few minutes to look ahead to the next week and plan out some menu possibilities, listing groceries you'll need. For some reason it's often difficult to discipline oneself to do this advance menu planning, but it saves a tremendous amount of time.

Keep your list topical. As you write down what you need,

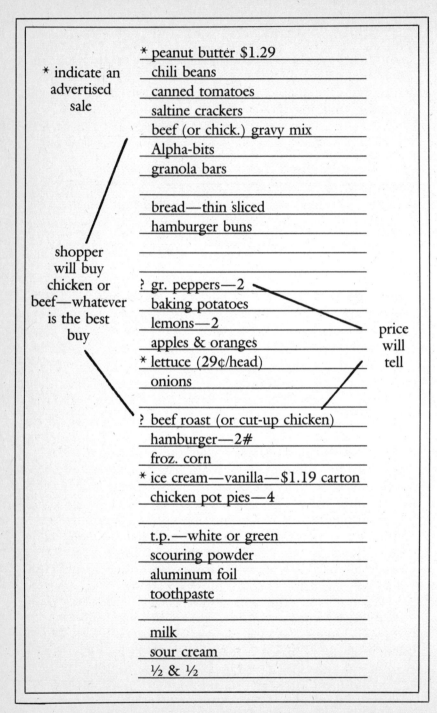

* indicate an
advertised
sale

* peanut butter $1.29
chili beans
canned tomatoes
saltine crackers
beef (or chick.) gravy mix
Alpha-bits
granola bars

bread—thin sliced
hamburger buns

shopper
will buy
chicken or
beef—whatever
is the best
buy

? gr. peppers—2
baking potatoes
lemons—2
apples & oranges
* lettuce (29¢/head)
onions

price
will
tell

? beef roast (or cut-up chicken)
hamburger—2#
froz. corn
* ice cream—vanilla—$1.19 carton
chicken pot pies—4

t.p.—white or green
scouring powder
aluminum foil
toothpaste

milk
sour cream
½ & ½

group like items: all the produce together, canned goods, non-foods, etc. The heavy hitters even put the list in the same order as the store in which they'll be shopping so they can go down their list exactly as they go down the store aisle. Wow!

If you're committed to buying everything on your list, it'll cost you. Some foods, of course, are essential; you can't face the weekend without a fair supply of Ho Hos and Ding Dongs, and no one expects you to. But others are negotiable—grilled steaks would be nice for Friday, but only if T-bones are reasonably priced. In which case, put a "?" by T-bones, with an alternative meat—probably turkey dogs—noted on the list.

Cross-check your shopping list with your store's newspaper ads and "*" the item that will be on sale, and make a note of other sale items you'll want to investigate.

The Hunt

Armed with your list, coupons, checkbook, or cash, you are ready to commence shopping.

If Saturday morning at 10:30 or Friday afternoon at 5:00 is your only free time, that's when you'll have to go—but I wouldn't recommend it. A weekday morning is great, a weekday evening is also good. After a few trips you'll figure out the best time to go. By going at a less-busy time of day, you'll have time to compare brands, sizes, and products so as to get the best value. It'll save money, so it's worth doing.

You approach the store. The electric eye isn't working too well, and you've gotten hit in the face with the edge of a 160-pound door. Not to worry. If it's really bad, remember that they have insurance for that sort of thing. If not, proceed.

Where will you start? There are several schools of thought. Some say you should start at the meat counter, buying what's cheap and building meals around that. Others like a sweep-left or sweep-right approach, beginning at one end of the store and ending at another, regardless of where the merchandise is placed. Still others adhere to the policy of filling the cart with nonperishable items first, produce and dairy foods next, and frozen foods last in an effort to keep the Eskimo Pies from melting into the broccoli. We'll leave it up to you.

Hungry? Stop right there, turn around, go home, and get something to eat. It'll be an expensive trip if you don't, because

184 ☐ FOOD, SHELTER, CLOTHING & MOBILITY

hungry shoppers are careless shoppers, very much inclined to fill their carts with unnecessary (and you guessed it—costly) items. (The only exception to the don't-you-dare-shop-on-an-empty-stomach taboo is when the store is offering free samples of tempting foods to shoppers, in which case you should skip lunch, head straight to the market, sample everything you can (get seconds if at all possible), buy only half of what's on your list, go home, don a disguise, return to the store, eat more samples and finish your shopping.)

You commence shopping. Start with your list, but be open to new ideas, especially those that are inspired by especially nice looking meat or produce, or dramatic reductions in price. You were, for example, planning on stuffed cabbage for Cousin Hortense's visit. But when you get to the store you see that the cabbage is hard, brown, and priced sky-high. The green peppers, on the other hand, are beautifully big, dark green, smooth, and shiny—and cheap! So now Hortense will be impressed by your lovely stuffed peppers instead of your lovely stuffed cabbage leaves. The filling is the same in either case.

Watch out for traps. These include samples of glazed donuts (eat the samples if you like, but *don't* buy the donuts), candy bars at the checkout counter, and big displays for merchandise that looks as though it's on sale but really isn't.

When buying produce, make sure you understand if the indicated price is a per-pound price, per-package price, or per-each price. There's a difference. When you buy prepackaged meat, make sure you don't confuse the price-per-pound with the net weight of the package. More than once I've bought meat that I thought was, say 2.99 pounds at $1.17 a pound, only to find out later that it was 1.17 pounds at $2.99 per pound! Ouch!

Watch the expiration dates on meat, dairy, and bakery products. Don't get anything that's just about to turn nasty on you and don't buy anything in a dented or bulging can—*never*, not ever, no matter what it is or how cheap they're selling it. If you dent it yourself on the way home, use it right away, or transfer the contents to another container, and save it in the refrigerator until you can use it, and don't wait too long. Salmonella and botulism are crummy houseguests.

Some supermarkets have little tags on the shelves that show the price-per-ounce of all their merchandise, and these will help you compare prices between sizes and brands of a food. Don't assume that a large package or an off-brand is always cheaper. Some large sizes are actually more-per-pound than smaller packages, and some generic foods cost more than name brands (rare, but possible). Remember that the large size is cheaper only if you can use it up before it spoils.

In a meat counter you will sometimes see "expired" meat that has been reduced in price. My experience has been that this is generally of an adequate quality, and I buy it all the time. When you get it home, either eat it or freeze it right away. Don't let it sit around in the refrigerator for days and days—it's already sufficiently aged.

Home Again, Home Again

If you've got perishables in your shopping basket, get straight home, especially if the weather is warm. Put the frozen foods in the freezer right away, the refrigerated goods next, and then take care of everything else. Don't let your groceries sit around on the counter in shopping bags any longer than necessary. It's depressing.

If the packages that your meat came in appear airtight, it's okay to freeze in them. You're likely to hear that all meat should be rewrapped in white freezer paper, but I don't think that's necessary, as long as any cellophane packaging is intact. But if there's even a little hole, the cold air will get in and give your meat freezer burn, which is an awful way to treat your meat— ruins it in fact. Rewrap if there's a hole, or if the packaging has been breached in any way.

Shake and shake
The catsup bottle
None will come
And then a lot'll.
Richard Armour

Before putting it in the frig, wash your lettuce and put it in a plastic bag; wash your apples and pears, too, so that when you want one, they're ready to eat. Do *not* wash your grapes, because that dusty stuff on them keeps them from spoiling. If you rinse it off, your grapes will be mush within twenty-four hours. If your pears are hard, your tomatoes and bananas green, put them in a window until they ripen—do not refrigerate.

Once you've opened a package, ask yourself this question: "If I were a mouse/cockroach/ant/rat/worm/spider, could I make a meal of this?" and "Would mold like to grow on it?" If the answer is "yes" or even "maybe," then transfer whatever it is to an airtight jar, a plastic bag that can be closed tight, a good canister, or simply put the whole thing in the refrigerator or freezer. The refrigerator is the place to keep flour, wheat germ, ketchup, syrup, and anything else that's dubious. It couldn't hurt.

Keep your food away from cleaning chemicals and other not-to-eat stuff. Maybe you've got a really small kitchen and are forced to keep the popcorn underneath the sink with the Drano —I understand that kind of thing. But keep them separate some way. Get a brown box for your cleaning stuff so that it's not side-by-side with your food. And if you have nieces or nephews or neighbor kids or anyone under the age of fourteen in your apartment at any time—or pets, for that matter—get those chemicals totally out of reach. This is important. Put them on the top of the medicine cabinet in the bathroom, or in the garage, or down in the basement, or on a high shelf in the coat closet.

You *Know* What Ralph Nader Would Do

Sometimes when you get home you find yourself disappointed with what you got at the grocery store. Those beautiful red apples that were advertised as being crisp and delicious are, alas, soft and mealy. The bacon has a purplish-blue cast to it. The Coke is flat, the mayonnaise didn't "whoof" when you opened the supposedly vacuum-packed jar, the chips are soggy, the pineapple is oozy, the cereal looks buggy, the furniture polish won't come out of the can.

Hey, you paid good money for that stuff. You don't have to put up with that! That's why you never throw away your cash-register receipts. You always fish then out of the bag, stuff them into the cupboard, and hang onto them until you're pretty sure that everything is alright. And if it's not, you put it back in the bag and return it. Okay, if it's just one apple you bought and it's mealy you might not want to bother. But if you bought a five-pound bag of them and paid $3.29, you've got every right to demand a refund of your purchase price—or a replacement of what you bought. It's like anything else. If it's not what you paid for, you don't have to keep it. And if it makes you feel any better, be assured that your local grocer will go ahead and get his refund from his supplier—the wholesale apple guy, or whoever it was that supplied him with the bad merchandise. So it's no skin off his nose.

Cooking at Home

There's a lot of ground to cover in this business of preparing food at home. First, there's the aspect of nutrition: calories, protein, carbohydrates, saturated and polyunsaturated fats, etc. For the sake of brevity, I'm going to assume that you know all about the four basic food groups (and, of course, the fifth group which includes coffee, tea, Mountain Dew, Hershey bars, and Vela-mints), that you know why extra calories mean extra pounds, and why it's important to hold the line on salt and saturated fat in the diet.

> *"I feel a recipe is only a theme, which an intelligent cook can play each time with a variation."*
> *Madame Benoit*

Then there's the matter of cooking skills. Novice chefs have many questions: How can fresh vegetables that are slightly *under-cooked* be at the same time *properly* cooked? What is a pinch? What is the difference between a blanched almond and a Blanche Dubois? Does the inside of a chicken *really* need to be cleaned out before cooking? Are aspic and lemon Jello the same thing?

If you are going to do any amount of cooking in your home, you will need more help than can be given here. These are required:

(1) **A general-purpose cookbook**. My favorite is the *Betty Crocker Cookbook*; the *Better Homes and Gardens Cookbook* is also good. Whatever you get, it should be topically

organized, beginning with "Appetizers and Beverages" and ending with "Vegetables and Special Helps."

(2) **A nutrition guide**. You can get a comprehensive one, or pick up those little pamphlets at the supermarket checkout counter—Calorie Counter, Protein Counter, Carbohydrate Counter, etc.

Add to this duo other cookbooks and cooking guides that suit your taste. You may want a health-foods cookbook if that's your thing, or a Mexican cookbook, or a Chinese cookbook, or a Crockpot cookbook, or a Microwave cookbook. May I also suggest the *More With Less Cookbook*, by Doris Janzen Longacre (Scottsdale, PA: Herald Press, 1982). It was sponsored by the Mennonite Central Committee, and contains hundreds of recipes and suggestions that help you get maximum cooking enjoyment with a minimum investment.

Some cookbooks have menu suggestions in addition to recipes, so you don't have to guess about which vegetable goes best with Indian curry (peas, no question) or what kind of condiment would enhance the pork chops (spiced apples or applesauce). A good cookbook will also give emergency substitutions (a tablespoon of vinegar in fresh milk will do if you don't have buttermilk on hand) and even show you where the knives and forks and spoons go on a properly set table.

Use your nutrition guide to make sure that you're getting some nourishment from your efforts. Okay, you take a multivitamin every day. But that doesn't address your need for adequate protein, or help you figure out the salt content of a dill pickle. Remember, you don't have Mom figuring all that stuff out for you; you don't even have the dubious food at the dining hall (it was horrible, yes, but it was somewhat balanced—in its own peculiar way). You'll have to know what you're doing because no one is going to do it for you.

Equipment

The equipment that you need to get started cooking at home will be determined largely by your tastes. I can't fix French toast without a French whisk, but have gone all my life *sans* electric can opener, which is standard in many kitchens. So rather than follow some kind of shopping list of essential items, my suggestion is to scrounge what you can and keep your eyes open for good buys on the equipment that you have a need for as time progresses.

Just so you don't starve in the first few weeks, here is an idea of what you might procure in the early days:

- Utensils that can be used to get your food into an edible condition: a contraption to open cans, some cooking pots, and a frying pan. Also the appliances you perceive as crucial; and a toaster, crockpot, microwave, pressure cooker, wok, waffle iron, fondue pan, crepe pan.

- Tools with which to manipulate food: sharp knives for cutting, big spoons for stirring and ladling, forks for stabbing, spatulas for turning and scraping, and the all-important French whisk for creating smoothe béarnaise.

- The wherewithal to get the food into your mouth: whatever assortment of plates, bowls, drinking glasses, hot-drink cups or mugs, and flatware you desire.

- Cartons in which to store leftovers: if anyone wants to know what they can do for you, have them throw a Tupperware party in your honor. This is the sort of thing you need to save leftovers effectively, preserving their integrity for encore performances. Lacking Tupperware or Rubbermaid-type storing containers (they tend to be a bit pricey), buy your margarine in reusable tubs, save your cottage cheese cartons, keep your bread sacks, and hang on to the empty peanut butter jars. If it held food once, it can probably hold food again.

- Paper towels, aluminum foil, plastic wrap, waxed paper, and plastic bags make the job easier.

- Dish cloths, dish towels, hot pads, and an apron are needed.

- A couple of good rubber spatulas or scrapers rescue food that might otherwise be wasted.

Gratefully accept the castoffs of generous friends and relatives (indeed, solicit them), mosey on down to the thrift stores and check out their wares, and look for foods that come in useful containers (powdered breakfast drink in a pitcher, saltine crackers in a canister tin, jelly in juice glasses, etc.).

Thinking long-term, you should seriously consider making an investment in high-quality cookware. When you are shopping, ask the clerk for recommendations, look for warranties, and try to imagine what fate might befall your cookware and how each piece will react to it: is there a handle that's bound to loosen over time? (Count on it.) Is that nonstick finish guaranteed against flaking? (It better be.) Will the enamel coating chip? (Yes.) Could the pan warp if it got really hot? (Imminently possible.) You might want to bypass the fancy designer goods and buy old-fashioned, no-frills cast-iron pots and pans. They're cheap, indestructible, heat evenly, become naturally nonstick over time, and give you a fair dose of your Minimum Daily Requirement of iron.

Stocking the Shelves

As for obtaining the basic building blocks of food preparation, the same goes here as for equipment: buy what you need on an ad hoc basis. It would be fantastically expensive to fill your cupboards (no matter how small they are) with all the so-called essentials in one fell swoop.

A better idea is to build up your stock of staples over a period of weeks and months. As you plan menus and get the needed ingredients, you will build up supplies. One spaghetti supper, for example, will leave you with a nearly-full jar of oregano or blended Italian seasoning, perhaps some basil and garlic powder, a half-box of spaghetti noodles, and a bottle of salad oil. Then you make chili, and now you've got chili powder, ground cumin, and a can of kidney beans you decided not to use. A batch of chocolate chip cookies and you have vanilla extract, baking powder, and brown sugar on the shelf.

As you shop, keep your eye open for special prices on items that will contribute to your well-supplied larder: sugar, flour, salt, rice, vegetable shortening, cocoa, and the like. If you make it a point to buy at least one new spice each time you go to the store, you'll soon have a library of seasonings with which to enhance your cooking efforts. Watch the life of your spices, though; they tend to lose flavor over a period of time, so don't buy more than you can use in a year.

Yeow!

(1) When washing dishes, never throw a sharp knife in the soapy water for soaking. Keep your hands on it at all times. Pick it

up, dunk it, clean it off, rinse it, and put it in the drainer—handle up.

(2) If you put a knife in the dishwasher, make sure it's handle up, or you might impale your hand when unloading. Keep sharp knives separated from other utensils (as in drawers).

(3) Don't have a smoke alarm so close to the stove that you set it off each time you burn a pizza. That will make you distrust your alarm. *Do* keep a fire extinguisher close by. Know how to use it (it's okay to practice a little outside).

(4) If a fire starts in your stove, don't throw water on it. Most likely it's a chemical or oily fire that won't respond to water. Use your fire extinguisher or, failing that, baking soda or flour. Do what you can, but don't take chances. Call for help if it gets out of hand.

(5) Keep hot pad holders and kitchen linens away from the stove; they'll land on a hot burner sooner or later, and will quickly ignite.

(6) If you have a gas stove or oven that must be lit manually, have your match (a wooden kitchen match, not a paper match) already lit before you turn on the gas.

(7) If you smell gas, open the windows and call the super, the landlord, or the gas company. Don't ignore a gas smell.

(8) When broiling, pull the oven door open a crack and keep your eye on what you're doing. Don't leave the kitchen when broiling.

(9) Don't keep matches on the stove.

(10) The food junk that accumulates in the drip pans of your stove can catch on fire. If it's burned through and through, there's little danger. But if there's some life left in it, you should wipe it out before you cook.

(11) Never use a wet hot pad holder to handle something hot. Water conducts the heat; you'll get burned.

(12) Before you sit down to eat what you've prepared, check the oven and stove to make sure all burners are off; check any appliances you used to make sure they're off as well.

(13) Don't go fishing around in your toaster with a fork or knife until you've unplugged it. Same goes with any electric appliance; cut off the juice at the plug (not just at the switch) before commencing an investigation.

(14) If the cord on an electrical appliance is frayed or if the switch is temperamental, fix or replace it.

(15) Make sure you've got the kitchen ventilated, especially if

you're cleaning out the oven with something caustic, or burning large quantities of food.

(16) Use pans that are big enough to accommodate the food you're cooking *and* any expansion.

(17) Don't leave the house with the dishwasher going, or with meat thawing on the counter. Stay around until the dishwasher has completed its cycle, and thaw the meat in the refrigerator if you can't keep an eye on it.

(18) Don't keep cracked or chipped drinking glasses around. Throw them away, or give them to the art department at the university so they can turn them into *objets d'art*. A cracked glass will eventually be a ragged, broken glass—it's just a matter of time.

(19) Don't store heavy items in precarious places. This means that cereal boxes should go on the highest shelves, and canned foods on the lowest, where they're less likely to fall. This advice comes to you after having recently dropped a twelve-pound crockpot on my head.

(20) Keep your cupboard doors closed.

(21) Keep poisonous chemicals away from your food.

(22) Keep your dog's bed out of the kitchen. Same goes for your cat, your hamster, your parakeet. The kitchen is no place for pets.

(23) Don't leave food out. If you even *suspect* that it's perishable, keep it in the refrigerator or freezer.

(24) If it looks bad, pitch it.

Eating Out

Even with all this great information about how to do grocery shopping, and how to navigate in the kitchen, you may have objections to the eat-at-home experience.

"Hey, I don't think I can hack it," you say. "It's too dangerous, for one thing. Not only falling crockpots and spontaneously combusting kitchen towels, but chicken salad that could put me out of commission for a week. And talk about expensive! You can spend a small fortune on a piece of veal that never turns into dinner, or end up losing your security deposit on account of a well-used oven. Not me, Jack."

Some people are just natural restaurant patrons; others are forced into that role by circumstances beyond their control: unexpected company demanding sustenance, roommates who eat up all the good stuff, or the craving for something more tantalizing than Kraft American Singles on Weight Watchers Rye.

And so they seek out a restaurant. Problems begin to present themselves right from the start. You live in a small town that boasts only one sit-down restaurant and two hamburger drive-ins. Or you live in a big city where the range of possibilities is daunting, to mention nothing of the cost of parking, snooty headwaiters, random spoons on the table, and meal checks that look like your weekly take-home pay.

Every person who's living on his or her own should know the restaurants that are accessible (within walking or easy driving distance, depending on your mode of transportation); affordable (you should have a range of possibilities, from Dirt Cheap to Within Reach); and appetizing (which has to do not only with the food served, but the ambiance of the place, the amicability of the waiters, and the cleanliness of the kitchen).

If you live in a big town, you can keep your eyes open for restaurant reviews in the local paper. Only in the larger cities will these reviews be reliable; if it's bad, they'll actually tell you so. In smaller cities, the restaurants under consideration will also be potential advertisers in the newspaper, so if the critic didn't find any virtues in the place, he's liable to invent a few.

Better yet, ask a friend or acquaintance for advice. Use your head; ask your doctor for a good coat-and-tie place, the carryout boy at the supermarket for the best burgers in town. If you live with other people, set up a system whereby a new restaurant visited by any one roomie is critiqued for the benefit of all. If there are criticisms, ask for specifics. George may say that he hated Duffy's on account of the coleslaw which was creamy as opposed to vinegary—but you love creamy coleslaw, so there.

If you are uninformed about the cost of eating at a particular restaurant, call them up. Don't identify yourself; just ask the price of the average entrée on the menu (an entrée is the main attraction). Is that a complete dinner that includes salad, soup, etc., or is it an *à la carte* arrangement (which means that everything you eat has to be ordered and paid for separately—very expensive)? Beverage included? Dessert? Do they have any specials (all-you-can-eat buffet on Thursday nights)?

Speaking of all-you-can-eat, make sure that you want to eat what's being offered before investing a hefty price in a bottom-less-plate buffet. If a buffet is really cheap, it probably is. If it's high-priced, it may still be unspeakable. It's perfectly acceptable to arrive at a buffet restaurant, eyeball the offerings, and then walk out the door and over to Taco Bob's. You are under no obligation to eat brown lettuce, greasy chicken, and oily three-bean salad. If it is a decent buffet, make sure you have arrived with an appetite so as to get your money's worth. Sorry, it's strictly déclassé to sneak food out of a buffet situation. Not even rolls.

On the other hand, at a sit-down-and-be-served restaurant, Health Department regulations often require that any food placed on your table which is not eaten by you must be discarded by the restaurant—it can't be served to other customers. In which case, if there are three pieces of cornbread in the basket, and two pats of (unwrapped) butter left after you've had your fill, it's okay to wrap them up in your napkin or request a doggie bag. Restaurateurs sometimes take this as a compliment to their cooking, and nearly always prefer it to having to throw out perfectly good food.

Restaurants characteristically offer better values on their lunch menus than their dinner menus. The taco salad that goes for $2.99 before 2:00 will cost $3.99 after 5:00. So you might want to make lunchtime your big meal of the day, and have your sandwich for supper. A few restaurants who wish to fill their tables in the later afternoon will give really cut-rates to evening diners who order before 5:00 or maybe 6:00.

If you're interested in eating well and eating cheap at a restaurant, skip the appetizers, and drink water instead of Coke. Order a modest meal, and then get as much bread to come along with it as you can. Pass up the temptation to order extra cheese on the pizza ($1.30 extra) or a side of guacamole and sour cream for the enchiladas (seventy-five cents each). Skip the Roquefort dressing (always extra) and have the bleu cheese instead (usually no additional charge). Sometimes the takeout menu offers the same food at a reduced price since table service is not provided. Bring your grub home and add your own salad and beverage and dessert. Cheap. If you're getting fast food, you can create your own menu. Take your car to the restaurant that has the beverage and french fries you like; then move on to the place with the best burgers, then to the best hot fruit pies. Do all this at the drive-up window.

Don't be a slob; if you got good service from your waiter,

give him a fair tip, especially if he got you all white meat on your chicken platter, or kept your coffee cup topped off. For lunch at a regular kind of place, it can be 10 percent—certainly no less for acceptable service. Fifteen percent is better. For dinner at an up-market hash house, it's got to be 15 percent—or more. If the idea of tipping sticks in your craw, confine your dining to self-service restaurants and cafeterias that don't demand it. But if you're getting service—like it or not—you're expected to pay for it.

Bumming Meals

Bumming meals is an important part of living well. There are free meals out there, and some of them are pretty good ones, too. Keep your eyes open, your stomach ready, and your thanks profuse.

(1) If you work in a job where you, your coworkers, or your business associates have access to expense-account lunches, take full advantage. Discuss the new contract with your client over lunch; let your boss take you out to dinner every night during the week when his wife is visiting her mother (only if you're a guy—females beware!); let that insurance agent who's always trying to sell you Whole Life put her money where her mouth is and buy you a decent breakfast while stressing the importance of adequate coverage.

(2) Go to church suppers—the Wednesday night potluck things. (Indeed, don't join a church until you're absolutely sure that they do indeed have good and frequent church suppers.) You will be expected to bring something, of course. Make a Stir-and-Frost cake, or bring a green-bean-and-mushroom-soup casserole, and then gorge yourself on lasagne, fried chicken, marinated mushrooms, and Boston cream pie.

(3) Go to Sunday morning worship services with an empty stomach. Sit next to a nice family, one that has a robust-looking husband and wife (indicating that they like to eat). Make no effort to cover up the sound of your growling stomach during the service (enhance it if you can). Be friendly. Let them know, somewhat wistfully, that you're living on your own. Hope for an invitation to dinner.

(4) Drop by at Mom's around dinnertime. Don't be proud. You can eat her food without losing face on this independence thing. If you are living in a town other than that of your immediate family, look up any and all (long-lost) relatives with whom

you can hook up. They will want to cook for you.

(5) Many charities use free banquets to raise funds. Wangle an invitation if you can. They pay for the eats, and hope you'll pledge to their organization. Eat for sure; give if it seems worthwhile.

(6) Eat at the supermarket.

(7) Never turn down an invitation to a party at which food will be served, no matter what. Eat and leave if you must; the important thing is to eat.

(8) Go to those cookware parties where a demonstrator makes a complete meal with his state-of-the-art waterless pots and pans.

(9) Attend grand openings—barber shops, car dealerships, supermarkets, computer stores, boutiques: they nearly always have something to eat.

"BROWN BAGGING"

There are many reasons for carrying your own lunch to work or school. You don't feel like you've really gotten full use out of the Partridge Family lunch box you've had since second grade; you adhere to a special diet that makes nearly every restaurant a danger zone; you prefer your own cooking to anyone else's; you are tired of paying an arm and a leg for runny spaghetti and soggy garlic bread; you prefer to eat in the open air where you can commune with nature while refueling.

Whatever your motivation, you can eat better and cheaper by bringing your own lunch. If you insist on eating every lunch at a restaurant you'll be over-junked on Whoppers, McNuggets, and Extra Crispy. Or you'll spend a weekly fortune in pursuit of balanced meals . . . not to mention the time investment of scoping out likely bistros, traveling to and from same, waiting for your order to be filled, and standing in line to pay the check.

Many companies, including lots of small offices, have recognized the need to accommodate lunch-toters, and provide refrigerators and microwave ovens for lunch storage and preparation. Unless you have a cool place to stash your lunch until it's time to eat, stay away from mayonnaise-based sandwich fillings that might go bad on you. Use vacuum bottles to bring hot soup and cold drinks. Don't confine yourself to peanut-butter-and-jelly sandwiches. Especially if you have a microwave, leftovers from the night before can be easily converted into today's lunch. Even a hot radiator will heat up a bowl of soup for you. (If you work in a foundry, so much the better.)

Don't feel self-conscious about bringing your lunch. It's cool. I have it from an excellent source that Richard Gere always brings his own lunches to eat on the set; he's somewhat of a food snob and shuns the commissary. Speaking of which, if your company provides a free lunch at an employee cafeteria, or even a well-subsidized one, take full advantage of it. Eat your big meal when it's cheapest to do so, be it breakfast, lunch, or dinner.

ANIMALS EATEN BY AN AVERAGE PERSON IN A 70-YEAR LIFETIME

14 cattle
12 sheep
2 calves
880 chickens
770 lbs. fish
23 hogs
35 turkeys

(From *The People's Almanac*, p. 1049.)

FRUITS THAT RIPEN AFTER PICKING

Apples
Apricots
Avocados
Bananas
Mangoes
Muskmelons
Papayas
Peaches
Pears
Persimmons

FRUITS THAT DO *NOT* RIPEN AFTER PICKING

Blackberries
Blueberries
Cherries
Grapefruit
Grapes
Lemons
Oranges
Pineapples
Plums
Raspberries
Strawberries
Watermelons

(From *The Book of Lists #2*, p. 383.)

17.

CLOTHES

Dressing for Work

There are precious few positions available to which you can wear Birkenstock sandals, khaki shorts, and a Mumford Athletic Department T-shirt (your student wardrobe); your backpack may be replaced by an attaché case, your poncho windbreaker by a London Fog trench coat, and your rainbow thongs by spectator pumps. It's the price one pays for taking home a paycheck twice a month.

Most jobs have a uniform, official or unofficial, and it is essential that you know this before you go spending a fortune on clothes. There are a few free spirits who dress as they please despite the rules, but they pay a price for their individuality. If you take your job seriously, you should also take the dress expectations seriously.

Some requirements are obvious: nurses, postal workers, police officers, and Federal Express drivers are locked into what they wear on the job. Other jobs require special attire: hard hats and steel-toed shoes for construction workers, leotards for Jazzercise teachers, or coveralls for housepainters. These uniforms just make good sense.

Those who work in banking, finance, insurance, and sales know that the way they dress sends a message to their clients, coworkers, and superiors. The gray flannel business suit is a Wall Street standard for men; a navy blue skirted suit with closed-toe pumps and fedora is the equivalent for women. John Molloy, who wrote *Dress for Success* and *The Woman's Dress for Success Book*, made this abundantly clear. Although there was initial resistance to the ideas presented in his books, they are now accepted as gospel by a generation of yuppies and yumpies who follow Molloy's directions to the letter.

Between the junior executives and the Easter Seals camp directors lies a tremendous no-man's-land, where millions of employees rise from their beds in the morning, gaze sleepily into their closets, and ruminate on the relative merits of wingtips, blue jeans, and dangle earrings. For this baffled horde I offer the following bits of advice, distilled from years of dressing for work:

(1) You are more likely to be singled out by your superiors for bad taste than for good taste. Exquisite taste in clothes is apt to be noticed and rewarded in some fields (the fashion industry, or garment retailing, perhaps), but it is generally enough to simply not be misdressed, and it is this situation that should concern you.

(2) You may choose to keep track of what you wear, and when, in hopes of not wearing the same thing twice within a given period of time (a week, two weeks, a month), but it is highly unlikely that anyone else is doing the same. This knowledge can free you from the burden of having fifteen different outfits in order to adhere to some arbitrary repeat pattern.

(3) Since you don't have to concern yourself with the matter of quantity, you can concentrate on quality clothes. This is a worthwhile pursuit.

(4) It pays to get the highest quality you can afford when buying clothes that will get a lot of wear. The cost of the garment, divided by the number of times it is worn, equals a Cost-Per-Wearing quotient that reflects the true value of your purchase. This is especially true of shoes that you work in or work out in. It's also worth your while to get a good quality coat or suit, confining yourself to classic styles that will last for many seasons.

(5) Don't invest your big bucks in five-inch French heels, gold lamé jackets, or any garment that will be worn infrequently. Get these things as cheaply as you can—from discount stores, secondhand clothing stores, or garage sales. Better yet, borrow

them from a friend. Remember: cost divided by the times worn equals Cost-Per-Wearing. The CPW will be high if you blow a bundle on a once-worn dress or jacket.

(6) Buy clothes that will be easy to maintain. Anything that says "Dry clean only" on the label should be purchased only if you are prepared to pay the cleaning bills. If the label says "Hand wash or dry clean," then you can get a bottle of Woolite or other cold-water cleaner and do it yourself, at considerable savings. Watch out for garments that will need a lot of ironing. Ironing is a time-consuming and tremendously boring activity. A garment that must be ironed will tend to look lived in after you've been wearing it for a few hours.

(7) Consider the part of the country you're living in. This is especially important if you've moved from Phoenix to Buffalo, or Anchorage to Tulsa. You may think you've just gotten yourself a perfectly serviceable winter coat, only to find that the open neck and wide raglan sleeves are an open door to icy winter winds. If you are unfamiliar with the climate you find yourself in, ask store clerks and friends and coworkers to advise you on what you'll need. As a general rule, buy clothes in the same vicinity as they'll be worn in.

(8) Pick a color scheme and stay with it. Your one pair of brown oxfords or black pumps will go a long way if you buy everything with respect to them. Shoes are really expensive, and if you insist on wearing every color under the rainbow in your clothes, you will be forced to buy a lot of shoes that will get little wear, or to wear shoes that kill an otherwise nice outfit.

(9) Buy clothes that are trans-seasonal. Stay away from those that can *only* be worn in the dead of winter or on a blazing summer day. A medium-weight suit can be matched with a sweater vest for winter wear or short-sleeved cotton shirt for the summer months. A seersucker suit, on the other hand, is dog-days only, and Harris tweed is strictly winter.

(10) Don't buy anything that doesn't fit just right; be sure not to buy a garment that's too small, with the intention of dieting to fit it. Diet first, then buy.

(11) Boots look terrible if you let them sit on the floor of your closet with the tops drooping down; boot-trees are also expensive. Roll up a section of newspaper, and stick these in your boots.

(12) Take care of your shoes. Vinyl is cheap, but leather lasts.

If they get wet, or get salt on them in the winter, or suffer other abuse, treat them as soon as you can with the appropriate remedy. A paste-type leather treatment is a good investment that will make your shoes last longer. Before consigning a pair of old leather shoes to the Goodwill box, take them into a shoe repair shop and see what can be done. They can be restored, dyed, resoled, reheeled, and revived. If the shoe fits, repair it.

(13) If you buy a garment that proves unsatisfactory, return it. You're not obligated to pay good money for colors that bleed, collars that pucker, shirts that shrink, or seams that split.

LABELS

The most obvious function of a clothing label is to identify the designer and/or manufacturer. Some labels have such status that they have been incorporated into the design of the garment, hence, T-shirts with "Esprit" silkscreened on them, or sweaters with the distinctive Bill Blass initials knit into the pattern.

Don't be misled by a label. Designers hire independent manufacturers to produce their creations with little attention to whether or not the manufacturer is doing a quality job. Consequently, it's possible to find a high-status designer's name on the label, and also to find poorly sewn seams, unclipped threads, machine oil smudges on the fabric, and mismatched plaids and stripes. So don't let the label be the last word on quality. Inspect every garment you buy to make sure it's up to snuff.

Bootlegging designer clothes is a big business. If you find a store that carries a lot of designer clothes, but whose quality is consistently substandard, it might be worth contacting a consumer protection agency about the situation. It's a crime, you know, and you're the victim.

A less appreciated but vastly more important label is the one that tells fabric content and gives instructions for care of the garment. Know this label lingo:

_____

Colorfast—the dyes are such that the colors won't run, bleed, or fade under normal circumstances.

Crease-resistant or wrinkle resistant—needs little or no ironing;

wrinkles that do develop will probably hang out overnight. This is *not* the same as . . .

Permanent press—if the garment is removed from the dryer immediately, *no* ironing will be necessary.

Drip-dry—will require little or no ironing *if* it is washed by hand and hung up to dry while still soaking wet.

Shrink resistant or preshrunk—laundering will not cause shrinkage beyond a specified percentage (usually 3 percent).

Soil release—a special treatment has been placed on the fabric so that greasy, oily spots will come out in the wash. Similar to . . .

Spot- and stain-resistant—which means that a surface coating will cause water and gunk to bead up so it can be easily wiped off.

Washable—you can throw it in an automatic washing machine. This is in contrast to *dry clean only*.

Dry clean only—is the only instruction on a care label that may not be true. Many "dry clean only" garments may be washed by hand *if* they're done in cold water, *if* a gentle cleaner (like Woolite) is used, *if* they are not twisted or wrung out, *if* they are dried flat, and so on. "Dry clean only" means that dry cleaning is the *best* way to clean, but not necessarily the *only* way.

Wash-and-wear—beyond washing and drying, little additional care is required.

Waterproof—the pores of the fabric are chemically sealed against (or naturally resistant to) water penetration. Scotch-guarding is a well-known waterproofing process.

Water-repellent—water will usually roll off before it is absorbed.

Laundry

Wash day! Since all your clothes are preshrunk, soil-resistant, and permanent press, this'll be a snap. We'll assume, for purposes of discussion, that you do not have your own washer and dryer. You will be patronizing the neighborhood laundromat, or the laundry room in the basement of your apartment building, or some other commercial concern.

The first thing you must do is scope out the territory and find the best possible laundry facility. The overall quality of laundromats varies from city to city. In Chicago, for example, I found that the quality of the laundromats was very high; a lot of people live in apartments, and their business inspires competition. In suburban East Memphis, the laundromats were the pits. Apparently most people owned their own machines, and the only people who patronized the laundromats were students and bag ladies. And me, of course—I was there.

Here's what to look for in a laundromat:

Location. Is it close? (If it's in your building, the location is obviously good.) Take into consideration the safety of the neighborhood since you're apt to be there at night, and the convenience of parking.

Ambiance. You're going to have to sit there for a couple of hours. Is it clean? Does it attract a decent kind of person? Are there unsavory types hanging around? Are there chairs to sit in, soft-drink and candy machines, piped in music? Is it a fun place?

Facilities. Check for the following: large surfaces for folding clothes; wheeled carts for transferring clothes from washers to dryers; vending machines that sell soap powder, bleach, and fabric softener; late model machines (should have automatic fabric softener and bleach dispensers and a variety of cycles—permanent press, delicate, etc.); a change machine that takes bills, or an attendant who will give change.

Cost. The cost of washing a load can be easily compared with other facilities. When it comes to dryers, the important thing to know is how long the dryer runs on a dime or a quarter or whatever. A good dryer that costs a quarter for one nice, long cycle can be more economical than an inefficient dryer that takes a handful of dimes to dry a small load of lingerie.

After deciding on the laundromat you're going to use, it's a good thing to patronize it regularly. If you know what kind of change you're going to need for your laundromat's machines, you can be saving it over the course of the week. If it has an attendant and you are recognized as a regular customer, the attendant might agree to do some nice things for you, like change a five, or watch your clothes while you're doing your grocery shopping, or even put your wash load into the dryer for you (a tip would not be inappropriate in such a case). Finally, if you're a regular you can get to know the other people who also come regularly. Since they're likely to live in your neighborhood—

maybe in your building—it's a good way to meet folks. Nice folks who do their laundry.

Basic Equipment

The basics of laundry equipment are pretty straightforward. Here they are:

Laundry baskets—probably two. You can use these as hampers during the week; put them in the bottom of your closet or at the foot of the basement stairs, and feed them your dirty clothes. Then cart your stuff to the laundromat in the same baskets. They can be cheap—often available for $1.99 at discount stores.

Laundry detergent. Naturally, this is a very personal matter. But if you have to cart your detergent around with you everywhere you go, there's no sense in buying a bulky detergent. Many of the newer brands take only a quarter-cup per washload, as opposed to a cup and a half or two cups of the old-fashioned kind. And the new ones might even have fabric softener in them, which is good.

Bleach. Most people will need an all-fabric bleach; if you have a lot of white Jockey shorts and sweat socks and bathtowels, you should also have a jug of chlorine bleach.

Fabric softener. Also very personal. Some people think it's a waste of money; others, fearing electrocution from static, swear by fabric softener. Softeners can be liquid preparations that are added to the final rinse cycle, or the sheet-things that are thrown in the dryer. Either way, they coat your clothes with something that makes them less likely to cling to each other, softer to the touch, and fresh-smelling. It's really up to you.

Measuring cup. You'll overuse detergent and bleach and fabric softener without the aid of a measuring cup.

Hangers. Once you've washed and dried your shirts and blouses and dresses, you're going to hang them up immediately so you don't have to iron them.

The Kill

Armed with your soiled clothes and your basic equipment, you set off to the laundromat. Chin up, head high, you will get them clean. In the space of an hour or two you too will say that dirt was no match for you.

You walk confidently to the washer(s) you wish to use. You make every effort to get a bank of washers all to yourself. You turn them on, measure in the detergent, and with great aplomb, proceed to sort your dirty clothes into the washers, grouping together dark cottons, permanent press, delicates and knits, clothes to be bleached, etc. No, you have not wasted time sorting clothes at home, or humiliated yourself by throwing your soiled clothes into piles on the floor of the laundromat. With one simple procedure you are now in possession of sorted clothes. (Remember to empty pockets as you sort.) Naturally, you want to get your money's worth when washing; nevertheless, resist the temptation to overstuff the machine. Fill it about two-thirds full of clothes.

Sorting is crucial to effective washing. A pair of new Levis thrown in with your white underwear spells D-I-S-A-S-T-E-R. If you have anything that's new, and are washing it for the first time, play it safe and let it have its own load. Think of it as a concession to being the rookie member of your wardrobe. Midway through the wash cycle, open the washing machine and take a look at the water. Dark blue? Dark red? Dark green? Uh oh, trouble. Wash it separately until the wash water tones down a little bit. Always refer to the care label inside each garment. If it says "cool wash" or "permanent press cycle" you'll do well to obey.

You are no dummy; neither are you afraid to look like a novice at the laundromat. Out of respect for your clothes you carefully read the information printed on the inside of the washer lid, or by the cycle settings, making sure that only those things that can stand a hot wash will get one, giving your fine clothes the care they need and deserve. Having successfully initiated the washing process of doing laundry, you gather up your paraphernalia (clothes baskets, hangers, and leftover detergent) and set about the task of amusing yourself for the next half-hour.

If there's an attendant on duty, you may have the luxury of leaving the laundromat to pursue other adventures—some browsing at the bookstore next door, a phone call to a friend, or grabbing a bite to eat whilst your clothes are frothing and churning. But don't take chances; most people prefer to keep a watch over their clothes, adding bleach or fabric softener at the proper moment, checking the suds level, and guarding them against theft.

So you read a book or a magazine, or count lint balls on the floor, or try to guess the name of each other customer's mother (first name only), or strike up a conversation with the hunk sitting next to you, or whatever seems appropriate.

Laundromats are a great place to meet people. It might be worth it to you to dress up a little—not heels and a feather boa, but you don't have to wear your rattiest cut offs, either (unless they're the only thing you have clean). Do *not* use this time to catch up on work from the office (ever-present danger of spills), polish your nails (they'll get smeared when you have to handle the clothes), or do an aerobic workout (obvious reasons). Remember that you are in a public place, and you have a job to do. Amuse yourself in a socially acceptable way.

Once the clothes are washed, they must be dried. If you have thrown your plastic shower curtain or rubber tub mat in with your terrycloth towels (which is a very good way to get them clean), remove them and let them air dry. The dryer is a hot place—don't tempt it with meltable materials.

You can usually get more than one wash load in a dryer. Let the dryer go for only one cycle. After it's done, check your clothes. Remove any that are already dry; you can fold these while the rest are getting done. Continue to check your clothes at intervals, removing what's dry and leaving the rest.

Superconfident types have no qualms at all about folding their clothes right there in the laundromat, in front of everybody. I have a grudging admiration for those clods who treat their fellow men to a view of their ripped underwear and sweat-stained undershirts. Most hurriedly stuff their clothes into duffle bags and slink furtively out of the laundromat, keeping the condition of their shorts a secret. You'll end up doing whatever you're comfortable with. But, if you have enough nerve to fold your sheets and towels, at least, and hang your shirts and blouses onto the hangers you brought with you, you'll prevent a lot of wrinkles.

Ironing

The big word in ironing these days is "don't." Don't iron unless you absolutely have to. Buy clothes that can be pulled out of the dryer and worn as is.

If you must iron, do it infrequently. An iron takes gobs of

energy to heat up, so once it's hot, press everything you've got. You don't need a lot of equipment to iron. Get a decent steam iron that you can run on tap water (distilled water is a waste of money). You don't necessarily need an ironing board; get a big beach towel or a couple of good-sized bathtowels and fold them into a pad that you can put on your kitchen counter and use for ironing. Check the condition of the counter from time to time. If you are doing a lot of ironing, you may find that you need to move your pad to a different location so the Formica can cool down.

If you're ironing a shirt or blouse, do it in this order: collar, cuffs, sleeves, back yoke, front panels, back. Deviate from this sequence at your peril; for some unknown reason it's the one that works.

Your iron will show you which setting should be used for what kinds of clothes. Again, read the label on your garment carefully so you don't burn a hole in a silk blouse on account of a too-hot iron.

A 100 percent cotton or linen garment can stand high heat, which is fortunate, because it'll take a lot of heat to get the wrinkles out. About an hour before you're going to iron, sprinkle your clothes with tap water—dip your fingers in a bowl of water and flick the drops onto the garment. Then roll it up and let the water make the garment moist. Your ironing will work better when the cloth isn't bone dry.

It might be wise to get dress shirts laundered professionally. It costs, sure, but it makes a big impression and it will save you a lot of time.

Don't waste time ironing sheets and tea towels. I don't care if your mother always did—it's ridiculous.

18.

TRANSPORTATION

One of the most challenging aspects of living on your own is getting around: getting from your place to Roger's place; getting to and from work; getting to the IGA; getting home for Christmas; getting to the lake for the weekend.

In America, you're nobody without a car . . . right? Having a car is everything. Thirteen-year-olds already know what sort of wheels they're going to get as soon as they turn eighteen. Receiving the keys to the family car is an important rite of passage. Having your own car assures a certain level of popularity in high school. Kids with cars are popular kids. Even if it's a barely ambulatory junker, you're still popular. If it's a '63 Impala convertible, you're admired. If it's a brand new Trans-Am, you're famous.

This is not fantasy; this is truth. There's no getting around it, cars are important. For that reason it's going to be extremely difficult to present a convincing argument against automotive extravagance, but here's my best shot:

The purchase of an automobile will be, even in the best of all possible worlds, a crap shoot. Careful consideration will often end in huge disappointment, because cars are unpredictable, and so are owners. This major commitment to buy is often, alas, an emotional decision. The car is seen as a means of ego-fulfillment—how else do you explain farm kids owning Firebirds and

Corvettes and city kids driving Jeeps, 4 x 4's, and vintage pick-ups? These vehicle choices have much more to do with the owner's self-image and personality than his or her transportation needs. So let's put the cards on the table.

Do you *need* a car? Do you need a *new* car? Do you need a big car? A fancy car? A sports car? Ask yourself these questions:

(1) How far must I go to get to work each day?

(2) Is there adequate accessible public transportation to work? What is the monthly cost of public transportation?

(3) Would a car be used mainly for in-town driving, or over-the-road driving? What kind of traffic would I encounter most often? Good roads or bad?

(4) How many miles per year would I put on a car?

(5) Am I usually driving alone, or would I be likely to have passengers?

(6) Is parking easy to find and affordable for the driving I would do?

(7) Would the car ever be used for cross-country or long-distance trips?

(8) Do I have a garage, carport, or other off-street parking?

(9) Do I need cargo space?

(10) Do I need Indy 500 performance, or something closer to "The Little Engine That Could"?

"Restore human legs as a means of travel. Pedestrians rely on food for fuel and need no special parking facilities."
Lewis Mumford

It's amazing how many people in this country drive huge station wagons to get themselves—and themselves only—to and from work, an approximate distance of about three-quarters of a mile; or how many own sports cars specifically designed to accommodate only one other passenger, when they are consistently called upon to carry more; or the number of drivers who invest in high-performance machines that never see the open road.

The fact of the matter is that you can vacation in Acapulco for two weeks every winter—airfare, hotel accommodations, food, and all the mariachi bands you can stomach, tax included—for the amount of money it costs to maintain the average car for four or five months. That's right! Even secondhand cars are expensive. You still have to buy, license and pay taxes on, keep supplied with gas, insure, house, maintain, etc., ad infinitum.

"Only 10,000 Miles on This Beauty . . ."

Okay, maybe I didn't talk you out of it. No matter what anybody says, you're going to buy the car of your dreams. You are *determined*. But perhaps at this point you'd be open to some good advice.

(1) Remember that new cars lose about 30 percent of their value the second they're driven out of the showroom. You paid $8,000 for a brand new car, but once it's in your driveway no one will give you more than $5,600 for it. Period. You lost $2,400 the moment it hit the street.

(2) The cost of credit varies. If it will take a bank loan to get you into the car of your dreams, call around—call banks, savings and loans, and your company credit union to see what kind of financing they will give you on that particular car. Weigh the advantages of larger downpayments and extended terms (thirty-six- vs. forty-eight-month loans). Get the best credit you can. (Don't get a forty-eight-month loan on a car if you've got a short-term or tentative work situation. A union contract up for renewal soon, the prospect of a layoff, a probationary job, etc. are all good reasons to stay away from *any* kind of installment debt.)

(3) Used cars are best bought from private individuals. Car dealers know exactly what they can get for a car, and charge it. There are few bargains to be had from dealers. They also know how to make a lemon look like a beauty. (You know, of course, that there are aerosol sprays that smell like "new cars"—new vinyl, new carpet, new paint—and these are widely used by dealers). If you *do* buy from a dealer, check with friends and the Better Business Bureau to see if he's reputable. The reputation of the dealer is more important than the make of the car he's selling.

(4) Any used car you are considering should be checked out by a mechanic you trust. Keep in mind how much you have to

lose if it's a lemon, and you'll be more willing to pay the mechanic's nominal fee.

(5) Once you have decided on the car of your choice, call the following people to see what the "hidden" costs are going to be:

- Secretary of State's office: get figures on licensing fees and taxes you will be paying. Will you have to pay sales tax?

- County clerk: what is the title transfer fee?

- Insurance agent: what will be your yearly premium? This will depend on the coverages you buy, your age and sex, and your driving record. Get at least three quotes. Sports cars cost more to insure than sedans and economy cars; ergo, your insurance quote may cause you to reconsider your choice of a car.

Add to that the per-month cost of fuel (estimated miles per month divided by estimated miles per gallon times the price of gasoline you'll need to buy), oil and filters, any amounts you will have to pay to garage your car and park while at work. Then, allow yourself some slack for repairs. If you are getting a brand new car, most repairs will be covered by warranty, but some will not. Used cars purchased from dealers may also be covered by a limited warranty (although you usually have to pay extra for it). You may get a good deal on a used car that you know needs work (a new transmission or new tires), and this, too, should be figured into your projections.

(6) If you put a deposit down on the car, get a receipt that says, "Buyer may forfeit deposit and withdraw." Otherwise your deposit is a binding contract, and you have to buy the car even if you think better of it later.

(7) A private owner may agree to a thirty-day or other short-term warranty on the car. It wouldn't hurt to ask. Refusal to guarantee the car doesn't necessarily mean that it's a bad car, though. (Would you guarantee a used car?)

(8) Take into consideration the upkeep of your car. Repairs and maintenance are highest on cars with lots of extras (electric windows, for example); high technology (fuel injection); limited popularity in this country (exotic foreign models—M.G.s, Rolls Royses, Saabs, etc.); discontinued models (an old Studebaker or Corvair).

(9) Keep looking as long as you can stand it. Car shopping can be exhausting, frustrating, infuriating, and exasperating. Give up too early and you'll probably pay too much for too little. The longer and harder you search, the better deal you'll get.

Luckily, there is mobility without motor cars. Remember: two weeks in Acapulco every winter—including airfare, luxury hotel, enchiladas by the dozen, mariachi band outside the window, tax and gratuity—is what it costs to maintain your own car, minimum. That makes looking at the options worthwhile.

Another One Rides the Bus

If you're lucky enough to be living in a large metropolitan area that isn't Los Angeles or Houston, you have at your disposal a public transportation system that can meet virtually all your needs. (Some small cities and towns also have good transportation, typically a bus system. Get a route map and schedule before moving into a new place, if you can; bus service in small cities tends to be quirky.) You can ride the train into the city from your suburban home, catch a bus from the station to the office, and take an elevator—the ultimate in public transportation (can you imagine how expensive it would be if everyone rode their own lift up to their office?)—to the forty-second floor.

The subway or el is fast and cheap. If you're a regular commuter, a monthly pass or multitrip ticket will save you money— you know that. Even the occasional cab ride, expensive as it seems, is pennies compared to the cost of owning a car, especially in the city, where parking, garaging, and unintentional damage (scratches, nicks, and fender-benders) are costly.

The greatest news in commuting is walkman radio-tape players (and their myriad imitators). What used to be unproductive windshield-staring time is now a prime entertainment slot; or an opportunity to listen to motivation tapes, or management training tapes, or any of a variety of talking books. The wearing of earphones is a strong message to your fellow commuters: "I don't want to talk," it says, and gives you privacy. If you want to let people know you are interested in conversation, carry a magazine or newspaper instead, and look up from time to time. Don't be afraid to catch a person's eye, or return a smile or nod of the head. But don't go giving your name or personal information to a stranger, either. Friendly caution—that's the thing.

Two Wheels Are Better Than None

In some climates, motorcycles, mopeds, and bicycles are more than recreational equipment—they're serious transportation. Lucky you, if you reside in the sun belt; you may be able to get by with two wheels.

I don't have much good to say about motorcycling as a sport; it's a costly and dangerous pastime. But as transportation, motorcycles are good, reliable, and inexpensive—but only if the owner is serious about learning how to purchase, maintain, and drive them to their best advantage, and do it year-round. The cost of owning a motorcycle that can be ridden only during the summer months, necessitating the use of a car for the rest of the year, is high. I don't care if you are getting one hundred miles per gallon, it's still expensive to have a road-worthy bike *and* a car. (In a cool climate, a motorcycle/bus scheme would be economical.) If you are living in a warm climate, if you can get safe parking for your vehicle at work, if your friends don't mind riding on back, and if you are willing to assume the safety risk (even with a helmet, you're twice as likely to sustain injuries riding your 'cycle as you would driving a car), then you might want to investigate motorcycles as serious transportation.

Since bicycles are cheaper by far than motorcycles, they may be a prudent supplement to car ownership. Even if you own a car that you use in inclement weather or for long trips, a good commuting bike—one which can be outfitted new for under $250—will pay for itself in short order. In other words, you don't have to live in New Orleans or Honolulu to get your money's worth out of a bicycle that you use even occasionally for trips that would otherwise demand the use of your car.

A good commuting bike will have: upright handlebars; three to five speeds (more than this is usually not necessary); a rearview mirror and front headlight; a way to carry cargo (bumper clips, or baskets); and a clip-on tire pump. A biking commuter will have a good backpack, a waterproof poncho, a lock, a working knowledge of how bikes are put together and the ability to handle road emergencies. These are necessities; if I were commuting with a bike, I would add a chain guard, a water bottle, a traffic flag, and a helmet.

Although bicycle riding has limitations when it comes to carrying cargo, or covering long distances in a short time, the cost savings and physical benefits of bike riding (as opposed to automobile driving) are so great that most people *should* have a bike, and use it whenever they can.

Between motorcycles and bikes are mopeds, neither fish nor fowl. Since they are motorized, users are apt to take little advantage of the peddling possibilities. But because the motor is so small, there is often not enough power to handle strenuous road conditions, much less avoid trouble. Mopeds have limited usefulness, and are excessively dangerous.

The main problem with any kind of two-wheeled transportation is that you get no respect. Cars are used to watching out for cars, not for motorcycles, mopeds, and bicycles—or pedestrians, for that matter. If you're in anything other than a big full-sized car, you have to take extraspecial care. If you're riding a bike and get hit by a Lincoln Continental, it'll be small comfort that the Lincoln should have been more careful—although you're bound to reflect on this fact during your prolonged hospitalization. If you're going to travel on two wheels, go into it knowing that car drivers will ignore you, cut in front of you, deny you a full lane, run you off the road, spray water on you, and resent you in a hundred different ways. And you will be nearly powerless against their carelessness and wrath.

"Beam Me Up, Scottie."

Walking is cheap. So is bumming rides. No matter how many cars, motorcycles, bikes, mopeds, unicycles, or transporter rooms you have, hoofing and mooching should be your first choice when it comes to transporting your body from one place to another. The thrill of crossing eight lanes of interstate highway on foot, of skillfully dodging cabs and articulated buses on a crowded city street, of confidently striding over hill and dale: what can match it? The social interaction that comes about as a result of imposing yourself on friends, the challenge of crowding yet another person into an overloaded VW, or finding a friend who is going as far as Arby's—these are priceless and precious experiences, the stuff that will comfort you in your old age as you reflect on your youth.

"Gee, Gramps, you mean that when you were a kid people were still driving around in cars? You could just ask someone you

worked with to give you a ride to a friend's house?"
"That's right, Cosmo. Ah, those were the days . . ."

"Natives who beat drums to drive off evil spirits are objects of scorn to smart Americans who blow horns to break up traffic jams."
Mary Ellen Kelly

Part IV:
Alive and
Well

19.

HEALTH

Button up your overcoat
When the wind is free
Take good care of yourself
You belong to me.

Oops. You live on your own now. You don't really "belong" to anybody (except perhaps to Uncle Sam for tax purposes). Mom isn't around to push chewable Vitamin C tablets on you when you start to sniffle. Student Health isn't around the corner, ready to dispense Ace bandages and knee braces to you, the weekend warrior. You don't even have a P.E. requirement to keep you fit.

Statistically, people who live alone don't live as long as those who live with a spouse or a friend. Why is this? Maybe it's a psychological thing—they don't have anyone to live for, so they give up earlier. But I suspect that eventually singles suffer for lack of a nagging spouse to enforce weight loss, a doting friend who will detect the first sign of an illness that needs treatment, an eating companion who cooks and appreciates being cooked for, or a live-in tennis partner.

The caricature of an overweight, heavy-drinking, chain-smoking, hardworking independent kind of guy—probably a stressed-out investigative reporter for a national newsmagazine—

epitomizes the at-risk single person. A spouse wouldn't stand for it; neither would a roommate or parent. But, without their input, health declines: exercise is infrequent, nutrition is ignored, and illness goes unattended.

Okay, you're going to live forever. You're young, and it's ridiculous to look so far ahead. But even without speculating on the future, it's easy to see how attention to the rudiments of wellness (they called it hygiene in high school) can make you healthier and happier now. You're in a different phase of your life. You need to set some standards for nutrition, exercise, and medical care that you can live with today and in the years to come.

Satchel Paige's Ideas for Staying Young

1. Avoid fried meats which angry up the blood.

2. If your stomach disputes you, lie down and pacify it with cool thoughts.

3. Keep the juices flowing by jangling around gently as you move.

4. Go very lightly on the vices, such as carrying on in society. The social ramble ain't restful.

5. Avoid running at all times.

6. Don't look back. Something might be gaining on you.

(From *The People's Almanac*, p. 1062)

To begin with, make it a point not to start anything now you're going to have to quit later. Try not to pick up any *new* bad habits, and quit those you do have. Don't start smoking. You're a big kid now: you don't have to prove anything. If you smoke, this is a good time to quit. It'll only get harder later. Drinking, especially excessive drinking, is not a healthy pastime. And drugs that are illegal in this country are illegal for a good reason: they're hideously dangerous, a serious public hazard, something on the order of playing chicken with diesel locomotives or diving into the shallow end. "Legal" drugs can be just as bad, especially when you pop a friend's Valium, or decide to fiddle with the dosage your doctor prescribed. Smoking, drinking, and drugs are all things that tend to get out of hand. Abstinence is the best insurance against addiction.

A much more subtle addiction is food. We're all addicted to food—no one can live without it. But you have to know when to draw the line. Lots of us don't; we're overweight. Some of us aren't overweight, but we're surviving on sugar highs, walking around with high cholesterol levels, suffering from anemia, or starving for protein.

Some people lose a lot of weight when they get out on their own. They're too busy or too unskilled to cook adequate meals for themselves; they might be high-strung and nervous and just plain scared by independence. They could be preoccupied with slimness, refusing themselves the calories they need to stay alive: they're anorexic (don't eat enough) or suffer from bulimia (eat and then vomit).

If you have trouble keeping weight on, see your doctor (more on this later). Try to get an extra hour or so of sleep at night. Eat before you sleep—something rich and fattening. If it's milk-based, that's even better, since milk helps you sleep. Drink whole milk. Use thick cream in your coffee. Put butter on everything. Put sauces on your vegetables and meats. Get the kind of bread that's high in calories, those big, heavy loaves.

But it's more likely that you're putting on weight. This may be a problem you've dealt with ever since you were a chubby little baby, or something that's snuck up on you in the past months or years. You need to know what's in the food you're eating. That's why you bought a nutrition guide and don't put a thing in your mouth until you understand what's in the morsel and how it will affect your eating regime. You have to do this all by yourself. No one is going to tell you if black olives are fattening or not; you have to figure it out.

Weight loss is a fine art, very difficult to master. The bad news is that most people who lose any kind of weight at all—ten pounds or more—are unable to keep it off for a signficant period of time, even a year. This has spawned a lot of theories on why we weigh what we do, and if there is really any way to change for the long haul. It's something that you should discuss with a doctor or a health care professional who knows what they're talking about. You should read books about it and keep up on all the latest information. If you're overweight, you're no stranger to diet books and diet programs. A support group like Weight Watchers is helpful; so is a good friend who cares about you.

Aside from the problems of underweight and overweight, there are other health conditions affected by diet: high blood pressure, high cholesterol, diabetes, hypoglycemia, kidney disease, and a host of other ailments. Now that you're buying your own groceries and cooking your own meals, you have to take full responsibility and make sure that what you're eating won't kill you.

"Another good reducing exercise consists of placing both hands against the table edge and pushing back."
Robert Quillen

Except in the case of strictly regimented diets, you will find it easier to think of your nutrition in terms of daily intake than per-meal intake. For example, it's pretty hard to devise a realistic breakfast that includes foods from all the food groups. That would mean you'd have to have something like fresh grapefruit, an omelette stuffed with sautéed vegetables, whole wheat toast, and a glass of milk—and this you've got to fix every morning. Most people aren't up to it.

"I'm not going to starve to death just so I can live a little longer."
Irene Peter

It's easier and just as healthful to assess the *day's* intake, and make sure that you had sufficient protein (this isn't such a big problem with the average American diet—you actually need less than you might imagine); some simple carbohydrates (bread, cereal, things made with grain); dairy products (less crucial than once thought, but it wouldn't hurt to have some yogurt or cheese every day); and plenty of fruits and vegetables: whole fruits are better than just juice, raw or slightly cooked is better than cooked to a gray mush, and lots of green leafies are required. If your intake for the day is good, then don't worry because lunch was just a salad (no protein), or breakfast lacked milk.

Chicken Fat

You probably don't get as much exercise now as you did when you were in school. Gone are the days of field hockey, intramural sports, bike tours and skateboarding. You drive a car to work, or ride the bus: an elevator deposits you on the eleventh floor; you plop yourself into a chair that's part and parcel of your anatomy until 5:00 or so, at which time you drive back home; you sit in front of "The Honeymooners" while eating dinner, settle back with a sixteen-ounce R.C. Cola and a couple of Moon Pies and read a book until bedtime. Wow, it's been some kind of day. Tired? You bet. Exercise? Forget it—no energy.

Of course the more you exercise, the more energy you have for it. You sleep less, you eat better (but without gaining), your outlook on life is sunnier, and you live without the guilt that comes with *not* exercising. But where are you going to find the time? What will you do?

Most people can find at least one activity that they enjoy which gives them a decent workout. This goes even for cerebral, sedentary types (they like golf). Some companies have exercise rooms that can be used before or after work or over lunch. If you've got access to one of these, you're in luck; in addition to getting exercise, you'll impress the higher ups. A fit employee is a productive employee is a promotable employee, to them.

Get involved in a church or company softball league, or a volleyball team. Join the racquet club, or a health club. Sometimes these places give discounts to groups, so organize your friends or coworkers and take advantage of the reduced fees. Find an apartment complex that has a swimming pool (make sure it's big enough to actually swim in) or tennis courts on the property. Invest in some weights.

Don't miss hidden opportunities to keep fit. Can you walk to work? Can you ride your bike? If you drive, park as far away from

EVERYDAY ACTIVITIES AND
THE CALORIES THEY CONSUME

Activities	Calories
Making mountains out of molehills	500
Running around in circles	350
Wading though paperwork	300
Pushing your luck	250
Eating crow	225
Flying off the handle	225
Jumping on the bandwagon	200
Spinning your wheels	175
Adding fuel to the fire	150
Beating your head against the wall	150
Climbing the walls	150
Jogging your memory	125
Beating your own drum	100
Dragging your heels	100
Jumping to conclusions	100
Beating around the bush	75
Bending over backwards	75
Grasping at straws	75
Pulling out the stoppers	75
Turning the other cheek	75
Fishing for compliments	50
Hitting the nail on the head	50
Pouring salt on the wound	50
Swallowing your pride	50

Throwing your weight around (depending on your weight)	50-300
Passing the buck	25
Tooting your own horn	25
Balancing the books	23
Wrapping it up at day's end	12

(From *Bulletin*, Columbus Industrial Association, July 11, 1977)

the office as practical, and walk the rest of the way. Same goes for anytime you've driven, to the shopping center, a movie, or a friend's house. Don't drive around looking for a close parking place; intentionally park a couple of blocks away. Meet the bus at the bus stop that's six blocks away, not the one that's right outside your door. Walk to lunch. Take the stairs instead of the elevator once inside the building; do it often.

If you're planning an evening out with a friend, build a physical activity into your plans: go bowling after dinner, play a couple of games of Putt-Putt golf while discussing the neighborhood clean-up, or simply walk while you talk.

Try not to let the day end without *some* kind of moderate exercise; over the course of the week, get at least three strenuous workouts. Don't let the change of seasons cheat you out of your exercise. When it's too cold to ride your bike, it's time to get out the snowshoes or cross-country skis; when three weeks of rain have spoiled your softball season, find an indoor gym where the team can shoot baskets.

If you're a solitary kind of person, you'll do well with running, walking, swimming, or weightlifting. If you're competitive, you'll enjoy one-on-one games: tennis, racquetball, handball, golf. If you crave camaraderie and teamwork, try touch football, softball, and rowing.

Feelin' Alright

When you're feeling well, you tend to be pretty unconcerned about your health. This is as it should be; feeling well goes with good health. Aches, pains, and discomforts are the built-in indicators that something's wrong. A fever, for example, means that there is an infection in the body; dripping nose means sinus infection; lack of energy could point to anemia, and so on. A person doesn't feel anemic; he feels tired, dizzy, easily exhausted.

So if you feel good, you're probably okay. But not always. High blood pressure is one fairly serious disease that rarely displays symptoms. Certain types of cancer can be present for years before the victim detects them on her own. Or it is possible for a person to have suffered from a condition so long that he doesn't even know he's sick, since sickness has been the norm. (I know a girl who had double vision for the first eight years of her life, never realizing that *everybody* didn't see in pairs.) While feeling fine is definitely a good sign, it's not the last word on health.

The kind of physical you get in a doctor's office can detect hidden problems: EKGs, pap smears, chest X-rays, and the like tell a lot. All your life you've been led to believe that regular physicals and a yearly checkup were essential to good health. Make that twice a year when you're talking dental care.

But the trend now is toward less frequent visits to the doctor if you're feeling okay. (Still twice a year to the dentist, though.) Some doctors even think that healthy people should stay away from clinics, since they're likely to come out sick even if they came in well—and when you see a bunch of runny-nosed little kids climbing around on the waiting room furniture, you can see why that might be a danger.

20.

THE HEALING ARTS

Health Care Delivery

Now that you know that you should have the periodic checkup, you need to figure out where to go. If you live in the same town you've always lived in, you can keep going to your old doctor if you like him or her. But maybe you want a different doctor, or you're in a new community.

All the books say to call the local medical society and ask for a recommendation, but just about every doctor in this country is associated with the AMA, so contacting them for a reference doesn't help much. Finding a doctor isn't easy; ringing up the AMA doesn't make it easier. Neither does calling a hospital; the fact that a doctor is on staff or has hospital privileges means nothing.

If the company you work for offers health care through a Health Maintenance Organization (HMO) or a similar program, you're all set. Under this scheme, an insured individual is given health care—both routine and extraordinary—by a group of doctors who practice together in a clinic setting. Instead of going out and finding all your own health care, it is delivered to you by the HMO. You will be assigned a doctor to handle your needs: a family practice doctor for routine physicals, OB-GYN for obstetrical and gynecological matters, and so on. The range of services offered will tie in to the size of the group. If you need treatment that cannot be offered by the HMO, you will be referred to a specialist, and the bill will be handled by the HMO. If you don't like the doctor who's assigned to you, you can usually ask for another one.

Barring that situation, you are still left with the problem of finding a doctor. You can go to the Yellow Pages. By studying the Yellow Pages you can at least find out where most of the doctors have offices (downtown? neighborhoods?), see what specialists are available, and get an idea about clinics in town (like HMOs in that they contain a number of physicians, usually specialists in various areas).

"My doctor is nice; every time I see him I'm ashamed of what I think of doctors in general."
Mignon McLaughlin

Most doctors have one or two hospitals that they work with. If you have a hospital preference, you should find out ahead of time where a potential doctor is authorized to admit and treat patients. If he or she isn't hooked up with your preferred hospital, keep looking.

Friends are often good resource persons when it comes to getting a doctor. Remember, though, that your friend's opinions might be colored. If Frank got some "Great, really great, man," pills from Dr. Feelgood, and if Dr. Feelgood prescribed these pills over the phone for Frank, without even examining him, then Frank's recommendation should be placed in proper perspective. And Jenny may have gotten good results from a terrific podiatrist when she injured her toe during the marathon, but you can't go to a podiatrist for a general physical. Friends *can* tell you if a doctor was courteous, understanding, concerned, and willing to explain all treatments given. A friend can let you know if the billing office is run by Ebenezer Scrooge, if the doctor keeps appointments on time, or if she makes house calls. Only a friend will tell you if she was treated like a real person or a bundle of symptoms. This is essential information when choosing a doctor.

For general care, you need a primary care physician, a doctor who can handle most of your needs. Years ago, nearly every doctor was prepared to treat a variety of illnesses and conditions for all members of a family, from little babies to pregnant mothers to aging grandparents. Then they found out that specialization was the key to modern medicine. For a while, it was nearly impossible to get any kind of comprehensive care: a woman, for example, would go to an OB to have a baby, a pediatrician for her children, a hematologist to treat her anemia, an orthopedic surgeon for a twisted ankle, and a dermatologist for heat rash. Which is very expensive, not to mention inconvenient. And the lack of communication between her numerous specialists often led to duplicate treatments, overmedication, and simple bad medicine. Patients got tired of the à la carte approach to health care and wanted their family doctors back.

So now family practice is a specialty, just like ophthalmology or dermatology. These doctors are trained to do general treatment. They can certainly do the basics of a physical exam, and handle about 80 percent of whatever's likely to go wrong with you. For the other 20 percent, they can recommend specialists— but you can still come back to your family doctor. If a good family practice doctor is not available, an internist (a doctor specializing in internal medicine, not an intern) is also good.

In addition to your friends, ask your minister, your boss, your professors, or your insurance agent for leads. Pick responsible kinds of people to ask, the kind who would insist on the best medical care. By and large, a physician with a good reputation is a good doctor who earned it.

Whatever route you decide to go—HMO, clinic, family doctor, or other—do ask around for recommendations (your old doctor, even if she's living in another town, is a good source of help). Weigh the recommendations you get against your own needs and the reliability of the people who gave them.

Once you've decided on a doctor that you want to try, call his or her office. Ask if Dr. So-and-So is board-certified. If she isn't, end the conversation—you're not interested. If she is, ask the receptionist to give you the fee charged for a physical, a checkup, or whatever you need; also ask about terms of payment. If the receptionist gets surly, or resents your questions, end the conversation—you're not interested. If the receptionist is helpful and friendly, Dr. So-and-So will probably be the same.

Bad Doctors Often . . .

1. Are aloof and unavailable; they don't return calls, are slow to relay the results of lab tests, and always look at you as though they've never seen you before.

2. Make a habit of keeping you waiting for an appointment. If you are left waiting in the reception area for more than twenty minutes, you deserve an explanation from the receptionist or medical assistant.

3. Have you in and out of the examination or consulting room in a matter of minutes (does not apply to brief follow-up exams for complaints under treatment).

4. View you as a set of symptoms, not a person.

5. Interrupt you when you are talking, cut conversations short, or have a detached look when "listening" to you.

6. Appear disorganized; allow bedlam in the waiting room; keep a cluttered desk and examining room; misplace your file and medical equipment needed for your treatment.

7. Allow examinations to be interrupted by personal telephone calls and nonemergency matters.

8. Continually treat your symptoms without addressing the disease that is causing them.

9. Insist that you leave the office with a prescription. They fail to explain the purpose and possible side effects of medications.

10. Diagnose and prescribe over the phone (except in the case of a chronic condition with which they are very familiar).

11. Show lack of concern for personal comfort during examinations. They are disrespectful of your privacy.

12. For women only: Bad male doctors perform pelvic examinations without a female nurse in attendance.

Good Doctors Usually . . .

1. Enjoy a good reputation in the community.

2. Are available and accessible. Any doctor can be booked up far in advance—most good ones are—but there will be a day-and-night answering service and provision for true emergencies and a good substitute to cover while on vacation.

3. Seem interested in you personally; ask your occupation, where you go to church, where you live, what your hobbies are, what kind of lifestyle you have.

4. Display a vital interest in your medical history; take a written or oral history; want to know about family illnesses, past illnesses of yours, etc.

5. Talk to you about smoking, drinking, drugs, diet, exercise, and stress; take their own advice in these matters.

6. Keep good files and remember your last visit; don't have to be reminded by you about your symptoms.

7. Show organization; have a comfortable waiting room; are well-groomed; know where things are; have a reasonably clean office; wash their hands before examining you.

8. Work hard. During a physical, examine every part of your body, ask a lot of questions, do a lot. Spend plenty of time with you, explaining procedures, answering questions, and listening to complaints.

9. Teach you how to be healthy. Talk about self-care, and stress wellness; explain medical terms; describe conditions you have—what they are, how they start, how they progress, how they are treated, what you can expect.

10. Prescribe cautiously, explaining the drug, the dosage, how it is to be taken (with meals, etc.), and possible side effects.

11. Admit it when puzzled, when lacking adequate training or facilities to treat your case; defer to specialists when

needed; confer with colleagues when unsure; welcome second opinions.

12. For women only: Good male doctors always have a female nurse present during pelvic examinations.

MEDICINE CABINETS

A well-stocked medicine cabinet develops over time. But you have to start somewhere. You should have just a few basic kinds of things on hand, because you're likely to come down with a sickness or incur an injury that will need immediate attention, and leave you dreading a trip to the drugstore to get what you need. You should have:

- Band-Aids in assorted sizes
- Aspirin or acetaminophene (Tylenol, Datril), or other all-purpose pain reliever
- Antiseptic spray (to cleanse wounds)
- Thermometer
- Pepto-Bismal, or other preparation for stomach problems
- Rubbing alcohol
- First-aid book (like the one the American Red Cross puts out)
- Home medical guide (a big fat book that tells you what you've got, and when it's serious)

You can get the rest on an as-needed basis from your pharmacist. Of course you should include an ample supply of any medications you take regularly or are likely to need, such as insulin, hypertension pills, or hay-fever remedies.

PHARMACISTS

Simple medications and remedies can be obtained from the supermarket or discount store, but there's no beating a local drugstore staffed by a licensed pharmacist. A short chat with a pharmacist can often save you a trip to the doctor. They know more than most doctors about over-the-counter medications. And, unlike many doctors, pharmacists seem to really like talking to customers and sharing their knowledge.

If you are having a prescription filled, ask the pharmacist about what you've been given. They will, free of charge, cheerfully offer great advice, such as: eat yogurt every day when you're on antibiotics; keep this in the refrigerator and it will be easier to swallow; apply salve with a gauze pad instead of directly to the wound. A pharmacist will tell you that if you're allergic to wool sweaters, you should stay clear of hand creams that have lanolin. They know what to put on a fever blister, which cough syrups have alcohol, which pain relievers have caffeine, how much vitamin A to take, and which kind of adhesive tape hurts least when removed from your skin.

A full-service pharmacy will take phone-in prescriptions from your doctor and deliver them to your door; it will set up a charge account for you in most cases, and have an emergency number for after-hours attention. Some will be open twenty-four hours a day, seven days a week.

Finding a good pharmacy and a good pharmacist is usually pretty easy, but well worth whatever effort it takes.

SPECIALISTS

THIS SPECIALIST...	DEALS WITH:
Allergist-Inmunologist	Asthma, hay fever, food, and other allergies; immune defects

THIS SPECIALIST...	DEALS WITH:
Proctologist	Diseases of the colon, rectum, and anus; hemorrhoids, rectal polyps
Dermatologist	Skin diseases; acne, psoriasis, seborrhea, skin cancer, infections, allergic reactions, moles
Family Practitioner	Well care, general medical care
Internist	Adult diseases, diabetes, hypertension, heart disease, emphysema, cancer, infectious diseases

Subspecialties include cardiovascular disease (heart), endocrinology (glands), gastroenterology (digestive), hematology (blood), nephrology (kidneys), infectious diseases, oncology (cancer), pulmonary disease (lungs), rheumatology (joints and muscles)

Neurologist	Brain, spinal cord, nerves; serious head injuries, epilepsy, brain tumors, "ruptured disc"
Obstetrician/Gynecologist	Female genital system; childbirth, infertility, birth control; diseases of the ovaries, fallopian tubes, uterus, and vagina
Ophthalmologist	Eye diseases
Orthopedist	Diseases of bones and joints
Otolaryngologist	Ear, nose, and throat disorders
Pediatrician	Diseases of children
Plastic Surgeon	Surgical correction of face, neck, body, and extremity defects; burn treatment
Psychiatrist	Mental and emotional disorders, especially those related to organic illness

Surgeon	All injuries and diseases requiring operative procedures
Urologist	Male genital system; kidneys, urinary bladder

All of these doctors have medical degrees. The following practitioners may also be consulted:

Chiropractor: employs manipulation of body joints, especially in the back, to improve nerve function
Podiatrist: foot problems—ingrown toenails, foot pain, hammer toes, bunions, calluses, injuries
Optometrist: visual refractions—can test eyes for disease and correct vision with glasses or contact lenses; cannot perform surgery
Dentist/oral surgeon: mouth and gums; may also correct defects of the jaw
Psychologist: mental and emotional disorders; may not prescribe medication or perform surgery

Naturally you want to do some homework, make an educated decision, and end up with Marcus Welby as your personal physician. That would be nice. But if you find yourself under the care of a bad doctor, you have no commitment to stay. Find another doctor. Have your medical records (containing the results of all those expensive tests) transferred to the new physician. You're paying good money for health care; get your money's worth.

Sick

If you are smart enough to make contact with a primary care physician *before* you get yourself into an emergency situation, unexpected illnesses and injuries will be easier to deal with. You'll have someone to call. Even if you suspect you have a broken leg, and you know your internist isn't going to be able to fix it for you, a call to that internist will get you a good referral and advice on what to do first (and what not to do at all).

Regular health care can also prevent emergency situations. Let's say that you are allergic to bee stings. The person who knows she's allergic can be given catastrophe-preventing help by her doctor; armed with adrenaline ampules, a syringe, and instruction on how to give an injection, she can handle a life-threatening situation. Otherwise an insect sting means an emergency trip to the hospital, and even then it might be too late.

So your ability to cope with an illness or injury—slight or serious—can be affected by how well you have attended to your routine medical care. If you find yourself in need of medical care for an acute illness or injury, you're always safe going to a hospital emergency room. Do this if you have no primary care physician to consult, no HMO connection, no accessible emergency clinic. Take yourself, have a friend drive you, or—in extreme cases—call an ambulance.

You are usually the best judge of whether or not you are sick, and whether your sickness merits professional attention. Same thing goes for injuries. A little booboo can be fixed with a Band-aid; a wrist swollen to three times its normal size should be lying on an X-ray table somewhere. You're not stupid; you can figure out the obvious stuff.

"I got the bill for my surgery. Now I know what those doctors were wearing masks for."
James H. Boren

Of course, there are the hypochondriac types whose idea of a fun time is spending the afternoon in a new specialist's office. There are also the macho types (male and female) who pride themselves on the fact that they haven't darkened the door of a doctor's office since they had their last tetanus booster when they were eleven. And all types in between. Most people tend a little toward the macho, and they are the ones to whom I address the following comments:

You tough it out with colds and flu; you go to work with a fever; you think little of hobbling around on a twisted ankle, and tend to side with those who believe that a Positive Mental Attitude will get you through just about any disease.

First of all, on behalf of all your fellow workers, the elevator operator at the department store, and your boss, I would like to thank you for spreading your viruses all over town. And don't think they don't appreciate it! They know who to thank when they come down with the exact thing that you were battling the week before last. They admire your courage and are always happy to share your diseases.

EMERGENCY!

IF YOU DISPLAY ANY OF THE FOLLOWING SYMPTOMS, CALL YOUR DOCTOR IMMEDIATELY, OR GO TO THE HOSPITAL EMERGENCY ROOM

- Fainting, coma, lethargy, or confusion
- Vertigo, dizziness
- Headache, with stiff neck
- Can't see, flashes of light, severe eye pain, or sudden double vision
- Can't hear, severe, sudden ringing in ear, severe earache
- Sudden weakness or paralysis in one extremity
- Seizure, convulsion
- Change in mental state or change in speech
- Sudden inability to defecate
- Severe abdominal pain
- Blood in stool (indicated by black stool as well as more familiar bright-red blood in stool)
- Inability to swallow
- Sudden, severe, profuse vomiting, with or without blood
- Profuse diarrhea
- Inability to urinate
- Blood in urine
- Profuse vaginal bleeding
- Inability to breathe

- Marked coughing, severe sudden cough with blood
- Severe and profuse nosebleed
- Marked discoloration of skin
- Chest pain
- Sudden rapid pulse rate
- Irregular pulse, particularly very slow pulse
- Sudden onset of black-and-blue marks in skin
- Marked, profuse, and sudden sweating
- Blue coloration of skin
- Sudden very high or very low temperature

(Adapted from *How to Choose and Use Your Doctor* by Marvin S. Belsky, M.D. and Leonard Gross.)

And now a word from your body. Your body is all for this PMA stuff, but it mentioned several friends (a liver in Kalamazoo, a spinal cord from San Luis Obispo) who were absolutely done in by their owners' refusal to wake up and smell the coffee—or feel the lump, or notice the bleeding, or take care of the ache. Your body knows that you get scared when something goes wrong, and often you'd rather hope that it'll go away than suffer through an expensive, time-consuming, and often embarrassing examination; but you wouldn't ignore a thud-ker-klunk in your gearbox, so why won't you give yourself the same break you do your car?

Oh yes, the doctors asked me to deliver this message: they're getting a little bit tired of removing whole breasts when earlier detection would have meant a simple biopsy; they wish they had known last year about your persistent headaches which are now diagnosed as meningitis. And your dentist told me to tell you that a root canal could have saved that tooth—if only you'd come sooner.

And finally, from all those who love and care about you comes this message: you're too precious to ignore. Your body is too wonderful to abuse. Your health is too important to neglect. If you have doubts about anything that's going on in your body—be it something on the outside or something on the inside of you, something in your mouth or on your skin, something vague or something obvious, something chronic or something acute—it would be greatly appreciated if you would err on the side of caution, consulting the appropriate doctor or health care professional for correct diagnosis of your condition and responsible treatment. Bodies are being handed out one per customer; better safe than sorry.

"You can only cure retail but you can prevent wholesale."
Brock Chisholm

Mental Health

Everyone is a little crazy, of course. Everybody gets carried away, loses control, gives up, or behaves peculiarly. Everyone, at various times, is apt to cry for no reason, laugh too loudly, get frighteningly sad, or unexplainably happy. But when it happens much too frequently or at the wrong times or for the wrong reasons, it becomes cause for real concern, and when that happens to you—get help.

Help can mean a lot of things. Help can come in the form of a call home, a heart-to-heart talk with a friend, a self-help book from the library, a visit with your pastor or rabbi or priest, a couple of days off from work, or counseling with a professional therapist.

Since help covers such a broad range of possibilities, the question "Do I need help?" is nearly always answered "Yes." But that's a very general assessment. A better way of looking at it is, "It wouldn't hurt."

Maybe you're just bored; you need a change. A coworker who stands next to you on the assembly line listens to your complaint and recommends a vacation—he had the same problem this spring and a week off did him a world of good.

Your problem could be stress; the many life changes you've had this year (new apartment, new job, new friends) upset the rhythm of your life. You need help coping with your present lifestyle; you need to find some routine in the midst of change.

"We are all born mad. Some remain so."
Samuel Beckett

Perhaps you're suffering mental or emotional anguish because of a physiological problem: low blood sugar, "iron-poor blood," overmedication, or a number of treatable conditions.

It's possible that unfinished business from the past needs to be dealt with—leftover guilt from when you were five, a hurt you've never forgiven, or a childhood trauma. A friend, therapist, or good book on the subject could help you identify the skeleton living in your closet.

But no matter what it is that's causing your problem, the fact remains that it's your problem. You own it. You have to solve it. That's the difference between being a child and being an adult. You're responsible.

Getting Help

If you think you need help, you're probably right. Knowing the early warning signs of mental and emotional distress will help you figure out if a professional opinion is called for in your case. If any of the following feelings or behaviors persist over a period of weeks or months and begin to interfere with your day-to-day functioning, it might be that something has gone wrong:

- Sadness, either over a specific event (a death in your family, a trashed love affair, loss of job) or for no "good" reason.

- Hopelessness, demoralization, a sense that your life is beyond your control.

- Violent and extreme mood shifts.

- Inability to concentrate on what you are doing, or to make everyday decisions.

- A sense that everyone and everything is against you, and out to get you.

- Trouble getting along with the people you come in contact with—family members, coworkers, neighbors, friends, and acquaintances.

- Severe marital problems.

- Sleep problems: insomnia, nightmares, excessive sleepiness, fear of sleeping.

- Sexual problems.

- Paralyzing fear of certain things or situations, like fear of dogs, airplanes, heights, or crowds.

- Self-destructive behavior: overeating, uncontrollable drinking and gambling, drug overuse (including legal, prescribed drugs).

- Frequent physical complaints for which medical causes cannot be found.

(Adapted from *The Common Sense Guide to Mental Health Care*, by Christina Ammer, pp. 18, 19)

If any of these statements describes the way your life is, get some professional help. Ignoring a mental or emotional distress is on a par with ignoring physical distress. Sure, you might grow out of it, or your symptoms might disappear on their own. But they might also get worse, and the time you waste could work against you.

Start with a medical examination. Go to your primary physician. Ask for a physical, telling your doctor about your concerns—physical, mental, and emotional. It might be that your doctor's examination will uncover the root of your problem. If it doesn't, the trip was still worthwhile. When physiological causes have been ruled out, other avenues can be explored. Your doctor can then recommend a mental health professional.

Other Resources

You may also make contact on your own with any of the following people or agencies. They are set up to handle your problem, or to refer you to someone else who can.

(1) **Clergyman**—if your own minister is too close to the problem, consult another in your community. Church membership is rarely a prerequisite for pastoral care.

(2) **Personnel officer at work**—large companies are set up to handle employee counseling.

(3) **Community Mental Health Center**—check the Yellow Pages in the phone book.

(4) **Psychiatrist or psychologist**—many of the criteria for choosing a primary care physician apply to choosing a psychiatrist or psychologist. See also the characteristics of a good and bad doctor; these pertain to psychiatrists and psychologists.

(5) **State mental hospital**—gives recommendations and information on state-supported programs you might qualify for.

(6) **Crisis hot lines**—usually listed in your phone book, they can handle crisis situations (rape, abuse, suicidal behavior) over the phone, and are good resources for follow-up care and counseling.

(7) **College and university-affiliated counseling centers**—even if you aren't a student, they will give referrals.

(8) **Local general hospital**—for referrals.

(9) Veterans can call the nearest **V.A. hospital**.

(10) **Self-help groups**, such as Alcoholics Anonymous, Gamblers Anonymous, Anorexia Nervosa Aid Society, Children of Single Parents, etc. advertise their meetings in the newspapers and are often listed in a special section of the telephone book. Your family doctor and community mental health center are also in touch with self-help groups in your community.

Part V:
The Material World

This Registers the amount of your Purchase.

21.

LIKE MONEY IN THE BANK

Forget the idea of banking; forget the idea of banks. We're talking "financial institutions." The government has been lifting many of the regulations from banks, savings and loan associations, and credit unions, so that the distinctions between them are fewer. Years ago they offered many mutually exclusive services, but not any more. Here are the major providers of financial services:

(1) **Commercial banks.** This is the traditional full-service bank. It has a name like First National Bank or Union Federal Bank and Trust, or Mudville Community Bank. Some commercial banks cater more to business customers, but nearly all are eager to have your consumer business as well. Commercial banks are insured by the FDIC (Federal Deposit Insurance Corporation). A bank like this can handle checking accounts, savings accounts, installment loans, mortgage and home improvement loans, credit cards (VISA and/or MasterCard), automobile loans, student loans, investment advice . . . and who knows what else. They're the supermarkets of banking.

(2) **Savings and loan associations.** Increasingly, an S & L can do just about everything a bank can do. The big news with S & Ls is that where they used to handle mostly savings accounts and long-term mortgage loans, they now offer NOW (Negotia-

ble Order of Withdrawal) accounts, which are just like a bank checking account with the exception that interest is paid on the balance you carry in your account. This makes savings and loan associations very popular with consumers. S & Ls are also getting involved in Individual Retirement Accounts and Keogh Plans, automatic account deposits and deductions, passbook loans, installment loans, credit cards—the whole banking banana.

(3) **Credit unions.** These are nonprofit savings and lending institutions—cooperatives, really—that are jointly owned by the "depositors," who share some sort of affiliation: they work together, are in the same union, belong to a common religious group, live in a certain area. Instead of receiving interest on deposits, credit union depositors receive dividends. Often the dividends exceed what might be earned in interest at a bank or S & L, since there is no profit component to a CU, and since CUs escape federal tax. CUs are strong on consumer loans and financial counseling, but they too are jumping into the banking game with mortgage loans, saving certificates, credit cards, and NOW-type accounts.

"The safest way to double your money is to fold it over once and put it in your pocket."
Frank McKinney Hubbard

Now that the players have been identified, it remains to identify your needs, so that you can match up with the institution that will suit you best. Every financial institution in your town wants your business. Each one has brochures and piles of pamphlets that describe the merits of the services they offer, including the fees for these services. So open your phone book to the Yellow Pages—start calling banks and savings and loan associations. Tell them you are interested in opening up a checking account and savings account. Ask them to send you some literature on the services they offer, making sure that you are also advised of current interest rates and applicable service charges on all accounts.

In a few days the mailbox will be crammed full of scintillating reading. You sit down on the living room floor determined to find the best institution for your needs. But what are your needs?

Checking services: Do checking account balances earn interest? Is there a minimum balance requirement for earning interest? Can you write an unlimited number of checks each month? Is there a charge for each check or each deposit made? A monthly service charge? How much? What about noninterest checking accounts? Is "checking plus" offered to protect you from overdrawing your account? Are blank checks furnished free of charge, or do you have to pay for them?

Savings accounts: What variety of savings accounts are offered? Competitive interest rates on short- and long-term deposits? Is access to your money restricted in any way? Will the institution transfer funds from your savings to checking account as needed? Is interest compounded daily? Monthly? Are interest penalties levied for certain kinds of withdrawals?

Safety: Who is insuring your savings? The FDIC? The FSLIC (Federal Savings and Loan Insurance Corporation)? The National Credit Union Administration (NCUA)? Some other state insurance?

Loans: Are bank credit cards offered? Will you receive preferential consideration when applying for a loan since you're a depositor? How do interest rates compare?

Convenience: Is there a branch location near you? What hours are they open? How about weekends and evenings? Will you get a statement every month? Will canceled checks be included in your statement? Can the customer service department be reached by phone, or will questions always have to be asked in person? How about automatic tellers? Are these available? Where? What kinds of transactions can they handle?

Other services: What incentives are offered for saving (appliances, gifts, etc.)? How about free traveler's checks? Can your paycheck be deposited automatically? Is electronic bill-paying available? Is there a travel service? Help with income tax forms? Group health insurance through the bank?

"Money is a terrible master but an excellent servant."
P. T. Barnum

248 □ THE MATERIAL WORLD

As you choose the institution that will get your business, put the various services offered into perspective. A bank that gives free traveler's checks and similar low-value inducements may be throwing up a smoke screen to hide their high service charges and low interest. Keep in mind what needs are the most basic for you—usually the cost of checking and the rewards for savings—and concentrate on the institution's performance in the most vital areas. A talking teller machine may be fun to use, but make sure your bank isn't charging you an arm and a leg to pay for such novelties.

Keep your eyes open for new services that are offered by your own bank and other banks in your area. If you become dissatisfied with your own bank, or if it changes the rules of the game to your detriment, then you should shop around again and get a bank that's good for you. Many financial institutions inspire awe and invoke respect from the customers. That's fine, it's part of the banking mystique. But don't forget that *you* are the customer, and they are the providers of a service, and in such a situation you are the one with the rights and they are the ones with the responsibility.

"My riches consist not in the extent of my possessions but in the fewness of my wants."
J. Brotherton

Troubleshooting for
Checkbook Balancing

You must balance your checkbook every month. This doesn't mean that you check your returned checks against the statement that the bank sends you—that's nothing. You have to check the bank's records against *your* records to make sure that no one's made a mistake.

The theory behind balancing your checkbook is this: You compare your balance with the bank's balance, taking into consideration any checks that haven't cleared, deposits that haven't been credited, service charges that were levied, and interest paid, in the course of a month's time. Beyond that I won't say much more about how to do the actual balancing. If you turn your monthly checking account statement over, there will be a printed form on the back along with instructions on how to balance your checkbook. You can follow those directions and do just fine.

But what if the two balances don't jibe?

(1) Make sure that the amount you recorded for each check is the same that the bank recorded. Sometimes a hurriedly written 6 looks like a 0, which will throw you off.

(2) Recheck your math in your checkbook. Get your calculator out and make sure you added and subtracted everything correctly.

(3) Make sure that you subtracted all outstanding checks from your bank statement. Don't forget those from previous months that still haven't cleared.

(4) Maybe either you or the bank transposed two numbers. When the difference in your reconciliation is divisible by nine, it's often due to transposed numbers (example: 86 − 68 = difference of 18, which is divisible by nine). I don't know why this works; it just does.

(5) The discrepancy should be checked against each item on the bank statement and your checkbook record, looking for an identical deposit or check, possibly one that never got recorded.

If you are having trouble balancing, you may walk the whole mess down to the bank and ask for help, which is customarily offered free of charge. A word of caution: don't go storming into the main office demanding to see the president because the bank made an error on your statement. They rarely make errors. In my personal experience, I have caught the bank being wrong only once—they transposed two numbers on a deposit. I, on the other hand, have erred countlessly. Save your outraged customer act for the moment when they admit their fault.

P.S. Balance your checkbook within one week of receiving your statement. It's difficult to find errors on a months-old statement.

THE DOLLAR BILL

The dollar bill is a piece of paper measuring 2 5/8″ by 6 1/8″ with a thickness of .0042″. The composition of the paper and ink is a state secret. New notes will stack 233 to an inch, if not compressed, and 490 notes weigh a pound. Every thousand notes cost the government $8.02 to print. At the same time, over two billion bills are in circulation, each with an average life span of eighteen months.

(Stephen L. W. Greene, in *The People's Almanac*, p. 340)

22.

CREDIT DUE

C redit is a product that is offered by a number of sellers. These sellers may be called banks, savings and loan companies, pawnbrokers, parents, the United States government, ABC Audio and Video Company, or Big Al's E-Z Term Loans & Used Cars.

The product (credit) is offered at a price. There is always a price, even if it's not immediately apparent. You may think that your roommate will extend you credit on your share of the rent until your income tax refund gets in, and do it without charging anything extra, but there's a price in such a transaction nevertheless. Your dad might be willing to make the monthly payments on your Camaro until you can pay him back—after you get your promotion—but there's a price. Once you've borrowed from a friend or relative, things are rarely the same between you.

Usually, though, the price is called *interest*. Interest is generally figured on a percentage basis: so much per month or year. There are a lot of places to get money (at least in theory), a variety of terms under which it can be obtained, and a host of reasons for obtaining credit. Some reasons are good, some are bad; a sensible credit purchase almost always begins with a sensible reason for doing so.

Good Reasons

(1) You have a true emergency that cannot be met by your current resources.

(2) You need money for educational expenses.

(3) A major purchase must be financed.

(4) A needed item is currently on sale, or will be sharply increased in price very soon; if you can buy it now, a great deal of money will be saved in the future.

Some examples? Let's say that you are laid off work because your plant has been closed for four months—bad economy for widgets, or something. You have a small savings account, but it is soon depleted, and you must pay your rent and bills until the factory is reopened and you get your job back.

Or you want to go to college, but your parents' contributions and the money you make at your part-time job do not cover all your living expenses.

You need a car to get to work. Very few people can afford to buy a car, especially a new or late-model car, with out-of-pocket cash.

Or the furniture you would like is half-price this week only, and you can save a bundle if you buy it now—even though you don't have the cash on hand.

Bad Reasons

Unfortunately, most of the reasons for obtaining credit and borrowing money are based on a very unsound philosophy of goods and services acquisition.

(1) You are infatuated with the idea of owning some unnecessary high-ticket item, and are unconcerned about the way it fits into your budget.

(2) You wish to increase your status by acquiring items you cannot afford.

(3) You are anticipating a raise in salary, a promotion, or some other financial windfall, but want the money now instead of later.

(4) You want money to participate in a risky financial venture.

(6) You must borrow in order to make payment on other loans.

Poor borrowing is evident in the person who has always wanted a Jaguar and is determined to buy it now and worry about paying for it later; in the person who maintains a day-to-day lifestyle that cannot be paid for out of current income; in the one who buys luxury items now because the proverbial ship is expected to come in; in the schmuck who borrows from a loan shark to play the horses, or borrows from a friend to invest in commodities; in borrowing for depreciable items like clothes, or even food; and in getting so deeply in debt that one has to borrow even more money to make the installments on existing loans.

If you can't afford it on your current earnings, you sure can't afford it on credit.

Except in the case of borrowing for genuine emergencies (number-one best reason for borrowing money), never get into a situation where you cannot liquidate and pay off all your debts if you have to. This means that your car loan balance should not exceed the value of your car should you decide to sell it; the same holds with furniture, appliances, anything.

Knowing good and bad reasons for obtaining credit, what are your options when you are faced with a true need, or a compelling reason to borrow money? The chart on the following pages covers your borrowing options: who to ask, *typical* loan maximums, annual percentage rates and maturity periods, and the advantages and disadvantages of each.

"So Worldly, So Welcome . . ."

Secured loans, home mortgages, student loans . . . these are the bread and butter of the lending world, but they're probably not what interests you right now. What *you* want is a credit card! You don't want to leave home without it. You want the world to be your oyster. You want to pay with plastic.

And why not? Certainly possession of a bank or travel and entertainment credit card is a great convenience. Purchases can be charged throughout the month and then paid off quickly and easily with only one check. This reduces the need to carry large quantities of cash or go through the hassles of check-cashing for every purchase. It also covers you when an emergency arises—

near or far from home—and makes it easy to shop by telephone. "My VISA number? Sure, I have it right here . . . 4401, 214 . . ."

Then there's the status. Nothing says it quite like an American Express Gold Card flopped nonchalantly on top of the dinner tab at the Ritz. And, if the advertisements can be believed, all the faceless celebrities have an American Express Card, Christie Brinkley is rich and beautiful because she has MasterCard, and if you pay for your pregnancy expenses with VISA, you're likely to have twins—a boy and a girl, no less.

All hype aside, a bank card or two can be of tremendous value, even if there is also a tremendous risk to having such easy access to money on loan. ANY CREDIT PURCHASE IS A LOAN. When you tell the shoe store clerk that you'll take those Capezios—both pairs—and tell him to "charge it," you're taking out a small loan for the price of those shoes.

It works this way: if the shoe store has its own credit card, and you use that card to charge your purchase, you will get to wear the shoes before paying for them. Maybe you'll pay at the end of the month when the bill comes in, maybe you'll pay a portion of the cost each month for a period of time. But the store is extending credit to you, loaning you the money you need to obtain the shoes you want.

If you pay for your shoes with a bank card, the procedure is somewhat different. The shoe store owner, at the end of the day, will take the bank card slip from your purchase to the bank card clearing center. Let's say the purchase added up to $84. The bank card clearing center will buy the ticket from the store owner, usually at a 5 percent discount. So the shoe guy gets 95 percent of $84 (which is $79.80) from the bank. Which he is glad to get, because now he has his money and he doesn't have to worry about your check bouncing or maintaining a store charge account for you.

The bank, now, will bill you for the purchase. If you pay in full at the time of the billing, they will consider themselves lucky to have gotten the 5 percent from the store owner for their trouble. But they'll consider themselves even luckier if you don't have quite enough to pay that bill at the end of the month, in which case you will choose to make a partial payment—and pay interest. Oh, joy! You're paying interest! The bank card people are happy and fulfilled.

Before you get too deeply in debt, let's back up a bit and see what kinds of credit cards are available, and what they mean for the possessors.

Personal cards at local stores. In the case of a personal account, your credit card is merely an identification card that lets clerks at a local store or local chain of stores know that you are a credit customer in good standing. When you charge a purchase, it is put on a bill that you receive monthly. Usually, you are expected to pay the bill in full; there may be terms available for extended payment, but the store would rather have the money than service your loan.

Single-purpose credit cards. An oil company, airline, telephone company, car rental agency, or department store may issue a card to their preferred customers. It's their own card; it cannot be used in any store or for any service besides their own. A Lord & Taylor card is no good at an Amoco station, and your United Airlines card is worthless at Hertz. Although a revolving plan in repayment is sometimes available, single-purpose credit cards are usually meant to be paid off at the end of the month.

Travel-and-entertainment cards. These are American Express, Diner's Club, Carte Blanche, and others. There is almost always a yearly fee for the privilege of using T & E cards; in return, customers may get travel insurance for using their cards, free traveler's checks, check-cashing privileges at hotels, monthly travel magazines, discount buying services, and other frills. But the card must be paid off at the end of the month. Some may offer extended terms, but not many. T & E cards are widely accepted by airlines, at restaurants, and increasingly at retail stores.

Bank cards. A yearly fee may or may not be charged; the issuing bank may choose to charge interest on every purchase you make as soon as it's posted, or defer the matter of interest until they see whether or not you paid your bill in full at the end of the month. Fees and interest rates vary, even on the same card, depending on which bank issued it. So a VISA card with one bank could cost considerably more than with another bank, and the same with MasterCard. Bank cards are widely accepted. You can charge your groceries in Llandudno, North Wales on VISA (I know, because I did it). You can get clothes at the downtown department store, gas at the filling station, medical care at the hospital emergency room, and tickets for Bruce Springsteen on a bank credit card.

Credit Begets Credit

It's a part of American folk wisdom that only those people who don't need money are qualified to borrow it, that you have to have credit to get any, and so on.

There is a large grain of truth in this. There isn't a bank in the world that wouldn't lend $2,750 to one of the Kennedys or Pillsburys or Gettys. And it is also true that once a person has a credit card, or a loan, it's easier to get another credit card, and another loan.

But a person without credit is not out of luck entirely. There are places to start in developing a good reputation with the credit folks, to establish your credit-worthiness with the people who can both give you credit and recommend to others that they do the same.

If you qualify, take out a student loan, even if you can live without it, or the amount is small. In the case of a government-insured loan for education Uncle Sam is agreeing to be your cosigner, which means that if you default he'll pay the bank what is owed. But the important thing is not to default. Pay the loan back when you should. Make sure that none of your payments arrive late. Don't pay it off before it matures: it's regular monthly payments that impress a credit bureau.

After your student loan is paid off, you will have an excellent bank reference that can be used to obtain other credit.

- Open a checking account. Make regular deposits. Never overdraw. A year's worth of conscientious checking will be worth something in terms of credit.

- Open a savings account. Deposit something every pay period, even if it's only five or ten dollars. The regularity of your deposits will impress your bank.

- If you have a job in which you do traveling, or have an expense account, apply for a T & E credit card through your place of employment. You can get a card (American Express is probably the best) where you are billed personally for all the business expenses you have charged, but for which your company has issued a guarantee of payment. When you receive your expense reimbursement from your employer, then pay off your outstanding balance. In this way you are using someone else's money (your employer's) to establish credit in your name.

A note of caution: use expense reimbursements from your employer *only* to pay off the amounts you have charged. You may get your expense check back from accounting before all your charges show up on your bill, tempting you to keep the difference, and worry about the outstanding charges next month. Wrong! Smart people send the entire amount received in reimbursement to the credit card folks, even it if exceeds the billed amount. There's nothing more depressing than paying off a business-related credit card debt with personal funds because you spent your reimbursement on a frivolous knickknack, or a cheap thrill.

- Buy a major appliance, piece of furniture, television, or stereo on time—even if you could pay cash. Many appliance and stereo stores are willing to let you pay in installments because they hold a lien on what you've purchased until the transaction is completed—they can repossess your hide-a-bed if you don't make your payments. Under such circumstances, they are often willing to sell "on time" to someone without a previous credit history since their risk is low. Their rates for carrying your account will probably be high, but this may be simply the price you must pay to establish some kind of credit rating.

If you have a job that pays a regular salary, and if you have a bank or savings institution that you are doing regular business with, you will probably have no trouble getting some kind of credit. If you are turned down for a credit application, you have the right to know why. It is possible that your circumstances were misunderstood by the person who processed your application, in which case you can clarify the situation.

It is also possible that a credit agency (a company that is in the business of keeping records on the credit-worthiness of citizens) has erroneous information about you, in which case you have the right to see your file and correct any mistakes that are in it. You'll have to document the errors; no one's going to believe you without proof.

Loan Source	Typical Maximum	Typical Annual Interest Rate	Typical Maximum Maturity Rate
Parents, Relatives	?	? may be as low as 0%	? may go on forever
Friends	?	? as above	? as above
Employer (advance against salary or loan)	?	Advances: usually no interest charged Loans: Negotiable	usually six months to a year, but may vary
Commercial banks and savings and loan associations			
—Personal loan	$ 20,000	18–21%	3–5 years
—Auto loan	10,000+	8–18%	3–5 years
—Check loan ("Checking Plus")	2,000	18–21%	???
—Mortgage loan	100,000+	10–14%	30–35 years
—Home improvement loan	20,000	12–16%	5–10 years
—Secured loan (collateral)	depends on collateral	10–16%	3–5 years
—Credit card loan (VISA, Mastercard)	2,500	15–21%	???
Ready credit (automatic line of credit with bank or credit card company)	$2,500– $5,000	15–21%	varies
Credit union	varies	varies—usually ¼% + below prevailing bank rate	varies
Licensed small loan company	$2,500	often twice bank rates	1–3 years

Advantages	Disadvantages
—no legal pressure —sympathetic lender	—embarrassing to ask for —lack of pressure to repay could prolong the indebtedness —may not get the exact amount you need; personal relationship could affect judgments on both sides
—as above	—as above —also, pressure of borrowing/lending can corrode a friendship in a way it probably won't a family
—money is available —employer may be sympathetic lender —interest rate and repayment period probably good —advances: borrowing from yourself instead of someone else	—may muddle relationship with employer —may subject your personal affairs to scrutiny of your employer —advance: means reduced or no paycheck in future
—simplicity of transaction —objectivity of the part of the bank —relatively inexpensive; competitive rates —full disclosure is required of the bank —friends and relatives are uninvolved —credit reference is established when loan is repaid	—may be difficult to qualify —penalties (often 5%) for delinquency —inflexible repayment schedule
—immediately available for urgent needs —charged only for use of money actually needed —can be used to even out cash flow	—not good for long-term loan needs —may be *too* ready and encourage overspending on nonessentials
—interest rates usually lower —dealing with fellow-workers or associates	—must be a member to borrow —funds often limited
—handle small loans —accept less "credit-worthy" customers —would rather extend a loan than sue for their money	—high interest rates —lend smaller amounts —may need a cosigner to qualify

Loan Source	Typical Maximum	Typical Annual Interest Rate	Typical Maximum Maturity Rate
Life insurance company (borrowing against cash value of whole life policy)	95% of policy's cash surrender value	5–8%	none
Pawnbroker	50–60% of auction value of the pledged asset	3–4 times higher than a bank	180 days
Loan Shark	none	500–2600%	none

If you are denied, say, a bank credit card, talk to the bank officer who made the decision and ask what you can do to reverse it. You might suggest that you be given a chance to prove that you can be trusted, by obtaining a card with a very low credit limit, or one in which your repayment terms are strict. If you are sincere in your desire to prove that you're a good credit risk, it is possible that you will encounter the cooperation of lenders.

Staying Afloat

If you use it wisely, credit can be a wonderful thing. It can pull your fat out of the fire in an emergency, allow you to incorporate the cost of major purchases into your monthly budget, and save you money as you make purchases when the price is right—as opposed to when you have ready cash.

But credit abuse, like other kinds of abuse, can ruin your life. Those who are especially susceptible to peer pressure will find themselves using credit to keep up with the Joneses. They will forget that their credit cards come with monthly statements that demand payment. They eventually find themselves unable to pay even the minimum monthly payments on their installment loans. They borrow money to pay back money they have borrowed. They throw away hundreds and thousands of dollars every year in interest alone without decreasing their total indebtedness. Juggling their debts steals time and energy away from other pursuits.

Advantages	Disadvantages
Life insurance company −cinch to get −low interest −no specified repayment time	−loan decreases your life insurance protection −absence of specified time for repayment may cause laxness in retiring the debt
Pawnbroker −complete privacy −immediate loan −possessions can be immediate collateral	−expensive −lose use of the asset pledged −can only get a fraction of what asset is worth
Loan Shark −none	−endless

(Distilled from *Sylvia Porter's New Money Book for the 80s*)

They become miserable and depressed; their personal self-esteem suffers. Family life can go down the tubes.

The advice given here about loans and credit is meant to give you some general information on an important subject, and to provide some early warning so that you don't get into debt trouble. If you can keep your head screwed on straight from the beginning—and this first venture at living on your own is definitely a beginning—you can avoid all sorts of problems in the future.

If you are already in serious trouble with your indebtedness, there's no time like the present to get right so the problem doesn't get any worse. It won't be easy. At a minimum it will probably entail spending at least a year making whatever payment you can on your current debt and not charging another thing, or borrowing another cent. And that's just for starters.

The following books are very good resources for learning how to manage your money. You can check either one out from the public library.

Sylvia Porter's New Money Book for the 80s by Sylvia Porter (Garden City, NY: Doubleday & Co., 1979).

Everyone's Money Book by Jane Bryant Quinn (New York: Delacorte Press, 1978).

23.

BUDGETS

Let us begin by issuing exemptions to the following individuals who neither need to originate nor maintain a budget. These lucky people are:

(1) The truly poor who have virtually no income and therefore no need to structure its disbursement.

(2) The truly rich who have virtually limitless income, and therefore no need to discipline its disbursement.

(3) The truly satisfied; those who have lived under present circumstances for a considerable period of time, having never (or at least rarely) been frustrated by savings or debt, excess or shortfall, plenty or want.

Those persons described above may make themselves a sandwich. The rest of you are going to hear about budgeting.

Budgets are very simply a set of figures designed to guide you in spending, saving, and giving away your money. It is only a set of figures, and it is only a guide. It's a personal thing—it reflects your aspirations, goals, and values. Your plans for your money say a lot about you.

Retroactive Budgets

A retroactive budget is based on a backward look at the money you received and how you spent it. On the income side, place everything you have received; on the disbursement side belong expenditures: housing, clothing, food, entertainment, business expenses, personal expenses, insurance, etc.

Retroactive budgets are good for learning about yourself. They tell you how much you're spending on your hobbies, what you have invested in your future, how much you spend on your friends, what you have given to the poor, and so on. And even a cursory glance through last year's check register can bring back waves of nostalgia—"Oh, here it is . . . $10 to Christa Whitling for Girl Scout cookies. And $2,430 to the Internal Revenue Service. What an audit that was! Boy, that $50 I used to repair the ski rack was the best bit of money I ever spent."

Retroactive budgets tell you if you are, on the whole, living within your means or beyond them. While week-to-week and month-to-month irregularities are common, a review of last year's total earnings versus last year's total expenditures serves as unimpeachable evidence of your ability to stay afloat.

Retroactive budgets help you plan for the days to come. By finding patterns in your past earnings and spending habits, you can make projections about the days to come. If you have never been able to keep more than $100 in a savings account, but you wish to build a substantial account in the next twelve months, your previous experience may guide you toward a system of savings or discipline that will work better than your previous ineffective plans.

When making such a budget, determine what you wish to learn from it and then devise your retroactive budget accordingly. Do you want a general idea of how the year went? Or just last month? On one sheet of paper list all income for the period, and on another all expenses—not individually, but in meaningful groupings. These could be housing/food/clothing/gifts/transportation/personal expenses; or maybe daily/monthly/yearly expenses. You can arrive at a method of categorization that helps you.

Prospective Budgets

The prospective budget looks ahead, naturally enough. It uses past information and combines it with projections into the future. It's the crystal ball of personal finance. Such budgets usually cover the next twelve-month period. On the income side, they take into account current earnings, expected raises (promotional or cost-of-living), gifts that might be received, interest from savings accounts and other investments, Christmas bonuses, outside income, tax refunds, and collectable debts. Every penny that is likely to come in.

All expenses must be noted, too. That's everything. Refer to the retroactive budget for guidelines. And then inflation must be taken into account, and higher tax brackets, and major purchases that are planned.

As a general rule, once you have figured your income for the next year, deduct 10 percent to get a working total. For expenses, figure absolutely everything and then add on another 10 percent, and you'll have a fairly accurate estimate. You're only going to disappoint yourself if you estimate income high and expenses low —it never, hardly ever, works out that way.

If expenses exceed income, you must find a way to decrease expenses or increase income. Either remedy is effective. If income exceeds expenses, you are the proud owner of what is called discretionary income, the goal of nearly everyone who has to live with money. Discretionary income can be saved, invested, given away, or squandered.

A prospective budget will help you realize goals that you have for the coming year. You might want to put a down payment on a house soon; you will use a budget to help you save a substantial portion of each paycheck for that goal. Maybe you want to give away more money to charities or the church, and by working with a budget you will find a way to set aside a set amount or percentage each month for that purpose.

As you put those figures down on paper, though, remember that you'll have to live with them. When faced with a monthly deficit, it's no good to say you'll spend half as much on food, or to determine to "make more money" unless you have a pretty good idea of how you're going to eat on half of what you're spending now, or exactly how you're going to bring in more money. Part-time job? Overtime? You'd better know the specifics.

Budgets can be tedious and ego-deflating if they are unrealistic and restrictive. Even if you must live on a tight budget, you should give yourself a pocketbook allowance: a modest amount of money that you can spend however you like whenever you like. It might be five dollars a week that you carry around in your wallet for gum and Cokes. Even a very small amount of pocket change will make you feel that you are controlling your money, rather than having your money control you and your life.

In time, a prospective budget must be viewed in retrospect. At the end of each month, look back on your actual expenses and reconcile them with what you had budgeted. How did you do? If you are consistently spending more on carfare than your budget indicates, change your budget or change your outlay. It makes no sense to have a budget that doesn't work. Revise and revise; if you do, you'll know where you stand, as well as where you've been and where you're going.

The Value of It All

The biggest value of working with budgets is that it opens your eyes to the dynamic effect of money in your life. And as with most problems, half of solving money problems is recognizing that a problem exists. Working with a budget can point out areas of weakness graphically so that you can work on those areas. On a more positive note, early familiarity with budgeting can prevent problems from getting out of hand.

Attention to your budget can help you anticipate big expenses that are looming on the horizon—a tax payment, insurance premium, or repair bill—so that you can plan now to cushion the blow later. It can put you in touch with your financial affairs so that you are not as likely to succumb to an impulse purchase (you know you can't afford it) or pass up the opportunity to buy or do something that is important to you (you know you *can* afford it).

Above all, let budgeting be your tool, not your master. It's good to budget, to know where your money is coming from and going to. Money has value; it deserves your respect and demands your conscientious care.

KEEPING TRACK

(1) The Sugar-Bowl Method. At each pay period, place the budgeted amount for each expenditure group in a marked envelope or broken sugar bowl or whatever. The envelope marked "FOOD," for example, will contain cash in the amount that you have budgeted for groceries (and maybe meals out). The envelope for "ENTERTAINMENT" has another amount. And so on. During the course of the month (or half-month or week) you will be able to clearly see how much money you have left for each budget category. You can also economize in any area and use the surplus at the end of the month for an unbudgeted item.

(2) The Check Voucher Method. If you can pay for everything by check (or with a credit card), you will have a clear record of each expenditure. Paying by check is a nice, clean way to handle your financial affairs, since all disbursements are known— there's no slush fund that mysteriously depletes itself. The disadvantage is that the stores in your area may not accept your check without a big fuss, and you can run up a lot of bank service charges if you write a check for every little purchase. The problem with credit card purchases is that you may not realize until the end of the month, when the bill comes in, that you have overspent your budget. Do keep your credit card slips so you know how much you have charged and can check them against your monthly statement

(3) The Ledger Method. More tedious, but extremely accurate and consequently very useful: you periodically record each expenditure, be it cash, check, or charge. With this system you get a ledger book, and note all income received, and all purchases made. You can keep a little notebook in your pocket or purse to record each expenditure as it is made, and then transfer this information to your ledger. It takes constant vigilance, but there's nothing like it if you're really serious about seeing where your money goes.

24.

FINANCIAL PRIORITIES

There have been allusions to saving money, making investments, and giving money away.

Some people have never done anything significant in any of
these three areas. They live hand-to-mouth, and are apt to spend
all that they receive on current expenses. They always have. They
view saving, spending, and giving as luxuries for the rich.

Others adhere to the golden mean of money management:
Give 10 percent, Save 10 percent, Invest 10 percent. For them, it
seems natural, whenever the paycheck is deposited into the
checking account, to immediately write a check for 10 percent to
their church or other charity, to transfer 10 percent to a passbook
savings account, and to put 10 percent into a long-term investment—stock, retirement plan, real estate, or cash-value insurance.

The problem in addressing this matter is that, obviously,
some people have no intention of saving, investing, and giving,
while others have already committed themselves to a strict formu-
la that is, after all, well beyond the norm for the average American.

Giving

If you are not the kind of person who sees the importance of
giving a portion of your income to the poor, to your church, or

to any other altruistic purpose, there is little I can say here to convince you otherwise.

I'd like to, though. I'd like to convince you because it's been so satisfactory for me for so long. I came from a family where we, as children, were taught to do what our parents did: give a tithe (10 percent) of everything we earned or received to our church, or missionary work, or local charities. I have done it ever since I was a little child who got a ten-cents-per-week allowance. I have done it as an impoverished student, and all throughout my adult life. A few years ago I felt that I wasn't getting as much pleasure from it as I once did, so I started giving more than 10 percent. And I continue to be committed to a yearly percentage increase in giving to the kinds of religious, charitable, and relief work I believe in.

I realize that it's hard for a nongiver to understand how in the world it can be fun to lop the top off a paycheck and struggle through on what's left. It is a challenge, of course. But the really great thing about it is that, even in times of no money, you sleep at night with the knowledge that you've given to others who have even less than you have. Such a realization helps put one's life and certainly one's financial condition in perspective.

If I can't convince you, I'll recommend to you that you at least give it a try. As you prepare your prospective budget, write in an amount that you would like to give away. It works best if you figure what you're going to give as a percentage of your income (even if it's just 1 percent) and pay it as soon as you get paid. Don't wait till the end of the month to make your donation if you're really serious about giving money away. You're bound to have thought of a million ways to spend any surplus you might have at the end of the month, and of course there is the distinct possibility that there just won't be any money to pay out. This takes discipline; all mature money management has a big discipline component. But I have found that I get more personal satisfaction from what I give to others than from what I keep for myself.

Saving

Saving money may be seen as either a luxury or a necessity. It's tempting to look at your monthly income and your monthly expenses and say, "Yes, I do wish I could afford to save something. I also wish I could afford to take a vacation in Greece this winter. A fur coat would be nice. But I don't have money for any of those things."

Again, this is a matter of personal priorities. What comes first? If you are inclined to think of savings as a priority, it is likely that you will always have enough to save. You will delay purchases that interfere with your savings program. You will obtain satisfaction from the knowledge that you have some degree of financial security.

But people commonly put hobbies, preferred entertainments, vices, and creature comforts above financial security. "Why save money? If I had a big savings account, I'd just use it to do what I'm already doing. I don't like money for money's sake. I'd rather use what I've got to do what I think is important."

That's valid. I don't see much point in amassing a lot of money, building up huge cash reserves for some unknown purpose, clinging Scrooge-like to every little penny while life passes by. That's no fun. And not very important if an individual has a steady job, adequate insurance to protect against financial calamity, and few personal obligations (such as children or other dependents). Savings can be superfluous to a happy life; they can even be a hindrance.

But you might want to consider briefly some worst-case scenarios. What would happen if you were laid off or fired? What if you got in a serious accident? What if someone you care about needed some financial help? What if you got sick for a long time? If the prospect of these situations makes you uncomfortable, you may choose to make saving money a priority so that you can have greater peace of mind.

And of course there is the obvious advantage and fun of saving for extras like a new car, a vacation, household furnishings, etc. Even a live-for-today type can see the sense in setting a little aside on a regular basis so that major purchases can be more easily made.

If you want to save but lack the willpower to do so, you can usually arrange to have a set sum deducted from each paycheck and deposited to the credit union, or your bank will automatically transfer funds from your checking account each month and deposit them into a savings account for you.

Investments

Investments are long-term savings. Often they are less "liquid" than the kind of savings that you have with a passbook account at the bank. This means that when you wish to get your money out of them, it will take more time to do so. An example of this is stocks. If you own stock in a company, you would rather not be put in a position where you have to sell that stock regardless of the condition of the market. You want to sell when you can make a profit on your investment. Or real estate. If you need cash in a hurry, you probably couldn't get it by selling a piece of land you own. It would take a long time to find the right buyer, close the sale, and get your investment back.

So whatever you put in a long-term investment should not be something that you're likely to need back in a hurry. This is why financial experts advise clients to build up adequate savings ("liquid assets") of two to six months' salary before addressing the business of investment. Sometimes you can borrow money from a bank and put your investment up as security for the loan. That works, and under those circumstances most investments—used as collateral—can help you get money in a hurry if you need to.

At this stage of the game, it may be too early to think seriously about investments. It is unlikely that you have hit your peak earning years. You have extraordinary expenses, in that you may be buying your first car, setting up housekeeping for the first time, paying off school loans, or starting a family. At this time in your life, you have high living expenses and low earning power.

Later that will probably change. When you're in your 40s and 50s, you may have a mostly-paid-for house, children that are grown, and the job you've been working toward for the last 20 years. In my opinion, that is the time to start looking at long-term investments. I wouldn't turn down a chance to get in on the ground floor of a great deal, of course, even if it involved some financial sacrifice to do it. But neither should you—if you're in your twenties or even early thirties—be overly concerned about saving for your retirement or your old age. There will be time for that later.

25.

INSURANCE

There are two philosophies of insurance.* One is right and one is wrong. They are:

(1) Insurance is an investment. It can turn calamities into windfalls.
(2) Insurance is protection. It can make calamities less devastating.

Statement 1 is wrong; statement 2 is right. And here's the reason why: if you are looking at insurance as an investment, any kind of insurance, you are looking at one of the worst investments in the world—in league with playing keno in Las Vegas. Keno is not a good investment; neither is insurance.

In the insurance investment game you, the insured, are betting that you will die/get sick/have an automobile accident/get robbed, or be victimized in some way, thereby collecting on your insurance benefits. The insurance company is betting against it. They're betting that you will live/stay healthy/avoid automobile accidents/escape thievery and remain unmolested by life's misfor-

---

*A cookbook of insurance coverages and terms is beyond the scope of this book. Please refer to Quinn's or Porter's comprehensive money books (see Bibliography) for a more complete discussion.

tunes, thereby continuing to pay your premiums like clockwork, releasing them from the obligation of paying benefits.

Now, really, who's going to win this game? The big multimillion dollar, multinational, diversified insurance company with its millions and billions in assets, with its highly trained actuaries, and its commission-fed salespeople who know the human psyche better than Sigmund Freud himself? Or you, Average Wide-Eyed Innocent? No, MegaBucks Insurance Conglomerate is not going to lose.

You're going to lose. You're going to lose if you collect on your benefits, and you're going to lose if you don't.

NEVER BE GLAD THAT YOU COLLECTED ON YOUR INSURANCE. It is true that an insurance benefit check can bring great happiness, but only because it arrives after great tragedy. It's what makes the pain bearable. But never look on it as a blessing, something that you're anxious to get your hands on. The price is too high.

"But I have an insurance policy on my life that will pay off even if I don't die! If I pay from now until I'm age sixty-five, it will give me a whole bunch of cash right on the spot." This is called whole-life or straight-life insurance and it does pay a cash benefit even if the insured has the bad fortune to live. But the insured is still better off without it, and there will be more about that later.

The Protection Philosophy

The right way to look at insurance is as needed protection. You need insurance because you do not have sufficient financial resources to protect you against unhappy twists of fate.

Look at it this way: a multimillionaire industrialist, J. P. Cashbags, does not have the same kind of insurance needs you and I do. A $322,578 hospital bill could be easily absorbed into the budget of someone like J. P.; so could a car accident that totals the Rolls and damages the neighbor's garage; if there's hail, he can afford to repair his tile roof damage without taking salt and pepper off the table; if he dies, his estate is large enough that his widow will be able to scrape up the money needed to pay for the funeral and live pretty much as she always has—with or without him.

It is those of us *without* such wealth who need insurance—as protection, not investment. Each individual should have sufficient insurance to cover the risks he faces—but just cover them, not turn them into financial windfalls. Overinsurance is a moral hazard; insurance companies realize this and don't like to get involved in it. For example, a single woman with two stepchildren, ages eighteen and twenty-one, who has a paid-up mortgage and a yearly salary of $32,000, and is insured for a whopping $2,000,000, is in a morally hazardous situation. Why so much insurance? Is she planning on committing suicide? Will her scheming stepchildren knock her off to get the money?

The same thing holds true for health insurance. Most people can get adequate health insurance coverage through their jobs. Because there is a deductible, and co-insurance (which means that the insured has to pay a percentage of all incurred expenses) there is a built-in deterrent to seeking medical care unnecessarily. After all, treatment will cost the insured *something* out of pocket, even though the insurance carrier is paying the bulk of the expenses.

But some people don't like that situation. So they add to their group health insurance coverage an individual policy that they pay for themselves. And then they buy daily-benefit insurance (advertised in the Sunday newspaper supplement)—a policy that will pay them up to $200 a day for being in the hospital. Now, obviously, a person with such coverage has a tremendous motivation to contract an illness, since she will make money if she can collect on her group insurance policy at work, on her individual policy, and on her daily-benefit supplement. And if she's been paying these high premiums for years, the first sniffle that comes along is going to look pretty serious to her, and she's going to try to get into a hospital to see what's the matter. She is viewing her health insurance as an investment.

Insurance is protection. You should have only the insurance coverage you need to protect you from what might go wrong, and you should make every effort to get it under the best possible terms.

Before buying insurance, know what your needs would be if problems arose. A good insurance agent will help you figure all this out: what the value of your personal property is, how much your car would cost to replace, what hospital costs are in your area, what financial obligations would need to be addressed by your family if you should die.

Remember, though, that insurance agents are salesmen. They

may call themselves financial counselors, or life underwriters, or insurance advisers. The door-to-door encyclopedia salesman may call himself an educational consultant, too, but the fact remains that the World Book dealer and the insurance agent are both salesmen. While an insurance agent has useful expertise that will be helpful in obtaining coverage, you should also be aware that he feeds his family on the commission obtained from your policies. He has a vested interest in your coverage that goes beyond what you need; it has a lot to do with what *he* needs.

Insuring Your Life

If you are looking at life insurance as an investment (which is the wrong way to look at it) you will be tempted to purchase what is called whole-, ordinary-, or straight-life insurance coverage. This is the kind that, in addition to providing a cash benefit on your death, also builds in intrinsic cash value. It is a combination of insurance and savings. The cash value increases over the life of the policy; if you live beyond a certain point, the insurance company will give you your investment back, with interest.

The problem with this is that the interest you are paid is close to nothing. Over the years it has rarely exceeded 3 percent. You don't have to be Milton Friedman to figure out that 3 percent is a lousy return on your investment. This cash build-up also works against you in that if you die after having paid in for years and years, you're really collecting (your heirs are collecting) on your *savings*, and less so on the protection provided by the insurance company.

Whole-life insurance is costly and bad money management. It continues to be sold because people like the idea of getting something back for all the premiums they've paid in; they also like it because the premiums remain level throughout the life of the policy. But the popularity of whole life has also been because insurance companies make their biggest profits from it and insurance salesmen make their biggest commissions off it, and consequently they have devised a thousand ways of convincing customers that it's their best product.

When I worked in insurance we had a saying, "If you sell term life you can't eat; if you sell whole life you can't sleep." Which means that the life insurance industry is living off whole-life money; salesmen who don't sell it don't do well financially. Salesmen who *do* sell it know that they aren't shooting straight with their clients, and they pay for it in peace of mind.

Term life insurance is pure insurance. With term insurance you pay a premium and collect a benefit in case of death, and only in case of death. There's no other way to get anything out of a term policy.

If the idea of throwing money away on term rubs you the wrong way, be consoled by the fact that term coverage costs anywhere from a fourth to a sixth as much as whole life. The difference in premiums, if deposited even in a low-interest passbook savings account, will give you a cash value far in excess of anything the insurance company would eventually pay you.

You can determine the amount of insurance you need by mentally anticipating your death and the impact it will have on your family. If you have no mortgage, no family and no large outstanding financial obligations, you could very well get by on a policy that would cover the costs of your burial and the settling of your affairs. Maybe your company offers group term insurance in a sufficient amount. But if you're twenty-eight-years old with a husband and a job and a small child and a mortgage and a car payment and a host of other obligations, your need for insurance is greater. Breadwinners need the most coverage. Your death would have a tremendous financial impact on your spouse and child; you need a relatively large amount of insurance to provide for those who would survive you.

Consult a competent life insurance professional for specifics. Listen to what he or she has to say. But make no mistake about it: that's a salesman on the other side of the coffee table. He's betting you'll live; you're betting you'll die. With that in mind, you can make prudent decisions about the coverage you need.

Insuring Your Health

Most employers offer group health insurance. There are almost no circumstances under which you should refuse it, even if its cost seems exorbitant. Group health insurance is the best way to protect yourself against medical expenses.

If you are married, you may elect to have family coverage. Your working spouse may do the same. Although the cost is greater for this option, the coordination of the two policies usually promises a 100 percent benefit payment (between the two of them) for all expenses. It's a judgment call: you decide if the added expense is likely to pay off.

If you cannot get insurance at work, you must shop for it yourself. This is very difficult to do. It often involves having a physical to qualify, paying high premiums, and getting minimum benefits.

The first place to look is to an organization you belong to, your bank, or savings and loan, or any other society that offers a group plan. In many cases it is worth joining an organization just to get the health insurance benefits. Investigate all avenues for group coverage before going on to individual coverage.

Individual coverage can be obtained through an agent. An independent agent can offer you the best coverage and premiums based on the carriers he represents. Call everybody. Get as many quotes as you can. Weigh the advantages of a high-deductible policy. If you could conceivably pay for the first $1,000 or even $500 in expenses each year out of pocket, you can get a lower-premium policy that will cover you in the event of really high bills.

Insurance is protection! Plan to pay as much as you can yourself and resort to insurance coverage only when it is beyond your means. Otherwise you'll end up paying a lot of money that you'll never see again.

HMOs are another alternative (see pages 227 to 229 on choosing a doctor). These may be available through your employer or individually. You prepay for services, and then have unlimited access to the services of a variety of health care professionals.

Living without health insurance is so risky you shouldn't even consider it. You must have health insurance. Each one of us is liable for medical bills in the millions, and your risk is as great as anyone else's. Even an ordinary illness or mishap—an appendectomy or sports injury—can put you in tight financial straits for years to come. It can make you a burden on your parents, put you at the mercy of the government, and cause you to be indigent for the rest of your life. Do whatever you have to do to get adequate health insurance.

MEMORABLE ARTICLES THAT WERE INSURED

1. The San Francisco-Oakland Bay Bridge ($40,000,000)

2. The *Titanic* ($3,019,400)

3. The voice of N.Y. Metropolitan Opera star Rise Stevens($1,000,000)

4. The legs of dancer Fred Astaire ($650,000)

5. The crossed eyes of comedian Ben Turpin ($500,000)

6. The ice skates (five pairs) of skater Sonja Henie ($250,000)

7. Comedy team of Bud Abbott and Lou Costello: against disagreement between them, for a period of five years ($250,000)

8. The legs of actress Betty Grable ($250,000)

9. Washington, D.C. shopkeepers against failure of Harry S. Truman to arrive for his 1949 inauguration ($200,000)

10. The nose of comedian Jimmy Durante ($140,000)

11. Loch Ness monster: its capture and delivery alive ($56,000)

12. Actress Julie Bishop took a seven-year policy with Lloyds against gaining four inches around the hips or waist ($25,000)

13. The Scottish Tailoring Mercery Co. of Sydney, Australia took a policy from Lloyds of London against "death caused by accident" due to the falling of a Soviet satellite ($22,400)

14. The special elasticized wool trousers (four pairs) of flamenco dancer José Greco ($3,920)

15. Talking myna bird in cookbook promotion ($500)

(Jeanne Lund Leleszi in *The Book of Lists*, pp. 474, 475)

26.

DEATH AND TAXES

Taxes

As a United States citizen, you are required to pay taxes. They may be taxes on your income, taxes on your property, taxes on your purchases generally, and taxes on specific luxury items—tobacco, gasoline, liquor, perfume; taxes on your car, taxes on your investments, taxes on the sale of your belongings.

If you're an average American, over two and one-half hours of your eight-hour work day are spent earning money to pay taxes, according to the Tax Foundation in New York City. Here's how they describe your day:

ITEM	HOURS AND MINUTES
Taxes, total	2 hours, 39 minutes
Federal taxes	1 hour, 41 minutes
State and local taxes	50 minutes
Food and beverages	1 hour, 5 minutes
Housing, house operation	1 hour, 32 minutes
Clothing	29 minutes
Transportation	39 minutes

Medical care ....25 minutes

Recreation ....19 minutes

All other (personal care, ...52 minutes
personal business, private education, savings)

You may argue that your income isn't distributed that way, but over the course of your life it probably will be. At any rate, the point should be taken: a tremendous amount of your time is spent earning money that will be paid in taxes of various types.

You can devote your life to the avoidance of taxes; there are limitless strategies for reducing the tax burden. Or you may resign yourself to paying taxes, giving little of your energy or attention to tax breaks. You may moan and groan about taxes, considering them life's greatest agony. Or you may think that the taxes you pay are fair exchange for the benefits you derive from the government in defense, income security, cross-country highways, local roads, space exploration, law enforcement, fire protection, and the entire host of tax-funded services.

Federal Income Tax

The biggest portion of your tax dollar goes to the federal government, and it is collected in the form of income taxes. Their current scheme is to charge taxes on a sliding scale, as a percentage of adjusted gross income. (Adjusted gross is the amount you made after any business expenses have been deducted from your total income.) A person who has a small adjusted gross pays a very small percentage of her adjusted gross in income tax; she may pay nothing at all if her earnings are sufficiently small. A person who makes a very large income, even after business expenses have been deducted, may pay up to 50 percent in federal income taxes.

The Internal Revenue Service has enlisted the aid of your employer to help them collect taxes. Every pay period, your employer deducts from your paycheck a prorated amount that is believed to have some relationship to the tax you will owe at the end of the year. How does she know how much to deduct? You give her a clue by telling her how many deductions you have (one for yourself, and one for each member of your family who is dependent on you for financial support); this is weighed against your earnings. The IRS provides nifty tax tables that advise your employer how much to deduct, and that amount is sent to the government on your behalf. That way the feds don't have to wait until the end of the year to get their money.

Eventually, a tax return is filed. It may be quite simple or terrifyingly complicated, depending on your circumstances. It tells the complete story of your earnings, your deductions, and the tax you should pay. Depending on how much tax you paid throughout the year, you will be entitled to a tax refund (when you have paid in too much) or liable for an additional amount (when you have paid too little).

Simple, right? Of course it's simple. The system is so well-established, and runs so smoothly, that the vast majority of taxpayers never have a bit of trouble with it, never question it, never stop to wonder if they're getting everything from it that they can.

But there are others, as you probably know, who have more complicated dealings with the IRS. They are represented by thousands of people who make a full-time job of trying to understand the hidden complexities of the federal tax system: tax analysts, tax consultants, tax lawyers, tax preparers, and paralegal tax advisors.

Presenting a comprehensive guide to the Internal Revenue Service is obviously beyond the scope of this book. Their codes fill volumes, and the written interpretations fill rooms. And every year Congress changes the rules, and every day tax courts reinterpret the rules. Keeping on top of all that is for experts.

Nevertheless, a basic knowledge of how the system works is essential for any taxpayer.

(1) You have a basic right to pay only the income tax you owe, and not one cent more. This right is, in theory and practice, honored and protected by the United States government, the Internal Revenue Service, and every legislative body and court in the land.

(2) The amount you are required to pay may, at times, be open to honest dispute. Which is to say that you and the IRS may have a genuine disagreement as to how much tax you owe and should pay. Surprisingly, such disputes can result in the realization that you owe *less* than you thought. Of course, it also happens that you may be shown that you owe *more* than you were prepared to pay.

(3) When you and the IRS disagree, the burden of proof is on

you, the taxpayer, to prove them wrong. This is exactly the opposite of how the legal system usually works; if you are accused of any nontax crime, it is up to the court to prove, beyond a reasonable doubt, that you are guilty. Your innocence is assumed. Such is not the case with you and the IRS. What they declare must be disproved by you.

(4) The IRS may exact high penalties and interest if you fail to pay your taxes on time or file your tax returns when you should. For this reason it is a good idea to deal with the IRS in a prompt, courteous manner. Pay your taxes when they are due; answer any and all correspondence you receive from the IRS immediately; never antagonize the tax man.

(5) If the powers of the IRS seem awesome, remember that this agency exists by a mandate of the people. They are hired by you to collect the taxes that are due from individuals and corporations. Viewed in this light, the IRS is seen not as an enemy but as a confederate.

(6) If you get a tax refund every spring, you are wasting money. In order to get a tax refund, you must overpay your taxes throughout the year, which is the very same thing as lending the government money, *without interest*, that they then repay at their convenience. A tax refund is not a bonus. It is merely a return of your very own money. You will be better off if you can work with your employer to adjust your withholding so it is more in line with the taxes you will owe. Have the difference automatically deposited into your credit union or bank savings account. Then your money will be earning interest.

(7) You need not figure out your tax returns all by yourself. The IRS can help you with tax questions at any time. Remember that they are working *with* you to make sure that everyone pays the taxes they owe but no more. You can call them or write them at any time during the year if you have a question. When it comes time to pay your taxes, you may call a toll-free number for help. Or you can take all your tax records down to the local IRS office and an employee will help you prepare your return. There is no charge for this service. You get it as a matter of course because you are a tax-paying citizen.

(8) If you have a complicated return, you can often do very well by hiring a qualified tax expert to help you prepare it. Do *not* seek tax help from a storefront operator who opens for business January 2 and packs up on April 16. These fly-by-night preparers

are often poorly trained and will be unavailable should you have questions later or receive an IRS audit.

"The only thing that hurts more than paying an income tax is not having to pay an income tax."
Lord Thomas R. Duwar

FICA

In addition to federal income tax withholding, you are subject to FICA (Federal Insurance Contributions Act) tax, which is the same as Social Security tax. It is a straight (not graduated) percentage that is taken out of your paycheck: a student making $3.55 an hour working in the Union pays the same percentage in FICA as a stockbroker making $28,000 a year. (When earnings go over a certain amount—the level of which changes every year—FICA is no longer deducted for the rest of the year.) The theory of FICA is that money is automatically deducted from your wages now, invested for you, and then paid back to you in Social Security and Medicare benefits when you retire. The sad fact is that the money you pay now is going less for your own benefits than for the population that is currently collecting Social Security and Medicare, but that's beside the point. You must pay FICA, whether you are drawing a salary or self-employed. If you draw a salary, your employer matches your contributions. If you are self-employed you match your own contributions, so your withholding rate is much higher.

FICA withholding is very straightforward. No over- or underpayments (unless someone, usually your employer, goofs up), no refunds, no arguments. You just pay it every year.

State Income Tax

Some states don't have income tax. If you are considering jobs in a number of states, it would be worth finding out if you could possibly escape state income tax.

Most states levy their income tax as a percentage of the federal tax you pay. Your employer withholds from your paycheck just as he does with federal tax, you file a return at the end of the year, and you are eligible for a refund or liable for additional payment.

Problems with state tax are almost always linked to federal tax. The booklet that comes with your state income tax return forms is self-explanatory. If you have questions or problems, you can get the same kind of help from the state that you get from the federal government. Remember that they are working on your behalf to collect taxes in order to feed the state treasury.

For Entrepreneurs

If you are in business for yourself (I know there are a few of you Harvard Business School graduates out there), your tax situation is somewhat more complicated. If you are a sole proprietor, you pay income tax on your earnings from the business—and these must be estimated quarterly. When and if you incorporate, your business will also be subject to tax.

Since you did graduate from Harvard you know more about taxes than I do, so I won't bore you. Get professional help in setting up books and figuring your tax liability. Apply the same information to your business that you do to yourself. Don't get cute with the IRS; stand up for your rights; pay what you owe.

SHORT FORM, LONG FORM

You may file a Short Form (1040A) if:

- you made less than $50,000 last year; *and*

- all your income was from wages, salaries, tips, and other employee compensation; *and*

- you do not wish to itemize deductions.

You MUST file a Long Form (1040) if:

- you have income from sources other than employee compensation, *or*

- you wish to itemize your deductions, *or*

- you contributed to an IRA or Keogh plan, *or*

- you made estimated tax payments, *or*

- your income was significantly higher this year than in previous years.

The Will

And, finally, there is the will—the last financial document you'll ever need. Even if you don't have a great deal in the way of property and financial assets, or if you believe that it will be a relatively simple matter to give what you do have to the "logical" person, you should have a will.

There's no guarantee that your money will go to the person you want it to go to unless you specify who that person is. If you are unmarried, have no children, and your parents are living, your property will go to your parents, regardless of their need. Your brothers and sisters will probably get nothing. Neither will your close friends, or your favorite charities.

If your parents are dead, your brothers and sisters will inherit. If you have none, it'll go to your "next of kin," which could be an aunt you've never seen or a grandparent who is estranged from you. Close friends will get nothing; other relatives will get all.

If you are married and have children, your spouse will get some and your children will get some. If you have stepchildren, they get nothing. No children? Part will go to your spouse, and part to your parents in most cases. Brothers and sisters may also get money that you intend for your husband or wife.

If you die without a will (*intestate*) and the court can find no relatives, the money will just go to the state. Now that's an unsettling scenario. No matter that you gave 10 percent of your income to your church all your life, or that you worked at a group home for three years, or that you have a special place in your heart for historic preservation in your community; any causes you had during your life that could be benefited in your death will be left out in the cold if you fail to include them in a valid will.

If you have a relatively simple financial situation you may be able to prepare your own will. This is *not* a few sentences on a cocktail napkin that you stuff in your desk drawer to be read by your family in the event of your death. Although informal, even oral, wills have sometimes made it through the courts relatively unscathed, it surely cannot be advised.

There are some books that can help you prepare a will. A good one is *How to Be Your Own Lawyer (Sometimes)* by Walter L. Kantrowitz, J.D., LL.M., and Howard Eisenberg (New York: Perigree Books/Putnam's, 1979). The chapter on preparing a will gives step-by-steps that any individual can follow in preparing a will that will stand up to probate and whatever the courts decide to throw at it.

If you are involved in any of the following situations, forget about preparing your own will and consult a competent lawyer. You need a lawyer if:

(1) You have wealth and property of sufficient size to be subject to federal inheritance taxes. This means $120,000 if you have no spouse, and $250,000 if you do. Sound like a lot? Think about your life insurance, your car, your home (if you own it), your personal property, and your Batman comics collection. It could put you over the limit.

(2) You are likely to leave behind unhappy and quarrelsome relatives who will dispute your will. The matter of your death, and who gets what, could cause a permanent rift in your family if you leave your wishes subject to challenge.

(3) You want to leave money in a trust. Sometimes a parent wants to leave money to a child, but the child is too young to handle it in a bulk sum, so a trust is set up to manage the money on behalf of the child. Husbands used to do this for their wives, too, but less so these days. (Remember "The Lucy Show," where the widow Lucy was in constant disagreement with her banker Mr. Mooney, who was the trustee for her inheritance? Maybe it makes a good sitcom, but it's rotten in real life.)

Don't be afraid to draw up a will. Some people are superstitious and think that if they make out a will, they'll die. This is obviously true; every single person who has ever made out a will did, or will, die—eventually. So will all the people who didn't make a will.

You're young, and you don't think much about dying. But most of you know or know of someone who died at an early age; maybe they were even younger than you. This is not a scare tactic, it's just the facts. You could die at any time. Think about what and who you'll leave behind; take into consideration the welfare of the people and charities you care about; execute a valid will (on your own or with the aid of a lawyer) so that your death doesn't cause a financial hardship for your loved ones.

Part VI:
The Important Stuff

27.

PERSONAL LIFE

Autonomy

On to personal autonomy. Not personal anatomy—mesomorphs, ectomorphs, and endomorphs—but the ability to function as an individual: autonomy. It has to do with being able to survive on your own, gain a sense of mastery over life, and the ability to enjoy yourself and pursue your own interests, with or without another person.

If you are married, or intimately involved with another person, or eagerly seeking such a relationship, you may think that autonomy is just for widows and die-hard singles who are facing a lifetime of loneliness and rejection—not for you. You have other plans for your life, and those plans include a husband or wife, a close family, someone to lean on and depend upon, someone who will make you a better person.

This is called Noah's Ark Syndrome: the assumption that if you're not going through life two-by-two, you are missing the boat. You have no value unless you're matched up with someone else.

But the gospel of autonomy is that no matter what else happens in your life, you must be able to live with yourself. The President of the United States, this year's winner in the Best Actor category, and even cartoon character Ed Grimley all have to live with themselves. There is no escape from this reality.

Even a happily married couple, the very picture of intimacy and mutual interdependence, must struggle through geographical separation, emotional distance, or ultimate parting. I've known married people whose lives virtually halt while a spouse is away on a business trip. During this period of temporary separation they accept no social invitations, eat no worthwhile food, work on no long-term project, and basically are content to merely survive until their spouse returns and life resumes. They can't handle even a brief geographical separation.

It is also true that even in the best of relationships there will be emotional distance. No matter how open the lines of communication, there will be feelings, impressions, ideas, and stirrings that are hard to reveal to one's husband or wife, and during these times the dependent partner (the nonautonomous person) may become very unhappy because he or she is emotionally unequipped to deal with significant issues on his or her own . . . or to accept the fact that his or her partner is doing so.

And although I don't think it does much good to think of it on a minute-by-minute basis, it is nonetheless true that each of us is only a heartbeat away from our eternal destiny, and separation from a most cherished friend, our closest brother or sister, or our husband or wife. The promise of ultimate separation—death—is with us at all times. It is the nonautonomous individual who is least equipped to survive such a crisis.

No matter what is going on in your life, and no matter what happens in the next few minutes, weeks, or years, it is absolutely vital that you develop a sense of autonomy—the ability to survive on your own, and to live life as an individual.

"I think somehow we learn who we really are and then live with that decision."
Eleanor Roosevelt

Basic Skills

How can this be accomplished? The first step is to learn the basics of day-to-day living. Most of this book has been dedicated to setting out the skills that one needs to have in order to live independently: everything from putting frozen food in the shopping cart last to finding a competent physician. This is because it's the little things that get people down. My first shopping trip—the one where I paid my own money for my own food that I would prepare myself and eat off my own kitchen table in my own apartment—had me in tears (real tears) as I drove home from the supermarket, wondering how in the world I had managed to spend $10.45 (it was a lot of money at the time) for two tough steaks, a head of iceberg lettuce, a few bottles of cleaning supplies, and a box of chicken Rice-a-Roni.

When you get down to cases with unhappy people, especially those who attribute their unhappiness to the fact that they are living without an intimate companion, the dissatisfaction, anger, and pain are likely to express themselves in such statements as, "It's when I have to put the storm windows on by myself that I really miss Dick," and "I never go out to eat because I don't want to eat alone," and "The apartment is always a mess because I don't have anyone to clean it up for." All these remarks have to do with frustration over not handling the simple day-to-day tasks with sufficient skill.

Some of you have fathers who would starve if your mother wasn't able to cook for them. She could be lying in bed with a 105° fever, and your dad wouldn't be able to do anything about his hunger except cajole her to rise from her sickbed and fix him some supper. You may have mothers who are in some sense like the socialites in the light-bulb joke: How many executive wives does it take to screw in a light bulb? Answer: Two. One to mix the martinis and one to call the electrician. Those are the stereotypes of your parents' generation.

The lack of simple coping skills has sent many of our fathers to cooking class and our mothers to powderpuff mechanics courses, because they are realizing that they need to be able to survive on their own. They need autonomy.

Mastery

After the basic skills have been obtained, there should be a striving for mastery of life skills. Because we won't be content to simply "get by" for long; eventually we want to be really good at something.

I vividly remember a feeling of mastery that I gained several years ago. I had moved to the Chicago area (after growing up in a small Midwestern city) and was working for a large corporation (yes, the same one that later fired me) in a job in which I did quite a bit of travel. O'Hare Airport daunted me. I had flown in and out of it several times, and something always went wrong: I went to the International Terminal when I should have been at the domestic one, I waited at the wrong gate and missed the plane, I thought there would be a meal on the flight and there wasn't, I couldn't find my car in the parking garage, etc.

I remember to this day a trip I took to San Francisco. No associate traveled with me—I went on my own. Instead of being driven to the airport, I took a limousine from the office. I got to the right terminal; I got in the right line to confirm my reservation and get my seat assignment; since it was a 727, I requested a seat over the bulkhead—my favorite. I got my luggage checked okay, and had enough time before the flight to buy a newspaper and some gum in the gift shop. I made it to the gate on time, boarded the plane, ate the lunch I knew would be served, and enjoyed a perfect flight. When I got to San Francisco I retrieved my luggage—all there, all intact—picked up my rental car, and had a blessedly uneventful drive from the airport to the downtown hotel where I was staying. Yes, they had my reservation. I accompanied the porter to my room, tipped the man, closed the door behind him as he left, threw myself on the bed, and screamed to myself, "You did it! You did the whole thing!"

> *"Only a person who can live with himself can enjoy the gift of leisure."*
> Henry Greber

I felt as though I had mastered business travel—and I had. After several trips I had finally acquired knowledge of the finer points of making reservations, dealing with airline schedules, tipping, and navigating a strange city. From that point on I no longer dreaded trips, wondering what ridiculous mistake I would make next or what outrageous act would be perpetrated upon me by others.

Some people are obsessed with becoming the absolute best at everything they do; I am not a proponent of self-indulgent expertise gathering. I am rather a believer in acquiring the skills needed to handle day-to-day situations and working towards mastery of certain skills that are most likely to be used often. It leads one toward autonomy.

The Alone Self

In acquiring autonomy, it is also important to spend enough time alone to get to know yourself. Most single people—unless they have too many roommates, or are terminally popular—have ample opportunity to be alone, and consequently to learn more about themselves. Married people should do the same, but it's often harder for them because it is expected that they will spend every waking minute together. This is smothering. It is vital that all people—whether married or single—have enough alone time to figure out who they are.

There are other ways to get to know yourself besides sitting in a room all alone contemplating your psyche. One of my favorites is to put myself in a novel situation and see how I'll react as my own guinea pig. I have learned a great deal about myself while traveling: put me in another country and I reveal to myself all sorts of hidden truths. Or try staying awake until 5 A.M.: what happens? I was surprised to find out, several years ago, that in a large college lecture class I was among the few who had nerve enough to ask questions of the professor, but that in smaller classes of twenty or fewer I *never* spoke up in class. And I've learned that I act differently when I'm wearing a business suit from when I'm wearing a sundress.

The person who is working toward autonomy should also make it a point to pursue interests and hobbies that are individual. Some people are so overloaded on group interests—softball, Creative Anachronism, partying, and community work—that they never have time to enjoy an activity that they do on their own. Every person should have something they enjoy doing that doesn't involve another person: crossword puzzles, refinishing furniture, painting, reading, jogging, and weight lifting are possibilities. Competitive types should strive not only against other people and external standards, but also seek the thrill of beating themselves.

While spiritual truths may be discovered with others, the disciplines of Bible reading and study, meditation and prayer are often solitary activities that bring one toward true autonomy. Skeptics may refer to religion as a "crutch" (which would supposedly work against autonomy), but in that case food, education, and our fellow human beings might also be called crutches. Since we have an inherent spiritual dimension, we will never be truly autonomous unless that dimension is explored and developed. The fact that the development of this aspect of one's totality includes belief in and, ultimately, dependence on God doesn't lessen that simple truth.

Introspection

The late comic Todi Fields, an overweight person, professed a need to come to terms with her body, accepting herself for what she was. A therapist suggested that she stand naked in front of a full-length mirror and write down every positive physical feature that she possessed, as a start toward appreciating herself physically. Ms. Fields reported that she stood motionless in front of the mirror for almost two hours, finally wrote down "good teeth," and hurriedly put her clothes back on. So much for self-disclosure.

You are likely to be drawn to books, friends, and situations that help you examine who you are. Self-help books exist in abundance (and some of them are even helpful). If you are lucky enough to have a friend who doesn't agree with everything you say and do, that's another valuable tool for establishing your autonomy. Professional counseling can be a great help if you have problems or obstacles to autonomy that you cannot deal with on your own—perhaps some past experiences that are troubling you, or assessments that are difficult for you to make on your own.

After sitting through a particularly grueling evening where a mutual friend poured out to a roomful of people his personal journey to self-understanding, my friend remarked that, while the unexamined life isn't worth living, the overexamined life isn't worth much, either. I suppose there comes a point at which too many questions are being asked, and too much personal dissection is taking place. But each person finds their own level of self-awareness. Don't be afraid to find out who you are, because once you know who you are you are well on the road to personal autonomy.

So you're autonomous. This is great. You can do it all on your own—at least you can do a lot of it on your own. What's next?

Intimacy

Intimacy is next, because it's the real goal of autonomy. No healthy person works on his autonomy in order that he can live his life in complete isolation—that's not the way we're built. We're built to be with other people, to be close to them, to be intimate with them. But in order to achieve this intimacy, we must first be autonomous.

The problem of tackling intimacy from a position of dependence is that the more we need the other person, the more they will resist us. An example is in order: let's say that there is a young woman (Sheila) who believes that she will find fulfillment in her life when she marries a successful man who will provide for her financially, will support her emotionally, and will fulfill her personally. Sheila is waiting, waiting for this young man to arrive in her life. Because she is convinced that it is the job of the mysterious Mr. X to deliver her happiness (when he comes), she neglects to develop in herself the very attributes that would attract such a successful, supportive person. (Such a person would be attracted to a mature, confident personality in most cases.) Each time she meets a man, Sheila thinks to herself, "This might be the one. Don't take a chance. Your happiness is riding on this relationship; go for it." She proceeds to smother him with kindness, demand a degree of fidelity he will not provide, and basically present him with the very picture of an emotional cripple. He can't imagine any enjoyable scenarios with her and refuses to get involved.

After many experiences like this one, she becomes desperate. Still neglecting her own autonomy, she lowers her standards. She is absolutely convinced that her happiness lies with a man. If he's successful and kind, so much the better, but since she has been rejected by this type before she revises her expectation; any male will do.

Now what kind of guy is interested in her at this point? Probably a domineering person whose self-worth lies in his ability to keep another human being completely subservient to him. The two meet. She's willing to take it; he's willing to dish it out. She wants to be happy; he's willing to promise to make her happy ("After all, who wouldn't be happy with a guy like me?" he asks rhetorically). It's a warped relationship, and its "success" depends on Sheila convincing herself that this is it (she's happy now) and the man believing that he can pursue his own concerns without any thought of her.

This happens in same-sex friendships, it happens between parents and children, and it happens between friends and spouses. The submissive person desperately clings to the beloved, and the object of his or her affection resents the intrusion so deeply that he or she pulls away. A father doesn't want his son to move out of the house, a woman becomes possessive of her friend, a man threatens suicide if his wife leaves him. Each one is like a crawling vine that chokes out the tree on which it lives.

The best way to commence the search for intimacy—which is what we all want—then, is from a position of personal strength. Only when we have the necessary degree of autonomy are we equipped to deal with the commitments and disappointments inherent in an intimate relationship. This seems contradictory, but it is a dynamic of life that is with us.

The autonomous individual is ready to reveal big chunks of himself to another person and to witness the same exposure in another person, prepared to risk rejection, and able to risk acceptance as well. He can explore the realms of trust and support; he can give and receive affection.

"In Genesis it says that it is not good for a man to be alone, but sometimes it's a great relief."
John Barrymore

It is possible to experience intimacy in each aspect of existence:

Intellectual intimacy. The two scientists who work side by side, day after day in a cramped laboratory, pooling their intellects to discover a cure for a dreaded disease are intellectually intimate. College students who stay up until 4:00 A.M. discussing Jungian synchronicity are intellectually intimate. They are sharing their ideas, their plans, their doubts, the workings of their minds.

DO NOT THROW
AWAY
CUSTOMERS
ORIGINAL PRINTS
IN THIS
ENVELOPE

FORM #669

Emotional intimacy. A family that shares feelings with each other is emotionally intimate: they laugh when happy and amused, they shout when they are angry and frustrated, they cry when they are sad. Each member of the family expresses his feelings freely and accepts that in others. Two friends who meet for lunch and express their mutual disappointment in another person or situation are emotionally intimate. They are sharing their feelings.

Social intimacy. Sixteen office workers jammed together in an elevator are socially intimate; the guests at a party are socially intimate; eighty-three thousand fans at a college football game are socially intimate. They are sharing space and experiences with one another. Their sheer proximity and involvement in a common event determine that they are intimate with each other.

Physical intimacy. A young mother and her nursing baby are physically intimate. So are the roommates who hug each other after being separated for the summer. The couple that makes love is physically intimate. They share their bodies.

Spiritual intimacy. Worshipers at a church service are spiritually intimate as they sing, pray, worship, and learn together. The man who shares his faith with his neighbor is spiritually intimate with him. The person who prays is spiritually intimate with God. They share their sense of place in the world with another.

Intimacy is achieved when one shares his innermost personal self with another person, and allows the other person to do the same. Some acts which might be intimate are not. The drunk who pours out his life story to the understanding bartender; the teenager who brags of sexual achievements with his friends; the soap-opera devotee who falls in love with the new doctor on "General Hospital" may all have a sense of intimacy by virtue of what they do, say, or feel, but intimacy demands reciprocity. Without sharing there can be no true intimacy.

And some acts that don't seem intimate in themselves become so because of their intent or context. When a father sings to his child, there is an intimacy that is not present when that same father sings in the shower or even in front of an admiring audience. Washing clothes isn't particularly intimate, but when done for a special friend it can be a very private, very intimate act.

We want this closeness. We want to give of ourselves and want to receive from others in the same way. We're looking for that. We can't live without it. Without intimacy we are depressed, alienated, and lonely. We cannot live for long in such a state.

---

*"The physical union of the sexes . . . only intensifies man's
sense of solitude."*
Nicholai Berdyaev

The Biggest Barrier to Intimacy

The biggest barrier to true intimacy with others is usually sex. Partly, it's a semantic mix-up; sex is almost synonymous with intimacy, since "They were intimate" means that they had sex. But we don't really know if they (whoever "they" are) were intimate or not. Sexual intimacy certainly suggests emotional, intellectual, and spiritual intimacy, but it is not—repeat, not—the same thing. The testimony of those who have awakened next to a total stranger with whom they have spent a night of lovemaking (and the total stranger can even be one's own spouse) is that sex does not equal intimacy. It seems like it should, because the physical revelation is so startling, but the mathematics of hearts and souls is different.

The testimony of millions who looked to marriage as automatic intimacy is the same: marriage does not automatically equal intimacy.

The biggest problem with sex (and marriage for sex) as the path to intimacy is not that it cannot *contribute* to intimacy, but that it is so often presented and accepted as the only way to get there. The consequence is that people tend to think that close friendships with same-sex persons should be carefully regulated so as not to become homosexual; marriages are neglected, and the idea prevails that the legal (and consequent physical) union has an intrinsic power to fulfill the need for intimacy; a generation of single people are looking to sex to define their relationships, deciding that if the sex is good, then the other aspects of the relationship are good; husbands and wives, friends and lovers with sexual dysfunctions or hang-ups have come to believe that they can never participate in intimate relationships; and (this is the one that bothers me the most) single people who live chastely are viewed as freaks. An unbearable burden is placed on sexual intimacy, that it must be *all* intimacy.

The Risk of Intimacy

If sex is the biggest barrier to true intimacy, the greatest threat is the possibility of rejection. It is entirely possible, and sometimes even probable, that the person who is open to intimate relationships—and consequently personally vulnerable —will be rejected. She will share an important secret with a friend, only to have that friend betray the confidence: "Gee, why are you so touchy? I only told Midge about it . . ." He will hug his friend only to experience the dreadful sensation of having his friend stiffen and pull away from him. "Uh, yeah. Well, hey, it's great to see you too, Tom." She will offer her opinions to someone who tramples on them, belittling her for her thoughts: "That's the most ridiculous thing I've ever heard. I can't believe that you believe it!"

The risk of rejection, when presented to a dependent, nonautonomous person, is so threatening that it can effectively cancel all potential for intimacy. "I can't take another rejection," says the person whose self-worth is riding on the acceptance of another.

But when working from a position of autonomy, the autonomous person knows that he will survive, more or less intact, even if faced with rejection. The potential for pain is still present, but the autonomous person knows that he will survive in his own life, and that he can enjoy himself and pursue his own interests, even if no one else does it with him.

An additional risk is that a person with whom you are intimate will not be able to relate to you on all levels—intellectual, emotional, social, physical, *and* spiritual. You may fear being torn in several directions. This is not unusual; as a matter of fact, it is fairly normal. Even in the best of relationships, intimacy on all levels is rarely achieved.

A wife would be jealous if her husband had physical intimacy with another woman, but very understanding of the fact that his needs for intellectual intimacy are most often met with his colleagues at work. Good friends are sometimes able to share their feelings, but not their thoughts with each other. Families may be emotionally close, but differing religious beliefs can keep them spiritually distant.

This is not so bad. It's normal. And it illustrates the importance of welcoming intimacy wherever it is to be found. Single people, especially, are likely to shy away from potentially intimate relationships because they believe they should save all that until marriage. And married couples tend to look to each other for fulfillment in every area of their lives, placing a tremendous strain on their relationship when they might better enlarge their circle of intimate friends who will support their marriage by offering an appropriate intimacy.

The Rewards of Intimacy

We are willing to take the risk of intimacy because we are enticed by the rewards.

With intimacy, you can be more natural. You are past the stage of testing, attacking, defending, or frustrating each other. You are comfortable with the other person, the other person is comfortable with you. You can let your guard down. You can relax.

With intimacy, you can be more honest. The honesty comes from your sense of acceptance. You know that you are beyond the point of having to exaggerate, belittle, deceive, or tell lies. In an intimate relationship these things all work against, not for, your relationship.

With intimacy, you can be more open to experience. Having already risked rejection, you now have the confidence you need to become involved, to experience new sensations, and even to be wrong or to fail. You feel confident about yourself and about the person you are intimate with, and this broadens your experiential horizons.

With intimacy, you can be more involved. Not only are you doing something that you want to do, and which you think is important—you're doing it with another person. This more than doubles your pleasure, and tends to telescope time while you are deeply involved in mutually rewarding activities.

With intimacy, you can more afford to fail or to be wrong. Since you know that—win or lose—you will still be perceived as a person of worth, you can let go a bit, be less cautious and conservative. You have the freedom to be wrong. Your welfare, and the welfare of your intimate, becomes more important than whether or not you were successful in a given venture.

With intimacy, you can be more accepting of others. Because you are accepted by your friend, you are anxious to show acceptance to others. Having experienced the warmth of security in this relationship, you are anxious to offer it to others.

With intimacy, you are more able to cooperate with others. The person who goes it alone in life must accomplish everything on his own. He has no one to help him and is unlikely to offer a hand to someone else. But the intimate person knows how helpful it is to have a partner, a friend who is willing to help because achievements are reckoned as joint efforts.

With intimacy, problems are solved. Human beings have a tremendous ability to sweep under the carpet problems, frustrations, and neuroses. Without another person to question the cover-up, and to provide the understanding support needed to handle problems, it is likely that they will never be confronted. Some problems are simply too painful to solve on one's own. With the help of an intimate, they can be confronted and tackled.

(Adapted from *Love and Intimacy* by Robert L. Coutts, pp. 195-199.)

These tremendous promises keep us going in our search for intimacy. We must have intimacy: we can't live without it. We enter into intimate relationships with our family, our friends, and with God. There is a need to be connected to other people and to our Creator, to share our most private places with others, and to accept them when they share with us.

Loneliness

Lonely people are asking for it—loneliness, that is. Inasmuch as we cherish our freedom, admire independence, and savor isolation, we are asking to be lonely.

Years ago, people lived in larger groups than they do today. Single people lived with their families (mother, father, siblings); married people sometimes lived in the family home, too. Widowed relatives were taken in by their families. Single people who maintained their own residences had boarders, or servants, or apprentices. This business of having your own place is pretty new. And it's a contributing factor to aloneness, which at some point leads to loneliness.

Loneliness is not a big problem until it gets out of hand. It's a lot like physical hunger in that it's a perfectly normal sign that a perfectly normal need is at this time unmet. In the case of physical hunger, a little bit of it can be a good thing, since it makes eating so much more enjoyable. The same goes with loneliness—just a bit makes the company of others more enjoyable.

But out-and-out starvation, or wholesale famine, is another ball game altogether—as is pervasive loneliness. Instead of indicating a need, it becomes a need in itself. And it's the sort of problem we all can live without.

If you've been lonely, you know what it feels like: it's a restless feeling, an empty place inside of you that begs to be filled, and echoes until it is. It may be vague—you can't exactly explain how you're feeling—or so strong, so unmistakable that you immediately know what the problem is, as you cry, "I'm so, so lonely! I can't stand it another minute!"

"One of the greatest necessities in America is to discover creative solitude."
Carl Sandburg

Filling up Holes

Nobody should be chronically lonely, but every normal person should sometimes be lonely. When it gets to be the hallmark of one's existence, then the hunger has gotten out of control.

In dealing with loneliness, that empty feeling, a number of remedies may be tried. Some are active: they involve getting semimilitant and doing something about loneliness. Some are passive: these are concerned mainly with just surviving the bout of loneliness. Can you identify the active and passive strategies from this list?

- eating
- drinking with friends
- drinking alone

- watching television
- shopping for clothes
- listening to music
- having sex
- calling a friend on the phone
- arranging a visit with a friend
- working on a journal
- composing a song, or a poem
- crying
- sleeping
- convening a party
- jogging
- volunteering

Eating, drinking, getting blasted, listening to music, crying: they're mostly passive (although they may call for a minimal amount of effort) in that they don't really tackle the emptiness— they just try to make it more bearable. Calling a friend, organizing a party, or volunteering to help are active; they start hacking at the roots of the problem. They put a lonely person in contact with other people, people who may be in a position to understand and help.

Some activities change character depending on whether or not they're done alone or with friends. As the list indicates, there's a difference between drinking in a social context and in doing it privately. I'm not advocating all of this as a cure for loneliness, but it should be pointed out that a drink with a friend is a whole lot different than emptying a fifth of Southern Comfort all by your lonesome while listening to the Dr. Demento Show.

But rather than deal with loneliness most of us would like to know how to avoid it in the first place—or at least keep from getting the megadoses of loneliness that can cause depression, despair, and sometimes the feeling that life isn't worth living if it has to be so lonely. (If you feel like this, skip over to page 239 immediately.)

Loneliness strikes on three fronts; it's a social condition, a personal condition, and a spiritual condition. One at a time.

Social Loneliness

This is largely a result of the society we live in. Because we're mobile, because it is expected that young adults should leave home and strike out on their own, because our culture idealizes independence and shuns interdependence, we find ourselves lonely in our society.

The first and most important thing that people who are socially lonely must recognize is that their condition is no reflection on them personally. For example, a young man who has been transferred by his company to Smallville, USA from New York City should not interpret his feelings of loneliness and his failed attempts at finding his place in a small town as a reflection on his personal attributes, or on his value as a person. It's merely the natural outcome of an unnatural action—moving away from something familiar and into something foreign.

Researchers say that almost everybody who moves is lonely—good and lonely—for about a year afterward. This can be of philosophical comfort to someone (like you) who has recently moved. The uprooted, lonely person can tell himself, "It's only natural—once I've been here for a while it will start feeling like home, and I'll be happier."

It can, and I think should, also be a warning: avoid excessive relocations. Let's say that after living in your apartment for a year your landlord decides to raise the rent rather dramatically and you believe that you should move out. Think, now. You might save a few dollars, but are you in a position to deal with the loneliness that's inevitable with any move? Taking into account your present state of mind, it could be smarter for you to (1) negotiate with your landlord on the rent, (2) pay the increased amount and consider it the price of stability, (3) take on a roommate (or another roommate) with a mind to decrease your financial responsibility and, incidentally, your loneliness. Staying with a job, keeping in touch with old friends, remaining in the old neighborhood—all these are useful in heading loneliness off at the pass.

If you have roommates, or live in a housing cooperative, or are on friendly terms with your neighbors and the shopkeepers in your neighborhood, if you're active in community affairs, you are less likely to feel lonely.

Personal Loneliness

Being hooked up with the community at large is fine, and it's important, but it doesn't necessarily help solve the problem of deep personal loneliness. Remember Richard Cory? He had it all—respected, well-known—but surprised everyone by putting a bullet through his head. It's not enough to be involved in church, community, and neighborhood affairs. When we lack personal intimacy we get lonely.

Since personal loneliness is so often thought to have as its cure sexual intimacy, I want to say once again that the problem of personal loneliness is not found in sexual promiscuity. In fact, the reverse is almost always true. C'mon, guys, didn't you see/read *Looking for Mr. Goodbar*? It's the worst way to go. If you try to fill up your personal emptiness with a casual liaison, you'll wake up the next morning worse off than before.

Seek friendship. Friendship is nearly synonymous with love. Whether dealing with those of your same sex, or opposite sex, you owe it to yourself and to those around you to look for friendship, to cultivate it, to nourish it, and savor it. Do for others; let them do for you. Be less concerned with what others have to offer you, and more concerned with what you can offer them. Some good friendships become romantic; that's something to be prepared for. But it's not something to count on.

Show affection—physical affection—to your friend. The handshake, sitting as it does on the far end of the physical affection continuum, is one way of having personal contact with a friend. Hugs are important (you need one or two a day just to maintain yourself; several if you want to grow); kisses are good.

Many of us were taught as children and preteens that we shouldn't touch our friends. It wasn't right. Maybe we even got the idea that it was perverse. Or we were told that it would lead to "other things." Dancing was really discouraged in my youth—it led to "other things." Holding hands, hugging, kissing: all these were on the road to "other things." So we were told at church and at church camp and in books that we shouldn't start something that we couldn't finish.

But I believe now that the need for physical contact is so basic to every human being that we should actively seek acceptable ways of getting it. I think that adolescents should dance; it's good for them. I think that friends—same sex or not—should touch, should hug, should be physically close. When it becomes unacceptable, or gets out of hand, you'll be the first to know—you don't need any arbitrary guidelines.

Maybe it doesn't come naturally for you to hug a friend—you flinch. But that shouldn't keep you from doing it. You may come to like it!

Spiritual Loneliness

Here's a mental picture for you: each person has a God-shaped hole right in the middle of him. The hole is pretty big, and uniquely shaped so that it's obvious to anyone who can see the hole that nobody but God will be able to fill it up.

I believe we all have God-shaped holes. We can try to fill them up with things other than God—materialism, self-indulgence, friends, or even ourselves—but in the end all our efforts will only approximate filling of the hole. The God-shaped hole is filled only by God. That's the way we've been created, and the sooner we realize our need for God and our innate longing for Him, the sooner we will deal with our spiritual loneliness.

Just buying into the concept of the God-shaped hole goes a long way toward filling it. We ask God to make us complete people by living in us. The natural outcome of this is that we want to know our Creator; and we do this through prayer, Bible study, meditation, private and corporate worship, and associating with other people who are also anxious to let God live in their lives.

"Loneliness can be conquered only by those who can bear solitude."
Paul Tillich

Spiritual loneliness is like all the other kinds: a little bit is a good thing because it points us to an area of need. But if it's prolonged and unattended it can cause the deepest kind of unhappiness that exists. It causes people with loving personal relationships and social belonging to cry out to the sky in despair. The spiritual loneliness of our society in general has made death our cultural taboo, religion an unmentionable subject, and faith such a personal matter that we're afraid to talk to each other about it.

Conversely, spiritual fulfillment can make all other kinds of loneliness bearable. When you have a good relationship with God, social isolation and turmoil as well as personal dry spots are put into perspective and become manageable challenges. Time and time again we hear people say, "If it weren't for my faith, I couldn't have survived," and "In spite of it all, I was happy because I knew that God was with me."

It's the most important thing.

28.

SOCIAL LIFE

Nearly everyone values (and consequently wants) for themselves an active social life. What actually constitutes an active social life is certainly open to individual interpretation, and depends in large part on one's inclinations and need for interpersonal interaction. There are those who are left reeling by three or four invitations in a year's time, and others who suspect that they have developed an offending body odor if two consecutive nights are spent without the company of others. And what is a social event? Breakfast at McDonald's with four other coworkers? Dinner at the Portuguese Embassy?

Social life has a lot to do with popularity (this is fairly obvious), and popularity has long been equated with personal value, which is why few people will admit to having nothing to do Saturday night, or to ever having thrown a party to which none of the guests came. This is unfortunate. An active social life has nothing at all to do with one's human worth; it's more a matter of opportunity and tenacity.

Although your social circle—those with whom you interact for the purpose of mere pleasure, as opposed to business or some other functional purpose—will probably include those with whom you are most intimate, it certainly isn't limited to your intimates. This too is a popular misconception: that each and every person you invite into your home, or spend an evening with, should be close to you. The fact is that your social circle should include those people that you enjoy spending limited amounts of time with. The fact that you wouldn't dream of entrusting them with a personal secret, or that they are definitely off the roster of potential marriage partners, shouldn't keep you from enjoying their company.

How to Begin a Social Life

We're social animals, and with a little bit of training we can be made sociable as well.

First off, accept invitations that are extended to you by others, no matter how unpromising. You're just starting out, remember. At such social functions, make it a point to learn the names (and, if appropriate, the addresses and phone numbers) of other guests that seem interesting to you.

Secondly, exercise initiative and entertain (my tried-and-true tips for successful entertaining follow). Instead of inviting the same crew of regulars, mix it up a little bit and throw in a few wild cards: a new neighbor, a guy you work with, or your second cousin who just moved here from Cleveland.

Show an interest (genuine, if you can manage it) in the people you live near and work with. Join volunteer organizations that include social functions on their slate of events. Quit avoiding strangers (except the kind that offer you candy or wear baggy trenchcoats and no trousers). Take a chance!

How to Maintain a Social Life

Having gotten a toehold, you must nourish your social life. This is largely a matter of manners and wit.

As for manners, you already know the basics, which have to do with showing simple consideration and shunning gaucherie. You RSVP when asked to do so, make an effort to keep your sleeve out of the cucumber dip, and do not spill anything of an indelible nature on the carpet.

As for wit, it is important to tell a story only once, even if you suspect that you *may* have a fresh audience on which to try your favorite old anecdote (the time you took the Greyhound bus to Sacramento and sat next to Bob Dylan). Come prepared with a few jokes—not ethnic, not lewd, not esoteric. (Such comedy rarely gets a laugh, and inevitably discloses more about your personality than you ought to exhibit at a social function.)

Party animals are in great demand these days, but you should be as willing to help someone in your social circle move across town as you are to eat and drink them into poverty. Try not to be a leech; contribute when you are asked.

How to Repair a Social Life

Practice the fine art of apologizing and asking forgiveness.

What It Is, Really

Social is an overworked word. There's social psychology, social work, social disease, social patterns, and the social register. Such technical handles tend to make the simple employment of social occasions with those who are in one's social circle, (i.e., social life) sound a bit more ominous than it really is.

Your social circle is your piece of the world. With the exception of Andy Warhol and perhaps Mick Jagger, nobody has a social circle that encompasses all of humankind. Your immediate social circle is the people who live near enough to drop by if you ask them to, or even if you don't ask them to. It's the folks that you think of more as people than as functionaries; when the gas station attendant becomes good old Joe, who is thinking seriously of playing soccer with you on Saturday, he has ceased to become a functionary (the nonentity who puts gas into your tank) and has made a leap into your social circle.

Your social circle is also your buffer against the world. It protects you. When you need companionship, support, or a ride to church, you can draw on your social circle for aid. These kind people make you laugh, don't care too much if you cry, and some of them will come through for you when you're in a bind. Which is plenty. Sometimes it's even enough.

Don't expect everyone in your social circle to be registered Democrats, to share your belief in eternal security, or to like ketchup on their eggs. It's too much to ask. You're not trying to live with them, just enjoy them. The more you can overlook, the wider your social circle and the richer your social life.

How to Throw a Party

People are always coming up to me on the street and saying: "Alice, you could do the world a big favor if you'd reveal your secret for all those fabulous parties you give. How about it, girl? Are you going to tell us how it's done?"

For years I have chosen to keep all my entertaining secrets to myself, but I now believe that the time has come to share with the teeming masses the expertise I have gained over the years—years spent eating, drinking, and making merry with my friends.

What follows are the philosophies and practices that have made me famous in every corner of the earth (what do you mean you've never heard of me before?) for my wildly successful (and sometimes just wild) parties.

(1) Remember that your guests are offering themselves to you as a gift, and you should receive them as such. Hey, they didn't have to come. They could have stayed home and watched "Love Boat." But they didn't; they agreed to accept your invitation, and for this act of kindness they should be treated with great respect and high regard. When they arrive, you're on hand to greet them; you look excited to see them (because you are), and you do everything you can during the course of the evening to let them know you're honored by their presence. When they leave, you thank them, thank them for coming.

(2) You extend to these good people unambiguous invitations. You let them know—either with a written invitation, a phone call, or in direct conversation—what the date of the gathering is, the exact time, what kind of food and drink will be served, if it's formal or casual, and if you want them to bring anything (besides themselves). Let me elaborate.

It's not too hard to get the date right. But I've gone to parties at what I thought was the appointed hour only to find out that I'm about two hours behind the other guests, or that the other guests won't be arriving until after lunch. That's no way to treat someone you care about. I have also worn a party dress when everyone else was wearing jeans. Once I arrived at a friend's house for dinner (I thought) only to find her putting the last of her dinner dishes into the dishwasher; I nearly starved that evening, and I'm ashamed to admit that I made a bit of a pig of myself when the pizza rolls were finally served around 10 P.M.

Some parties require guests to bring some kind of food or beverage. Although many people resent this, I tend to think it encourages more entertaining because the host assumes less of a burden in terms of time and expense—and the more parties the better, as far as I'm concerned. If you want your guests to bring something, be up-front about it. If they ask, then you simply need to tell them what: "Oh, thanks, Janet—I appreciate your offer. How about making some of that incredible artichoke dip that you served last summer? Sure, if you'd bring the crackers for it that would be great!" If no offer is made, you may say something like this when issuing the invitation: "I'm going to be making a huge birthday cake, but several people have offered to bring munchies, and if you'd like to bring something I'd appreciate it."

Maybe your guests have children. At my parties, other people's children are always welcome, because they're not my responsibility. If kids are being encouraged, you say, " . . . and I hope you're planning to bring Tiffany—Sam Piper said he's going to do some magic tricks and I know she'd enjoy that." Remember, though, that sometimes parents need a night off. If they say Tiffany will be going to Grandma's for the evening, don't push it. To discourage kids, you say, "Tiffany is welcome, but I thought you might like to know that Frank and Barbara and the McNeils have decided to get sitters for the evening."

My family orientation causes me to believe that children may be discouraged but never forbidden at a party. Nursing babies and toddlers with separation anxiety belong with their parents, and parents shouldn't be isolated socially because of it. And the cost of sitters—ay-yi-yi! Let 'em bring the kids if they like—it's their decision. You can live with it.

Whatever the occasion, it's better to spell out the details than leave them to chance—out of respect for your guests and concern for the success of your party.

3. Take stock of your house or apartment and plan a suitable function on the basis of your facilities. Don't invite twenty-eight people to a fancy dress ball at your small efficiency apartment (at least don't invite *me* to something like that). If you've got a mosquito-infested swamp for a yard, skip the cookout and go for something inside. If your apartment is on the condemned buildings list, have your party in a park.

Space is often a problem, so put what you've got to good use. You can put your bed up on its side, move the kitchen table into the bedroom, and serve the food in there; this leaves the living room clear for mingling and keeps people out of the kitchen. I've put a punch bowl in the hallway before, just to spread out the guests at a rather large party, all forty of whom would have congregated around the kitchen sink if they hadn't been forced to trot to the other side of the house for a drink. I've also moved the dining room to the living room for a sit-down dinner.

Before the party, bring your apartment to the level of cleanliness that makes you and your guests comfortable. Don't kill yourself waxing floors and cleaning windows; you'll be too pooped to enjoy yourself when your guests arrive. But you should clear out the dangerous filth and enough of the simple debris so guests can find a place to sit. Peg Bracken (author of the classic *I Hate to Cook Book*) advises hosts to skip the general cleaning, but always dust off the telephone before a party. If the phone's clean, the house seems clean. Candlelight, she says, is also a great idea for parties held in dirty houses.

Improvise. I read an article in *Glamour* a few years ago that suggested using overhead light fixtures (the shallow dish-types) as potato chip bowls. If the *Glamour* girls are doing it, who are you to object? Use your imagination.

If you are convinced that your living quarters are absolutely unsuitable for entertaining, hook up with a friend who has better digs and offer to co-host a party. He provides the space, you bring the food. You should also offer to help clean up the place beforehand as well as afterward. Invite some of your friends, some of his friends, and you're off.

(4) Which brings up the matter of how to make your guests feel comfortable and welcome. You're already off to a good start because you realize how valuable your guests are (1); you have extended a cordial and specific invitation (2); and you have made your living space as conducive as possible to fun (3). Of course, my guests always feel perfectly at ease, and have a wonderful time. Here's how I do it.

I start off by inviting people who will know each other, but try to make sure that not everybody knows every other person. Which is to say that I don't have a roomful of strangers, but I don't restrict the guest list only to people who already know each other to death. I try to include someone who's new to the group. It's best if this person knows a few of your other guests, but not essential.

With one or two newcomers you—the host—may (and should) spend quite a bit of time introducing them around. A new person is definitely to be treated as the guest of honor. You make a big deal of him. "Folks, I'm really excited that James could come tonight. He's usually not free on Saturday evenings, but he got tonight off work, so this is special. James and I went to grade school together, and I hadn't seen him since sixth-grade promotion, and then we ran into each other at the Traffic Violations Bureau." That'll do for a general introduction. Then you take good old James around to every single person there and introduce him, and you try as hard as you can to make connections between James and each other guest. "James, this is Missy. I work with Missy. Missy, James. Missy's really active in historic preservation programs in the neighborhood. She's trying to find a buyer for that old house on the corner of Elm and Watkins—you know, the one with all the beveled glass. James is in real estate, Missy . . ." Let them take it from there. If a conversation gets started, you can move on. But keep your eye on James! If you see him sitting around looking like a strip of wallpaper, you're back on duty and must introduce him to someone else. During the course of the evening he should have met everybody there.

Obviously this is a lot of work, which is why you can't afford to have too many Jameses at any one party. Keep the number manageable.

(5) Be aware of the practices that can kill a party. They are:

- having the television on. Everybody will watch the tube; nobody will socialize.

- playing stupid party games. Games are for Tupperware parties. (There may be a possible exception for a "game party"—such as a Trivial Pursuit party—but that's stretching it.)

- holding out on the food and drink until some arbitrarily appointed hour. The party starts when the refreshments are served, so have them available as your guests arrive. If you're going to save the cutting of the cake, or the pouring of the champagne, or serving of the enchiladas until later, when everyone has arrived, no problem with that. But your guests should have something to munch on (even crackers) and something to sip while they're waiting.

- putting a bunch of folding chairs in a circle for guests to sit on. Keep your furniture arrangement the way it usually is. Hosts sometimes want to create group cohesiveness by placing a ring of chairs around the perimeter of the room, which gets a bunch of people sitting too far away from each other to have a conversation. So they just sit and stare at each other.

- insufficient quantities of ice.

(6) My own world-famous parties are enhanced by:

- good music. Borrow a stereo and records if you must, but music is essential. A radio can be used if you have a good FM station in town. Since I have a tape deck, I like to program party tapes by assembling my favorite cuts off my favorite albums into one fabulous hour-and-a-half of programmed music. Sure it's a lot of work, but we're talking about parties here—no effort is too great.

- plenty of food. I usually plan what I'm going to serve to eat (and drink, for that matter) and have that laid out for guests, but also have extra in the cupboard or refrigerator that I don't need to serve (that is, it won't spoil if kept for a while), but can if we run low: extra bags of potato chips, cookies, etc.

- high spirits. There was a time when I got so bogged down in preparations that I couldn't enjoy myself when it was time to party. No more. I do only as much as I must, and save the rest of my strength for fun. Try to get a good night's sleep the night before, or take a nap in the afternoon.

- surprises. Figure out what your crowd usually does, and then try something different. Every summer, I host a breakfast picnic in the park—we all get to be outside before it gets too hot. When I turned thirty, I had a ceremonial burial of all objects typifying my youth: a Van Halen album, puka shells, Mickey Mouse watch, college diploma, hardbound copy of *Everything You Ever Wanted to Know About Sex, But Were Afraid to Ask*, bikinis, etc. C'mon, shake it up a little!

So there you are, world. My secrets are out. I am not prepared, at this time, to divulge the recipe for my Danish Puffs, or to tell how it is that I was able to remain calm when a guest spilled picante sauce on the beige carpet in the dining room. These are all for another book. You have enough at this stage to get started; just remember, I like to attend as much as I like to host, so don't forget to mail me an invitation.

Shyness

Probably one of the biggest barriers to a satisfying social life is shyness. It's estimated that 5 percent of the population is crippled by shyness, and about 40 percent of us are shy in certain situations: at a party with strangers, during an oral examination in front of five academics with no sense of humor, or at any function where you're expected to sing along (one of my social embarrassments).

So one out of twenty of us is dangerously shy, which is sometimes confused with being dangerous. Every time a sniper positions himself on the top of a state capitol building and empties his submachine gun on a bunch of government employees, what do people say about the guy? "LANDLADY SAYS TITTLE WAS QUIET, SHY," read the newspaper headlines. Which does nothing to further the cause of the shy; for weeks after every bizarre terrorist event, shy people of honorable intention and pure heart are shunned by their landladies and everybody else who misinterprets their reticence as psychosis.

All the time you hear people say about their friends, "I know Janelle seems shy, but once you get to know her she isn't that way at all!" or "He would die if he ever had to send back an underdone steak, but get him up on a stage, and he's the funniest guy I've ever heard!" Which is a clue to the fact that shyness is something that comes and goes for most of us; some situations make us shy, and others don't. There are movie actors who won't do live performances—they're too shy. There are preachers who shy away from one-to-one contact with their parishioners, but think nothing of doing something that would throw the average person into a sweat, namely, speaking in front of hundreds of people (for a living, yet!). There are also brilliant conversationalists who become semicatatonic when a beautiful woman or handsome man walks into the room.

What's shyness, then? What's it all about?

Mainly it's about lack of skill. Shy people aren't sick; they aren't psychopaths; they aren't abnormal. They are just unskilled in certain areas, the areas that they're shy in.

Usually their lack of skill has to do with the inability to talk or act spontaneously. The shy person walks away from encounters saying, "I wish I had remembered to tell him . . ." or "What I should have done was to . . ." or "If I had just had a minute to think about it, I could have . . ." Since it's clear by now that we've all had times when we felt like that, let's start talking about shyness in the first person plural: we're shy guys, you and me.

Every time we talk to another person, or take action, we are performing. So shyness could be called a fear of performing. When the fear is great enough, we just cancel the gig. We know we're going to mess up and be miserable in certain situations, so we refuse to get involved. We turn down invitations to large parties where we'll come in contact with a bunch of people we don't know; we don't attend churches where the pastor says, "And now, while we're waiting on the choir, let's take this opportunity to greet the people sitting behind, alongside, and in front of us" (at least not more than once); we don't enter occupations that require public speaking; we don't go out dancing or attend sing-along concerts or participate in political rallies.

This is all okay—why should we traumatize ourselves? If we don't look out for us, who will?

The problem is that most of us can't avoid every uncomfortable situation and still live the kind of lives we want to; so we end up suffering for our shyness. By necessity, we are forced into situations that make us sweat. The problem of shyness deserves attention.

Here's my eight-point plan for combatting shyness. If you (and I) follow it, we're bound to notice some improvement in our condition.

(1) Recognize that shyness is not a disease, but simply a lack of basic skills with which to deal effectively in a number of varied situations. Make a list of your Waterloos: every situation, every person, every condition that brings out your shyness.

(2) Looking at your list, decide what you can do to educate and train yourself to deal with the situations more effectively. For example, if you listed "I'm afraid to go out to eat at a restaurant," it's possible that you feel this way because you never learned good table manners; so instead of enjoying the food you're preoccupied with the plethora of flatware, the distinct possibility that you will spill your ice water, and the question of whether it's

okay to pick up your T-bone so as to get that especially tasty meat next to the bone (it isn't). Good news, though: it's not too late to polish up on your manners. Or to learn public speaking, or to improve your grammar, or to improve your coordination, or to make small talk with a beautiful woman.

(3) Once you've figured out what action will help, pursue it. You can take formal classes for some things; or subscribe to magazines that will help; or join a support group that will assist you. The ability to participate in a conversation is lacking in most shy people. This can be helped by talking to yourself when you're alone—and answering yourself. Or by watching television shows and movies and analyzing the dynamics of successful conversation, how it works and how you can participate in it. Play old conversations back to yourself: he said, you said, he said, you said. Oops! What *should* you have said? Say it—out loud. Next time you might remember to say it when the time is right. Football players watch films of their games; why can't you mentally, at least, replay your performances and see where improvements can be made?

(4) There's an English television and radio personality named Clive James. He is a truly funny guy, and by watching his television show, in which he interviews guests, you could learn a lot about the fine art of conversation. He disclosed on one show that he was forced to become good at talk because he thought he was physically unattractive to women. Not willing to do without the company of the fairer sex in his life, he decided to relate to them through what they heard, not what they saw. He believes that there's an inverse relationship between looks and the ability to converse: gorgeous people don't converse well because they don't have to—their beauty speaks all. Plain-looking people must display their nonphysical attributes in order to attract people, and he thinks that the plainer the better when it comes to ferreting out an interesting person at a party: always hook up with someone homely if you want witty repartee, says Clive James.

There's some truth to that, of course. But it's also true that many people are shy because of their looks, and they are unable to break out as he did and develop their other strengths. Is that you? Are your looks keeping you on the shelf? Don't agonize over the things you can't change, but you could take a minimal interest in your appearance so that you don't embarrass yourself. Try to wear clothes that are appropriate for the occasion; make sure that your personal encounters are prefaced with a bath, brushing of teeth, combing of hair, and zipping the fly. Why defeat yourself? When in the midst of a shy attack, when you think you're really dying, all you can think about is that you might have spinach on your teeth or a piece of toilet paper stuck to the bottom of your shoe, or that your mascara is probably halfway down your cheeks. All these things can be quickly and easily checked beforehand (and in between times) so that you can concentrate on other matters.

(5) Avoid superstressful situations, and embrace those that offer a framework for growth. Let's say you're afraid of public speaking (most people are). Your pastor calls you up and says he'd like you to give a fifteen-minute report on the activities of the Mission Committee at the morning service two weeks from now. I personally wouldn't do that: it's too stressful, likely to throw a shy person over the edge. But you might do something in your church that could stretch you a little without snapping you, such as chairing a committee, singing in the choir, or teaching a small Sunday school class.

Why go to a large gathering of rich, effete snobs if you know you'll spend the entire evening sitting in the bathroom? Let that invite go by; attend instead a small gathering of friends and set some personal goals in terms of how many people you'll talk to, or how long you'll try to sustain a conversation with one person at that small party. It's a framework for growth, not a leap off a high cliff.

(6) Set realistic goals for yourself. As with the small party, where you are determined to talk to a certain number of people or for a certain period of time, decide ahead of time what you wish to accomplish and devise a specific plan to reach your goal.

Let's hypothesize a situation in which you are enrolled in a university class that has only twelve students in it, and you learn on the first day that you will be graded partly on your participation in class discussions.

Argh! Class discussions—your bane! You can drop the class, but you can also decide that the class provides opportunity for growth and use it as a vehicle for overcoming your shyness of talking in front of others. So you set out a plan of attack for the semester.

Week 1: I will speak with the teacher after class about some matter related to coursework.

Week 2: I will ask a question in class, either of the instructor or another student.

Week 3: I will share an observation I have made during the course of a class discussion.

Week 4: I will respond to another student's observation.

Week 5: Same as week 4, except that I will respond to another student's observation each time that the class meets.

"WHAT ARE YOU THE MOST AFRAID OF?"

(based on responses of 3,000 United States inhabitants)

FEARS	PERCENT NAMING
1. Speaking before a group	41
2. Heights	32
3. Insects and bugs	22
3. Financial problems	22
3. Deep water	22
6. Sickness	19
6. Death	19
8. Flying	18
9. Loneliness	14
10. Dogs	11
11. Driving/riding in a car	9
12. Darkness	8
13. Elevators	8
14. Escalators	5

Sunday Times, London, October 7, 1973. Quoted in *The Book of Lists.*

Week 6: I will engage in a discussion in which I make statements or ask questions two or more times.

Week 7: I will introduce a topic of discussion.

Week 8: I will ask a question or share an observation at least
once per session.

And so on. Such a plan needn't throw the shy person into a
panic. It's very simple, and can be taken one week at a time. You,
the shy guy, by the time the semester is over will have progressed
from asking the teacher a question after the class has adjourned to
actively participating in classroom discussions. That's improvement!

(7) Cultivate a friendship with another shy person who also
wants to change. The last thing you need is to spend all your time
around someone who has no idea why you can't stand up and
speak your mind (or sing your song, or play your part, or whatever). No, you need to have at least one friend who understands
what it's like to get numb when called on to speak during a
departmental meeting. You will need each other's help and encouragement. Share your failures and share your successes with
each other.

(8) If shyness is having a debilitating effect on you, get the
kind of professional help you need. You can start by reading an
excellent book entitled *Help for Shy People (and Anyone Else Who
Ever Felt Ill at Ease on Entering a Room Full of Strangers . . .)* by
Gerald M. Phillips (Englewood Cliffs, NJ: Prentice-Hall, 1981).
There are plenty of books that give a psychological and sociologi-
cal treatment to the matter of shyness, but this particular book is
filled with the kind of help you need to tackle the problem.

Sex

After a rather complicated discussion of autonomy, intimacy,
loneliness, social life, and shyness, we're now onto the subject
that we've all been waiting for, which can be nothing other than
sex. Aside from a few circuitous references that were absolutely
necessary, I've been avoiding the subject up until now. This is not
due to prudishness or modesty on my part (I confess to being
neither), but because putting sex before autonomy, intimacy, and
the rest would be like spreading the butter before the bread is out
of the bag.

Here's the truth about sex: nobody ever died for the lack of it. A few subcultures have died out (through attrition) for lack of it, but no individual has ever forfeited life for lack of sex. (Please send the details of cases that contradict that statement in care of my publisher—I can't wait to hear how it happened!)

This disclosure is not unimportant. There are those who would have you believe that one cannot live without sexual intimacy, and that to practice sexual restraint can be damaging in a very ultimate sense. But the truth is that, though no one ever perished for lack of sex, many have died for lack of love. Do you remember hearing about orphanages where infants were fed, clothed, changed, treated for all their medical problems, but failed to thrive because they lacked TLC—tender loving care? Many of the babies died for simple lack of affection.

Intimacy is vital; touching is vital; tenderness is vital. When a relationship contains these vital factors, then sex has meaning—but not before. And since sex is such a dynamic drive/experience, it should be the capstone for a relationship, not its cornerstone.

With all that by way of introduction, I am now prepared to share with the world in general, and with you in particular, my best advice about sexual relationships.

(1) All relationships with fellow human beings should be established and maintained with respect to the original establisher and eternal maintainer: God. As children of the same father, every interaction we have with our brothers and sisters should be subject to God's will. This includes relationships within the family, with same-sex friends, opposite-sex friends, business associates, etc.

(2) You don't need to spend a lot of time wondering about what it means to have a romantic relationship that is acceptable to God. Read the Bible; it clearly explains what God demands of our relationships.

(3) Actively seek intimacy. Since sexual intimacy can dominate a relationship (not unlike the effect of garlic in marinara sauce), it should chronologically come after social, spiritual, intellectual, emotional, and nonsexual physical intimacy. (I offer no advice on the order of those—any way you like it is fine with me.) Sex has the power to inhibit the development of these other kinds of intimacy, and this is the reason it should come last.

As proof of this (as if I needed proof), may I cite the tremendous disappointment that many married couples experience in their first year of marriage. Traditionally, this twelve-month period has been devoted to sex—morning, noon, and night. Many married couples have found that sex in the early months and years of marriage has been so overpowering that they have nothing to share emotionally, intellectually, or any other way. Once the fever subsides, however, they are ready to resume a more normal relationship that recognizes sex but isn't controlled by it. Some couples find that brief, and even extended, periods of celibacy during their marriage serve to help them grow closer in other areas.

(4) When a relationship is developing social, spiritual, emotional, and intellectual intimacy, and begins to move toward sexual intimacy—then it's probably time to think about moving toward the altar. You have the start of a terrific marriage!

(5) If (make that when) you violate your own standards concerning your sexual behavior (which are, I sincerely hope, based on your commitment to bring all your relationships in line with your Creator), don't despair; pick yourself up and try again.

You may think that what you have done puts you beyond hope; you may think that you have failed so many times that you can't possibly change. But let me assure you that no matter what your besetting sin is, and no matter whether it's heterosexual or homosexual in nature, you must not resign yourself to failure.

I am firmly of the opinion that there is such a thing as illicit sex. Illicit sex isn't right (that's why it's illicit), but it isn't unforgivable, either. It's not beyond God's forgiveness, and if He's willing to forgive and forget, there's no reason why you should continue to hate yourself for doing something that you think is wrong.

"As to marriage or celibacy, let a man take which course he will, he will be sure to repent."
Socrates

(6) No matter how confused or frustrated or wild-eyed you get about it, your sexuality is worth celebrating. It's who you are. It's one of life's mixed blessings, to be sure, but surely you don't

want to do without it. Some people choose celibacy as their life's vocation; most do not. But celibate or sexually active, your sexuality is a big part of who you are.

And that's the truth about sex. Thanks for listening.

Dating

Here are my tried-and-true (I tried a few of them; the rest are reportedly true) directives for having a successful date:

(1) Don't look at each date as the proving ground for a lifetime partner. Such an outlook is pathetic and off-putting. Even if you suspect that the longing of your heart will be fulfilled by the young woman who has asked you to her apartment for dinner on Thursday night, it's best—imperative, actually—to keep your suspicions to yourself. Project an image of the interesting individual who is anticipating an evening of scintillating conversation, hearty laughter, and general sociability over dual Hungry Man Dinners—but never let your date suspect that you're sizing him/her up for a tux/wedding gown.

(2) Man or woman, boy or girl, guy or gal—Hallelujah! These days it doesn't matter what your sex is; you may initiate a date. These are indeed wonderful times we live in.

(3) Refusing a date is sometimes a good idea. I must confess that I have refused fewer dates than I should have. (See Preface to this book; of approximately 258 dates, almost 100 were doomed from the start.) I further confess that in the past I have encouraged friends to accept dates that they should not have accepted. Trudy, who is now my sister-in-law, got some of my poor advice when asked on a date by a guy she knew she didn't like. I told her to go: it was a free movie, right? She took my well-meant but wrong-headed advice and ended up paying for her own admission, her own popcorn, her own Dr. Pepper—everything—and suffering through a terrible evening with a mismatched suitor.

Sometimes you know that the date isn't going to work. Why waste your time and money (not to mention your date's) on a sure miss? Again, this is not to say that your date must be your heart's desire, but you have your standards, you know what they are, and you are in no way obligated to spend an evening with someone you detest.

(4) Furthermore, it is sometimes acceptable to end a particularly terrible (not merely disappointing, but out-and-out terrible) date before the appointed hour. If you find yourself out with someone who is threatening in any way (physically, psychologically, emotionally), you have a perfect right to end the date by whatever means seems most expeditious. This is because truly harmful occurrences are possible on dates. Nobody should be forced to finish out the evening with a drunk, a letch, a negligent driver, an intimidator, a dopehead, or anyone who is not playing by the rules—which you set, of course.

(5) Know ahead of time what the evening will consist of. This is important. If the planned activity is inappropriate, it's better to know before you've accepted the date than after you've been admitted to the mud wrestling tournament at the Civic Auditorium. Ferreting out the plan for the evening is not difficult.

"Hello, Richard? This is Elaine."

"Hello, Elaine! I'm glad to hear from you again."

"Richard, I was wondering if you're free to go out on Friday night?"

"What do you have in mind?" (Notice that Richard has left his options open; he's going to find out what Elaine's up to before saying "yes" or "no.")

"I was thinking we might go over to my sister-in-law's house and help her clean out her chinchilla cages."

"Oh, Elaine, that would probably be a lot of fun, but I'm allergic to chinchillas!" (Richard doesn't put Elaine down, or criticize her idea of a good time. He states a simple fact that, coincidentally, serves to get him out of an obnoxious task.)

Of course, if you *want* to clean cages on Friday night, then you could accept the invitation. "Clean chinchilla cages! Wow, love to! I'm so happy that you thought to invite me!" At any rate, you'll know how to dress for the occasion, and your expectations for the evening can be in line with the reality of the event.

(6) If you want to go out on a date, but are less than enthused by the activity being suggested, there are ways of making alternative suggestions without spoiling the invitation or seeming impolite.

"I was thinking that we might go over to my sister-in-law's house and help her clean out her chinchilla cages."

"Oh, Elaine, that would probably be a lot of fun, but I'm

allergic to chinchillas. I am free on Friday, though, and had thought of going to the opera. Does that interest you?"

In this way, Richard bows out of cage duty gracefully, communicates to Elaine his willingness to do *something*, and carefully suggests an activity that's more to his liking—hearing Pavarotti in *Die Fledermaus* (preferring, as he does, bats to chinchillas). Elaine is free to counter the offer—she could suggest a movie or hitting a bucket of balls at the driving range—or can decline the counteroffer.

"Gee, I'm sorry that you're allergic to chinchillas. I'm afraid that I couldn't go to the opera; I really did promise my sister-in-law that I'd help her on Friday night."

(7) If the situation warrants it, you might do some homework prior to your date. This can be anything from a predate phone call to clarify the plans ("I can't remember if you said we were going to the *opera* or *Opry*—which was it?") to some research into ethnic customs (if a friend has invited you to his cousin's bar mitzvah, you might want to bone up on the protocol for that important rite of passage so as not to make a *schlemiel* of yourself) or a crash course in your date's greatest interests (she's an art historian and all you know about art is what you see at the "Starving Artists" sales at the Holiday Inn parking lot; or he's the co-captain of the soccer team, and you don't know a soccer ball from a volleyball).

Remember that shyness can usually be attributed to lack of skill in a given situation; if you're prone to shyness, then do yourself a favor and learn a little bit about your date, his or her interests, and what you're going to be doing beforehand.

8. In most cases it is acceptable to suggest that another couple be included, especially if you are terrified to accept the date on any other terms. Of course, if you fear for your safety, you shouldn't involve another couple (assumed to be friends of yours) in a potentially dangerous situation. But if your fright has more to do with lulls (long lulls) in the conversation and embarrassment at your own (or your date's) awkwardness, then you may wish to say: "Elaine, cleaning chinchilla cages sounds like a whale of a good time! I'd like to do that with you on Friday evening. Do you think that we could invite Doug and Diane to join us? Doug is crazy about animals, and Diane is wild about expensive furs . . . "

Elaine may decline, but it never hurts to ask.

(9) When the date is over (or sometime during its course) the askee should find some way of communicating to the asker that he/she had (or is having) a grand time. Assuming, of course, that a grand time is in actuality occurring. This is the askee's way of letting the asker know that he/she would like to be an askee again. Another way of communicating interest is to switch roles and reciprocate the invitation. So Richard says, after a fabulous evening of cutting newspaper to size, "Elaine, I haven't had this much fun since Sparky, my pet canary, died. If you're free next weekend, I'd like to take you out to the animal shelter and introduce you to a friend of mine who works there . . . maybe we could go out for hot dogs after that."

If you have been the asker for a date, look for some sign of life and interest before initiating a follow-up invitation—either in your date's apparent enthusiasm or an outright invitation to get together again sometime. And if you are the one who has been asked, be sure to give such a sign.

RUDOLPH VALENTINO'S TEN ATTRIBUTES OF THE PERFECT WOMAN

1. Fidelity

2. The recognition of the supreme importance of love

3. Intelligence

4. Beauty

5. A sense of humor

6. Sincerity

7. An appreciation of good food

8. A serious interest in some art, trade, or hobby

9. An old-fashioned and wholehearted acceptance of monogamy

10. Courage

(Cleveland Amory, quoted in *The Book of Lists #2*, p. 318)

Help from Miss Manners

Dear Miss Manners:

What suggestions can you offer to a "social klutz" who absolutely dreads going to parties and social events where I will meet new people? I get so uptight about saying the wrong thing that I usually do. I am fine around people who know me and I'm a fairly successful hostess, but am a terrible guest.

Gentle Reader:

Most people develop clever opening lines for such events. If you let them deliver these statements and say only, "How interesting—tell me about it," you will soon have a reputation as a charming person and a fascinating conversationalist.

Dear Miss Manners:

What do you say if someone you don't like gives you a compliment?

Gentle Reader:

"Thank you."

Dear Miss Manners:

With the advent of telephone answering machines, a problem of etiquette has arisen. What should one do upon reaching one of these electronic marvels? I hang up whenever I reach an answering service, as I hate talking to a machine. I know this is not proper, but what is?

Gentle Reader:

It is perfectly proper to hang up on a machine. In fact, the whole concept of proper and improper behavior does not apply between people and machines. Miss Manners has enough trouble getting people to be polite to one another, without worrying about whether they are treating machines with consideration.

Dear Miss Manners:

My boyfriend is very shy, and we never seem to have anything to talk about. On the phone—he calls me every night before bedtime—the silences are awful. Can you suggest something I could say to him?

Gentle Reader:
"Do you have any nice friends?"

Dear Miss Manners:
When I have soft drinks at the movies, I often have to get up about halfway through the picture and excuse myself. The people in my row seem annoyed when I go past them, first in leaving and then in returning. I only block their view for a minute. Is this inconsiderate of me, really?

Gentle Reader:
Perhaps. But, then, so is the alternative.

Dear Miss Manners:
Your views on the propriety of applauding in church would be timely. It seems to me that whatever talent one displays in church—musical or oratorical—is offered up to the glory of God, not to solicit the admiration (true or feigned) of one's fellow sinners.

Gentle Reader:
Even when ecclesiastical oratory was more stirring than it usually is nowadays, it was never received with applause. If God wishes to applaud in church, He may, but it is inappropriate for anyone else to do so.

Dear Miss Manners:
I'm having a somewhat unusual disagreement with my new roommate on a point of etiquette. We share a dormitory room. It is my habit to pray (silently) each evening before retiring. Whenever I try to do so in our room, however, my roommate throws things at me or chases me out of the building. He says it's rude to carry on a private conversation in the presence of a third party. I say he's full of it. What do you say?

Gentle Reader:
A person who attacks violently one who is engaged in prayer is obviously a great authority on etiquette, whom it

would be futile, and probably dangerous, to contradict. However, Miss Manners would point out that your room-mate is perfectly free to join into the conversation with the Third Party, provided he observes the convention you do, of doing it in silence.

Dear Miss Manners:

As a smoker, I am constantly having run-ins with non-smokers who want to tell me when and where I can smoke. Are there any legitimate rules about this?

Gentle Reader:

Yes, and they never should have been abandoned, as they were when women began to smoke, which never should have happened, either. Smoking should be confined to certain parlors to which the smokers may retire from the sensible people and make their disgusting mess. One should not smoke at the same table where others are still eating. If you wish to smoke in the presence of clean peo-ple, you must ask their permission and be prepared to accept their refusal to grant it.

Dear Miss Manners:

Is it so awful not to be able to remember people's names? I've tried all kinds of systems, and it never seems to work. I find that if I fake a person's name when I don't know it, I get caught, but I'm afraid to admit right off that I don't know a name because people get insulted.

Gentle Reader:

We have a great deal of admiration in this country for people who have the ability to remember names. It is con-sidered enough of a talent to qualify an otherwise undistin-guished person for public office. If one votes for a candi-date because he has remembered one's name from one minute of a campaign appearance to another, it is not reasonable to expect such a feat from every private citizen. Miss Manners promises not to be offended if you ask her what her name was again.

(From *Miss Manners' Guide to Excruciatingly Correct Behavior* by Judith Martin)

29.
A STAB AT MATURITY

Balanced Life

When you were just a little squirt you learned to walk, to talk, and to go wee-wee in the potty, which delighted your parents to no end. Inspired by their ecstatic acclamation, you proceeded to learn your ABCs, your 1-2-3s, and geometries. When you came home from school talking about arcs, tangents, and planes they were transported.

But there was also that "citizenship" grade on your report card; over the years you learned to be polite, to share, and to keep your mouth shut while the teacher was talking. You learned to play tennis, to embroider handtowels, and to cook some basic meals.

At some point you started to concentrate on learning the kinds of things you needed to get along in the real world of work —zero-based budgeting, underground sprinkler system installation, and dictaphone operation.

You sense now that your learning years are behind you; it's time to *do* something. And you intend to spend the next forty years or so working, putting everything you've learned to some practical—not to say remunerative—use.

And when you retire from all this, you'll move to West Palm

Beach, Florida (or Sun City, Arizona), you'll play golf, eat All Bran for breakfast, go fishing, putter around your pink bungalow, and generally enjoy yourself; in other words, you'll play.

Retired is being tired twice, I've thought,
First tired of working,
Then tired of not.
Richard Armour

These are the three boxes of life—work, play, and learning—and most of us are trapped in one of them. (All this is based on Richard Bolles's fine book *The Three Boxes of Life*, which is recommended reading.) We tend to be wholly devoted to either work, play, or learning, and the result is that we feel trapped by them.

Think about it: grade school was okay, but you lived for recess, right? Remember your first after-school job? And how good it felt to get back to school in the fall after a summer of nothing but loafing? These were all signs of trying to break out of the box you were in. Recess was a bit of play in the middle of learning; your job was a taste of work; and returning to school was the promise of learning after too much play.

We are better off if we can integrate play, learning, and work—every day, every week, every year, and throughout our lives. Sometimes just grasping the dynamic between play, learning, and work is enough to spur action. It was for me. Because I'm primarily involved in the work stage of my life, this recognition helps me keep learning and playing. So I make it a point to read a lot (learning) and to indulge many of the interests that I once thought were time-consuming and wasteful (play).

"We work to become, not to acquire."
Elbert Hubbard

Assuming that you too are pretty much trapped in the work box, here are some ideas for activities that might help you break out:

Give room for play by:

- celebrating achievements
- taking up a sport
- "wasting" time doing nothing
- watching television, listening to records, going to movies, plays—generally pursuing entertainment
- dancing!
- socializing with friends
- reading for pleasure

Give room for learning by:

- subscribing to a newspaper or newsmagazine . . . and reading it
- subscribing to a professional journal in your field—or in a field that you know nothing about
- watching documentaries on television
- taking a night (or day) class
- attending seminars
- reading for information
- meeting new people

Some activities do double duty, such as:

- learning a new skill (archery, knitting) that is recreational
- meditating, or daydreaming
- talking to friends, which is fun and enlightening.

Bolles's book is the definitive discussion of this matter of the three boxes of life. If you suspect that you're trapped in one of the boxes, and would like to get out (or would like to avoid the trap altogether), do get a copy of it (publishing information is in the Bibliography).

"One ought, every day at least, to hear a little song, read a good poem, see a fine picture, and, if it were possible, to speak a few reasonable words."
Johann W. von Goethe

Time Management

Do you hate to stand in line when you get your license plates; or sit in a doctor's office waiting for your appointment; or be put on "hold" when you make a phone call; or spend thirty-six hours working on a project that a professional would have completed in thirty-six minutes; or get stuck with a bore who drones on and on about her exciting trip to Toledo; or sit in a class and listen to an instructor who knows less about the subject than you do?

Good! That's good—you're a prime candidate for a short course in time management, because you already have the most important quality that is needed: you think time is important—so important that you hate to waste it. And waiting is wasting, there's no doubt about that.

Any situation presents the possibility of wasted time, and there are two ways to work around that possibility: avoidance and alternate activity.

Avoidance consists mainly of steering clear of situations that are probably going to waste your time. You can avoid wasting time by eating at fast-food restaurants, or those that accept (and honor) reservations; by scheduling doctors' appointments for the beginning of the day, when there's less chance of an accumulated delay; by refusing to be put on "hold," or buying a microwave oven, or cutting off long tedious conversations before they get going.

Alternate activity has to do with making the best of a bad situation. No matter how you try to avoid them, there are bound to be times when you're stuck waiting, and there's nothing you can do about it, aside from making your time useful. Possible activities include reading (always have a paperback with you); writing letters (carry stationery); doing exercises (there are a number of body-building exercises that you can do in virtually any situation without anyone noticing); memorizing (names, Bible verses, class material); handiwork (needlepoint, knitting, whittling). Since phone conversations can be long, it's not a bad idea to get an extralong cord so you can dust, defrost the freezer, or paste trading stamps in books while involved in lengthy discussions.

Again, it's a very good thing if you hate to waste time—it's as much a virtue as hating to waste money and being nice to the elderly. It indicates a healthy respect for an important, nonrenewable resource—time.

"Those who decide to use leisure as a means of mental development, who love good music, good books, good pictures, good plays, good company, good conversation— what are they? They are the happiest people in the world."
William Lyon Phelps

Once the problem of wasted time has been addressed, you can organize what time is left—which should be a considerable chunk. These suggestions will get you started:

(1) Make lists and keep a calendar. You're bound to get too busy on some days and have other periods of activity drought if you don't write down what you have to do and when you're going to do it. Your calendar should be marked with all your commitments that are set in time: appointments, deadlines, etc. Your to-do list(s) should be more specific about what needs to be done each day in order to keep your life running smoothly.

(2) Organize your time in such a way that urgency is avoided. Whenever you have an urgent item on your to-do list, you have sacrificed your freedom and are less flexible. Anticipate your deadlines and necessities in such a way that you aren't continually faced with must-do-today tasks.

(3) If an activity or task remains undone day after day, week after week, you're either procrastinating or the task isn't very important. If the latter is true, scratch it from your list. If you're procrastinating, try to figure out why you prefer to be hounded by a task as opposed to actually *doing* it. Procrastinators can often benefit by the next suggestion:

(4) Break up big and/or undesirable activities into smaller, manageable pieces. You can bet that I've never put anything as big as "Write *Life: An Owner's Manual*" on a to-do list. What's the point? Daily items that work toward that big task might be:

(1) Create outline for chapter on time management;

(2) Library research on time management;

(3) Read books and articles on time management;

(4) Write first draft on time management chapter;

(5) Review and edit time management chapter.

Faced with the responsibility of writing this whole book, I could become paralyzed. But creating an outline for this chapter, doing the library research and so on, are all management tasks of which I am capable.

(5) Learn to say "no." On the basis of your to-do lists and your updated calendar, you have the information you need to assess your workload and say "no" to requests that will prevent you from accomplishing your primary aims. If you are bothered about the selfishness of saying "no," remember that you have your limitations. If *I* were recruiting volunteers for a project, I would much rather get an honest "no" than a "yes" from an overworked friend who is either going to kill herself making good on her commitment to me or let me down by not following through. Some people keep a "Say No!" sign next to their telephones to encourage them to be honest about their capabilities and limitations.

(6) Plan to do at least one thing each day that can't be undone. If every day is filled with activities such as preparing food (which is quickly eaten), washing clothes (which are soon soiled again), cleaning house (it will get dirty in short order), opening mail (there will be another batch tomorrow), or answering telephones (the calls never quit!), there tends to be a developing hopelessness, a sense that nothing of lasting value is being

accomplished. So in every day there should be activities that last. Reading a book lasts; so does working on a craft project, making a repair or improvement, or working on a long-term project.

"One of the greatest labor-saving inventions of today is tomorrow."
Vincent T. Foss

There are a lot of good books about time management available now—you can check them out at the library, or buy them at the bookstore. Most of us could benefit by some training in organizing our lives and our time. It does seem that the people who do the most have the most time left over; this is because they are organized. So if you value your time, quit frittering it away. These words from Charles Spurgeon should inspire you.

FILL THE SPACES

Select a large box, and place in it as many
cannon balls as it will hold, and it is,
after a fashion, full; but it will hold more
if smaller matters be found. Bring a quantity
of marbles; very many of these may be
packed in the spaces between the larger globes;
the box is now full, but still only in a sense;
it will contain more yet. There are spaces in
abundance, into which you may shake a considerable
quantity of small shot, and now the
chest is filled beyond all question; but yet
there is room. You cannot put in another shot
or marble, much less another ball; but you will
find that several pounds of sand will slide
down between the larger materials, and, even
then between the granules of sand, if you
empty yonder jug, there will be space for all
the water, and for the same quantity several

times repeated. Where there is no space for the
great, there may be room for the little;
where the little cannot enter, the less can
make its way; and where the less is shut
out, the least of all may find ample
room. So where time is, as we say, fully occupied,
there must be stray moments, occasional intervals,
and bits of time which might hold a
vast amount of little usefulness in the course
of months and years.

C. H. Spurgeon

(Quoted in *Sidetracked Home Executives*, p. 40.)

Crisis

Even in the best of times, there are hard times. Things don't go
according to plan. You get passed up for a promotion; your best
friend leaves town; your apartment building becomes overrun
with mice; you break an engagement; your parents split; there are
problems at work.

Hard times are a part of your life, and even though they can
be pretty unexpected and can throw things into a tailspin, you
have a sense of being able to cope. You can see yourself surviving
the setback, and you have some ideas on how you'll handle the
situation. You turn to tried-and-true ways of getting by—you call
a friend and cry on her shoulder; you go to the gym and work
out; you take off work and catch a matinee; you kick the cat. It's
worked before, and in hard times you feel fairly certain that it will
work again.

But sometimes hard times become crisis times. The old coping skills don't work. You can't visualize any way for the situation
to be resolved satisfactorily. Your life is not just interrupted—it's
in jeopardy. You're in a crisis mode.

When you're dealing with a crisis, you face three outcomes.
You can let it debilitate you. You can die. Or you can grow.

Debilitation is all too common. One hears of rape victims
who are permanently scarred by the trauma of their ordeal. These

women are disabled by their fear, anger, and humiliation. Others never recover from the death of their spouse, or the death of a parent or close friend.

Some people die as a result of a crisis. Even though the crisis itself doesn't kill them, they take their own lives, or live so recklessly that they are victimized by "accidents."

Happily it can be said that the majority of those who experience a personal crisis grow through it. They recognize that the opportunity to put their shattered lives back together does exist, and that they can even rebuild their lives to be better than they were before the crisis.

Psychological First Aid

When one has experienced a crisis, he must receive first aid, the same as someone who's been in a car accident or some other physical trauma. The long-term rehabilitation comes later; the first step is to make sure the most urgent needs are met so that the victim survives.

Tears, anger, loss of appetite, insomnia, fear, isolation—these are all normal reactions to a crisis. If you have lost a parent, or been victimized by another person, or have had your world shattered in some way, it's absolutely normal to cry, to quit eating, to stay up nights, to be afraid, to spend hours staring at a wall. If you accept the naturalness of such behavior, you're doing fine.

If you have thoughts of ending your life, or someone else's, don't ignore them. Although life-threatening thoughts are common, they're not unimportant. You must seek help immediately; a counselor or a close friend can help you at this point. If you are close to danger—have a gun in the house, a cache of pills, or a cupboard of alcohol—get rid of the danger. Give the gun to a neighbor; flush the pills and booze down the toilet. Don't drive. Protect yourself.

Remind yourself that these feelings don't last long, that they will change. The important thing is to keep your options open, and you can't do that if you act on suicidal or homicidal feelings.

Once you're in control of your most basic fears, you can begin to devise a plan for making it through the day, and the days to come. Begin by making a list of your thoughts, feelings, questions, worries, and frustrations. A person whose best friend has been killed in an auto accident might make a list like this:

Do I have to go to his funeral?

I wonder where his body is now.

Was he alone? His mother didn't say.

I bet he wasn't wearing his seat belt.

I always knew he'd get in an accident someday; he was a lousy driver.

Why did he do this to me?

Now what am I going to do?

I wish it had been Bob that died instead.

What a stupid way to die.

I wish I had been at his party last Sunday.

I think he was ready to die.

Writing all these thoughts and feelings down helps clear the confusion in your mind and heart. Once you've got a list, you're on your way to regaining control.

Now scan the list for items of high priority. Is there anything on it that, if left unattended, will reduce options for the future? You want to keep yourself as flexible as possible. A guy who's heard that his parents are getting a divorce, and who experiences that news as a crisis event, should refrain from saying anything to either one of his parents that would permanently damage his relationship with them. In the case of a rape, the victim should get to a hospital for medical examination; if she doesn't do this, she will not be able to support her case in the event of criminal prosecution.

"A problem well stated is a problem half solved."
Charles F. Kettering

Working with the list, make your best move. It may be a little thing, but if it's important for the future it should be done first.

Finally, draw on all your resources. This is the time to call on your friends, to use whatever reserve of physical strength you have, to accept help from God. This is no time to go it alone. You're in a crisis; you need help.

Growing Through a Crisis

Once the first aid has been administered, you face the task of putting your life back together again. It is hoped that during this time you can grow through the experience and use the opportunity to become a better person than you were before.

Take care of your body. If your body is not functioning up to par, you will be hard-pressed to solve any of your other problems. As mentioned before, you must protect yourself from harm. This means staying away from bad chemicals, avoiding dangerous situations (driving is usually dangerous for a person in crisis), and getting professional help if you feel self-destructive.

Then you must find ways to improve your health so that you have the strength and stamina you need to meet the challenge of rebuilding your life. If you ever gave a thought to nutrition and exercise, now's the time to really concentrate on it. Eat as well as you can. If you can't bring yourself to cook for yourself, accept the invitations of friends for meals, or eat in a restaurant that serves nutritious foods. Take a daily vitamin supplement. Get some exercise. This is a bad time to quit exercising, and an excellent time to pay more attention to your level of activity. Long walks are something most people can handle physically, and have a benefit that goes beyond physical exercise—they can provide a chance to think through your problems.

Does eating well and exercising seem self-indulgent? It isn't. It's self-preserving. The first thing you must do is take care of your body.

Manage your painful feelings. There are four steps to accomplishing this task.

(1) Identify your feelings. Put a name on them. How are you feeling? Angry? Upset? Depressed? Abandoned? Tired? Frightened? Write down all the words that apply to how you are feeling.

(2) Express those feelings. You can lock yourself in a room and talk to the doorknob; or pick up the phone receiver and imagine a sympathetic friend on the other end that you are un-

loading on; or ask a friend to listen while you vent your anger, your frustration, your questions. You probably have a crisis hotline in your community. Call the number and talk to the person on the other end. They want to hear how you're feeling.

(3) Analyze the feelings. Why are you feeling as you do? In analyzing your feelings, you're putting a thought or perception alongside your feeling. You might make statements like, "I feel abandoned because my father died last week," or "I feel depressed because I can't visualize my life without this job," or "I feel humiliated because I was attacked."

By analyzing your feelings in this way, you have moved your problem somewhat from your heart to your head; and feelings are a little easier to deal with when they are understood.

(4) Control your feelings. This doesn't mean that you should keep a stoic face in spite of everything that has happened—that's not healthy. Controlling your feelings means that you quit being controlled *by* them. You don't want to be shoved around by these powerful emotions; you're looking for ways to get the upper hand.

Try exercising, and relaxing. Laughter is a great way to counteract painful feelings—go ahead and watch that old "Honeymooners" rerun, or go to a funny movie. Read the comics in the paper, or pick up a Gary Larson or Garrison Keillor book at the drugstore.

You can also take a break from your crisis. Sometimes it gets too heavy, and you feel like you can't take it anymore. You don't have to. Take a break—go on a weekend trip, or take a night off, or just mentally check out for a few hours or a day. Take it from me: the problem will be there when you get back, but you'll be in a better position to deal with it.

Finally, you can gain control over your feelings by telling yourself, "This, too, shall pass." A little philosophy can go a long way when you're battling with your emotions. You're not going to feel this way forever. Your body won't let you exist endlessly in this crisis mode. Eventually you come to realize that it will be over at some point. "This, too, shall pass."

Change your mind. If you're going to grow, you'll need to change. You don't want to have a gut-wrenching feeling every time you recall what's happened. You want to get beyond that.

Sometimes you need to get more information; you need to find out what happened. As you get more in control, you can do this. The man whose friend died in the car accident may want to ask a police officer exactly how the accident occurred. It could be that not knowing is bothering him; and even though the answer he gets may be disturbing, he finds that this is easier to take than the questions.

You need to find out what it all means. How does it fit together? If your parents get a divorce, does it mean that you failed them in some way? If you have been shunned by a lover, does that mean that there's something wrong with you? If your friend was killed, does that mean that God didn't care about him? If you have been raped, does that mean that you deserved some kind of punishment?

The questions that must be asked in order to make sense out of what has happened are often painful, but they are a necessary part of working through the crisis. Unless they are brought to the surface, they will fester underground and cause untold problems in the future. The trauma of crisis events causes the individual to wonder all sorts of things about himself, about other people, and about what's going on in the universe. If these problems can't be dealt with honestly, they become insidiously ingrained into our thinking and feelings, causing us to form perceptions that are often false and harmful.

Finally, you must revise your beliefs. This is where the real growth takes place. The crisis event has made everything strange because it has challenged your beliefs.

You always thought you were the kind of child who had two parents—now, due to an accident you have none. You must change your belief about yourself.

You thought that God would protect you from danger; but you have been brutally assaulted. You must change your belief about God.

You thought that the world was a pretty friendly place to live in. But the people close to you have been unspeakably cruel. You must change your belief about the world.

This is not to say that you become cynical or jaded or adopt a nihilistic attitude that says, "Everything is nothing. It's a rotten world. God is a hoax." Rather, it means that you expand your beliefs to encompass a recognition of what has happened to you. You come to a different understanding of yourself, God, and the world because of what you have experienced. Perhaps you come to see that you were Pollyannaish before: you failed to take into account the possibility of human suffering when you thought about your life. This is your growing edge.

Your changed beliefs will help you account for what has happened, and will also equip you to deal with the future. By expanding your definitions and including this crisis in your resumé of experiences, you have a broader base from which to operate in the future.

For example, a young man who is involved in an accident that leaves him paralyzed must change his mind about several things. He may once have thought that his happiness was dependent on his ability to move about, to participate in sports, to go where he wanted when he wanted. Now he must change his mind about that; he must come to believe that he can have a full life in spite of his disability. He must look further than physical ability and discover the strengths he possesses to sustain himself. He will change his mind about how much help he should accept from others, and how much he does for himself. In light of his experience of physical disability, he has to grow and change his beliefs so they can account for what has happened to him and help prepare him to face his future.

"It isn't that they can't see the solution. It is that they can't see the problem."
G. K. Chesterton

Adjust your behavior. Once your mind has been changed, then your behavior can change, too.

As always, you have to handle first things first. If you've lost your job, you need to figure out a way to pay the stack of bills on your kitchen table. If you've been kicked out of school, you need to find a way to get moved out of the dorm. If you've learned of the death of your mother, you need to make arrangements for the funeral.

When the urgent matters have been taken care of, then pause to take an inventory of your life. What's it like? What's going on in terms of work? In terms of day-to-day living? What about relationships? Your health? Your leisure time? Write it all down—

the way it is. You might want to put a + next to the things that are strengths for you (such as having a good job, having a network of supportive friends, or free time to handle difficulties) and a – next to the things that are working against you (such as poor health, a lack of financial resources, or distance from family and friends).

Use your inventory sheet to set some goals for yourself. Play to your strengths—capitalize on them, rejoice in them. And when it comes to your weaknesses, and difficult tasks that have to be done, break them up into little pieces so that they can be easily accomplished. Goals like, "Put my life back together," or "Get a terrific job" are too cosmic to tackle in one go. Smaller goals, such as "Talk to Stacey about Dad on Tuesday," or "Get a library book on how to write resumés," is more realistic.

Find a place to start and begin in a small way. If looking far into the future is still scary, then don't do it. Look as far ahead as you're comfortable with. Do little things, and then reward yourself for the little successes that you experience. Pat yourself on the back for your bravery, your determination, your composure, and your persistence. Sometimes just getting out of bed in the morning is worthy of note. Since you know how hard it is for you to handle these things, you should be the first one to congratulate yourself when you triumph—even if the victory is a small one.

Keep a journal, or some kind of log that will help you chart your progress. Write down everything that you're doing right, and make special note of your achievements. "I was able to talk to Sid today," or "I finally got up enough nerve to drive past the hospital," or "Today I thought about Tammy, but I didn't have that same depression that I usually have." Such statements show growth; they show that you're working through your problems and are taking positive steps toward recovery.

Although it is not possible to protect yourself against the possibility of a crisis in your life, it is to some extent possible to conduct your affairs in such a way that when crisis does come you'll be in a strong position to survive, and even grow, through it. Just as a savings account makes the crisis of being fired from your job easier to withstand, a network of supporting friends can make emotional crises easier to bear.

In the end, though, crises are something that you must face by yourself. And how you get through a crisis will be determined by the decisions you make. The strength that you get from yourself, from others, and from God will help you through.

(The contents of this section are based on *The Phoenix Factor*, by Dr. Karl A. Slaikeu and Steve Lawhead. This book on surviving and growing through personal crisis is recommended reading for anyone who is facing a crisis or wishes to be of help to a friend who is in crisis.)

You think you've got it bad; so many people are afraid of these things they've even got a name for the phobia it represents:

Anthophobia: fear of flowers
Arachibutyrophobia: fear of peanut butter sticking
    to the roof of the mouth
Ballistophobia: fear of bullets
Belonephobia: fear of pins and needles
Clinophobia: fear of beds
Ergophobia: fear of work
Ombrophobia: fear of rain
Optophobia: fear of opening one's eyes
Pantophobia: fear of fears
Sitophobia: fear of food
Sophophobia: fear of learning
Taphephobia: fear of being buried alive
Trichophobia: fear of hair
Verbophobia: fear of words
Vestiophobia: fear of clothing

Success and Failure

Are you not ashamed of heaping up the greatest amount of money and honor and reputation, and caring so little about wisdom and truth and the greatest improvement of the soul?
Socrates

Everybody wants to be a success. We are willing to admit that there might be different definitions of success, but we're agreed that it's the thing to be—successful. And the opposite of success is, of course, failure. If you're a failure, you can't be a success.

Actually, the opposite of success is probably closer to despair, or apathy, or giving up. These are the real roadblocks to success. Failure, on the other hand, is an integral part of succeeding.

Before we go any further, let's make sure that when we talk about success we've gone beyond money, power, popularity, and vocational achievement. After all, this isn't a handbook for Yuppies. We're concerned with matters other than knowing the last good year for Piesporter. Our definition of success is more inclu-sive.

And so must be our view of failure. If failure is confined to getting an F in Microbiology, getting the boot at work, or not finishing a marathon race, it's too narrow a definition. Feelings of failure can come out of losing a job, to be sure; but failure also comes with bungling a relationship, finding one's goals unreachable, violating one's personal standards of behavior, or ignoring a noble calling. Failure can penetrate every area of life.

"Success is a journey, not a destination."
Ben Sweetland

So success and failure are very relative terms. And they have more to do with your perception of yourself—based on your assessment of your abilities—than actual events that may have transpired.

How else can we explain the fact that many accomplished people who have "succeeded" in very competitive fields—including movie actors, concert pianists, and Nobel Prize-winning scientists—still feel that they have failed? We are led to believe that these high achievers often are profoundly disappointed in themselves and the way they have conducted their lives. Contrast these against the Average Joes who see themselves as successes because they've been able to barely keep their families together, or hang on to a menial job for thirty-five years.

All of this is folklore, probably: the frustrated genius, the fulfilled peasant. But we know intuitively that feelings of success and failure are not entirely based on objective standards.

You have a right to come to your own understanding of success. And it is my belief that we should strive for success in our lives, insofar as success means that we have satisfied ourselves and our Creator with the way we have lived up to our potential. Failure, under such circumstances, is woven into the fabric of success. It's what we must do to succeed: fall down a few times. Any success that doesn't include some disappointments, some wrong turns, some setbacks, some falling short, is hardly worth having. If it's so easy, where's the fun in going for it? People who succeed have had their share of failures for the simple reason that they've been trying harder than most folks (the apathetic types who have decided that anything's better than expending an effort in hopes of some achievement).

For example, if you want to have a successful devotional life—which means, for you, daily time set aside for prayer, meditation, study, and the consequential spiritual enrichment that brings—you will fail before you succeed. There will be days, weeks, months that you won't remember to pray; there will be times when you go through all the motions, but don't get the spiritual enrichment you want; there will be times when you disappoint yourself. But these "failures" are leading you to success. When you do get to the point where you are consistently spending time for devotional improvement, you will know that you have been successful at it because it was hard to do.

"How can they say my life isn't a success? Have I not for more than sixty years got enough to eat and escaped being eaten?"
Logan Pearsall Smith

On the other hand, if you set out to be a success at, say, eating regularly, but you're the kind of person who wouldn't think of ever missing a meal and consequently you never fail to eat, then you can hardly look back over years of eating three square meals a day as a triumph. Big success? Big deal! It wasn't hard for you; that's the only reason you didn't fail—and it's also the reason that you can hardly take pride in your achievement.

Keeping Failure Constructive

Having said that failure is vital, it should also be said that failure can get out of hand. Sometimes the failures we experience are so appalling, so devastating, and so persistent that we start to think that we can't do anything right, that we'll never be free of the failure trap.

That's bad, naturally. Nobody should think that they're a failure. Remember—success and failure are individual kinds of things. So forget everything you've thought about what it means to succeed, and what it means to fail, and follow these steps for getting out of the failure mode:

Get a sane estimate of your abilities. Ask a close and understanding friend to tell you what you've got going for you, and what your weak areas are. Or take a mental step away from yourself and try to figure it out yourself. You could come up with a list something like this:

Going for me:
  B.A. in Human Relations
  physical strength
  can figure people out pretty well
  willing to work hard
  really like to be with other people
  care about other people

Going against me:
  Liberal Arts degree that isn't worth much
  talk too much
  lonely a lot of the time
  tend to be pessimistic

You don't have to show your list to anyone, so you can be really honest with yourself. Maybe it hurts to face your weak points, but that should be offset by being pleased with your finer qualities!

Understand your environment. Who is circling in your

personal orbit? Where are you from? What is limiting you from
the outside? What does all this have to do with you? Again, you
can make a list of positive and negative forces in your environment that affect your success or failure:

Positive Forces:
    good relationship with my dad
    supportive church family
    job with opportunity for advancement
    live in safe neighborhood, big city with
      lots going on

Negative Forces:
    Mother is alcoholic
    unemployment is very high in the city
    live far away from the people I'd like to socialize with

Maybe you've never thought before about how your environment can hold you back. This is not to say that you should blame
external events and situations for your disappointments or that
external factors can't be overcome—they most surely can be. But
you've got to know what's out there.

Analyze your expectations. What are your expectations,
really? How did you get them? Are they realistic? You can analyze
your expectations with this chart:

EXPECTATION	SOURCE	EVALUATION
Become President of the United States.	My dad always told me that I could be President if I really wanted to.	Probably not too realistic, although not out of the question either.
Work my way up in the company.	This company is full of people who have been here a long time; many of them started out with menial jobs and have worked their way up.	With my education and willingness to work hard, and given the size of the company, I could probably stay here until retirement and have a number of interesting jobs.

| Get married. | I think that society expects me to be married. | Most people get married; I don't see why I should be any different. |

| Have children. | My mom taught me that the most important thing a woman can do is have children. | Can't have children before I get married, and I'm not married yet. If I want to work my way up in the company, that could conflict with having a family. |

. . . and so on. Some expectations are very unrealistic, so bizarre that they can never be reached. By analyzing where they came from and giving some thought to how realistic they are, you can weed out the probable from the probably impossible. As with the person above, she might want to give up the idea of being President of the United States—which is based mostly on a patriotic ideal of her father—and concentrate on something she can do, which is to work herself up in the company she's already with.

Pipe dreams are good; sometimes they come true, and I wouldn't want to discourage anyone from aiming high and going for a significant goal. But it is good to know what is required in terms of personal ability, commitment, and opportunity.

Generate some goals. Look over your list of expectations and see which ones you want to concentrate on. Let's say that, even though it's a long shot, she sets a goal of becoming President of the United States. Why not? It's not out of the question. (She considers who has held the office in the past, and is reinspired to give it a shot!) Becoming President has moved from vague expectation to concrete goal.

Formulate intermediate objectives that will help you reach your goals. To be President of the United States, you might have these objectives:

(1) Read one book on American history every month.
(2) Volunteer to work on a local political campaign this year.

(3) Visit Washington, D.C. within the next two years.

(4) Work on a national political campaign in 1988.

(5) Subscribe to a weekly newsmagazine; read it cover to cover each week.

(6) Make contact with another person who is active in politics and try to establish a mentor relationship with him/her.

As these objectives are accomplished, new ones will take their place, more ambitious goals such as running for a local office or managing the campaign of another candidate.

Tackle these intermediate objectives one at a time. If you tend to go overboard and think yourself a failure most of the time, you should be sure to reward yourself whenever you do well. Put a silver star next to each item you complete, or treat yourself to a pat on the back when you succeed. If you are apt to ignore the handwriting on the wall, you should take a different approach to these immediate objectives. Be more critical of your performance along the way. In this way you will keep from jumping too far ahead, leaving important matters undone.

If you fail, try to learn from what happened. Analyze the situation. "I volunteered to work on the Hudson campaign, but dropped out after spending an afternoon leafletting in the neighborhood. I got exhausted walking from house to house, and was afraid of all the dogs."

From this experience, we know that our Presidential hopeful may lack the physical stamina needed to conduct a campaign, and is rather easily discouraged. On the other hand, there's more to running for political office than tramping up and down stairs and getting chased by domestic canines.

The experience may be enough to discourage you from your goal, or to encourage you to revise your intermediate goals. Whenever you perceive a failure in accomplishing one of the goals that you have set, go back to the beginning of the process: re-estimate your abilities—maybe you really weren't up to the challenge. Reassess your environment: it may have been more hostile than you originally supposed . . . and so on.

Failure will happen. But if it's happening to you, it's happening to everybody else, too. As a writer, I've always found comfort in the fact that some of the most successful books ever written were rejected by scores of publishers before they found a home. I also know that many of the world's best books are the most unpopular, and best-sellers are often literary trash.

"If at first you don't succeed, try, try, again. Then quit. There's no use being a damn fool about it."
W. C. Fields

The Key to Success is this: Know what it is. If you can develop your own standards of success—based on your abilities, your environment, and your expectations—you should be able to meet them.

Involvement

Forgive me if I reminisce . . .

I grew up in the golden age of involvement. My friends and I marched against war and for peace. We demonstrated on the Capitol steps for any and every cause that struck our fancy—equal rights, equal pay, the impeachment of Richard Nixon. We read *Ramparts,* Saul Alinsky, and *Rolling Stone* (some of us still read *Rolling Stone*). We listened to Pete Seeger and Peter, Paul, and Mary and Jefferson Airplane (before they graduated to Starship). We wore black armbands as protest against the Vietnam War, just as you and your friends tied yellow ribbons on trees for the Iranian hostages.

We made fools of ourselves, we did things we shouldn't have, we fought for causes that were only minimally just and some that were completely lost. Some of our activities were futile, and some of our leaders were corrupt.

But they were still the golden years, because we had a vision—even a blurred vision—of a better world. Some of us were Jesus Freaks, too; we combined our faith with our politics and social concern and tried to change the world on all three fronts.

Many of that generation have now given up. They worked hard and got very little for their trouble. They have lost their vision and can't see any hope in trying to change the world. A few have persevered: they are still working in legal aid clinics, doing social work in Watts, or writing revolutionary propaganda for the *Village Voice.* Most of us have incorporated ourselves somewhat to the mainstream of society. We have families, daytime jobs, nd Volvo station wagons. But at night we close the shades and play our old *Woodstock* album and sing along with Country Joe McDonald and the Fish.

We vote in every election—even the bond issue referendums —and we are active in our neighborhood associations and our churches and various civic affairs. We give modest amounts of money to national political campaigns. We read the newspapers a bit more thoroughly than we might otherwise have done, and know who Thomas Eagleton was . . . and is. We recycle our aluminum cans and look for the union label on our lettuce. We boycotted Nestlē, and we don't let our kids play with guns.

Out of the '60s and '70s, Into the '80s and '90s

It's obvious that the activism of the '60s and '70s won't cut it in the '80s and '90s. But it's also clear that people need to be active in their communities and in the world, and that it generally falls to the younger people to provide the idealism that will inspire the rest of the population to get off its collective can and do something.

So that's you—the younger generation. I think that there are more opportunities today than ever before for each individual citizen to plug into some kind of group or movement that is working to effect change. And you don't have to grow your hair or wear funny clothes to participate. You can keep your job. My, these are wonderful times!

If the generation of peace and love died out at Altamont, and if the "me" generation perished when the Iranians took American hostages, I think it can be said that the Yuppies breathed their last during the Live Aid concert. It's okay to be involved now. It's acceptable to spend vast amounts of time and give money sacrificially in order to help others—even others you've never seen, on the other side of the world. A lot of things are okay now: it's okay to get worked up about justice, it's okay to drive American-made cars, it's okay to work for the phone company, and it's okay to be involved in political and social issues.

With the opportunities so great and the needs so pressing, there's no reason why each of us shouldn't indulge our longing to do something of lasting significance for the people who live close to us, or on the other side of the world. There was a time when indulging your altruism meant that you might have to join a commune, quit taking a bath, or—this was the worst—eat granola for breakfast. The price was too high for some people in those days.

But not any more. Where does your heart lie? What do you care about? The people who live on your block? The policies that your city council has been setting? The mayor's downtown redevelopment program? The tutoring program that your church sponsors? Boy Scouts? The family farm? Corruption in the statehouse? The quality of air and water? Nuclear buildup? Abortion? Human rights issues? World hunger? Illiteracy? Apartheid? Unemployment? Conditions in state hospitals? The plight of the aged? Parks and city beautification? Quality of education? Abused children? Evangelism? Legal rights for the poor? Refugee resettlement? No matter what it is, there is a place where you can plug in and start helping.

"Once you accept your own death all of a sudden you are free to live. You no longer care about your reputation . . . you no longer care except so far as your life can be used tactically—to promote a cause you believe in."
Saul Alinsky

Locally

Local government and local affairs provide the greatest opportunity for direct involvement and influence. In most cities, the city council or board of aldermen is required to have public hearings on issues that affect the public, and any citizen has the right to stand up, make a statement, ask questions, and express his point of view.

At the local level, those who are concerned about hunger issues can be personally involved: disabled and aged persons need someone to pick up government food commodities for them when they are distributed; food banks need people to donate food, repackage it, and serve the people who come in for food.

A single individual can have a tremendous effect on local policies simply by writing a letter to the editor in the local newspaper, or running for public office, or becoming active in a neighborhood organization, or forming a task force to study a problem and recommend solutions to the governing body that can effect a change.

It only takes one really dedicated person to mobilize a church to initiate an evangelism emphasis, a tutoring program, a day-care center for single mothers, or a support group for grieving parents. And in any community there are usually a number of churches that have programs already in place, and need workers to help maintain them.

The day-to-day lives of people are usually more dramatically affected by the policies of local government than those of the federal government. A local zoning policy can loom large with a homeowner who sees one morning that a gas station is going in next door—larger than a federal policy on strip mining on government land. Not to say that the strip mining issue isn't important—it's important for all of us—but it is fortunate that we are able to have direct input where we need it most, at the local level.

State and National

Let's back up a step. You *are* registered to vote, aren't you? This, of course, is absolutely essential. While an individual vote rarely turns an election, your elected officials are unlikely to listen to the complaints and advice of a person who is not a voting constituent. By registering to vote, you endorse the democratic process—however flawed it may be—and indicate to yourself and your fellow citizens that you care enough to let your voice be heard at the ballot box.

So you're registered to vote; not only that, you do vote—at every election. Do you know who your representatives are to the state legislature, and to the Senate and House? Every now and then a television reporter decides to stop people on the street and ask them who their senators are. It's usually good for a laugh. Years ago Chicagoans were asked who the state's senators were, and not one in four could name both of them. At the time they were Charles Percy and Adlai Stevenson, two well-known figures that anyone—Illinoisan or not—should have been able to identify. (I'm sure that if these Chicagoans had been asked who their mayor was they could have named Richard J. Daley to a man, which only proves that city government is more influential than federal government to most people.)

Since you know who your representatives to the state and local legislature are, and since you're a voter, there's no reason why you shouldn't have a nice little correspondence going with your elected representatives (even if you didn't vote for them yourself). By all means, let them know how you feel about the issues that concern you. If you think that your solitary voice isn't audible above the din of others, then you can hook up with a lobbying group that is representing your point of view. Whatever you might think about powerful special-interest lobbies—sure, they've gotten out of hand—the simple fact is that they give voice to people who otherwise would not get a hearing. If *you* want a hearing, you may find it necessary to band together with others and designate a lobbyist who knows the ins and outs of government and who can get your point across.

In many places, those who have a cable hookup can view the state legislative sessions. This is a good way to keep current on what's happening. Is your representative in his/her seat? Is he/she present when there is voting? All this is a matter of public record; if it isn't obvious to you by watching the sessions, you can request an accounting—and, consequently, accountability—from your representative. Remember, you elected this person (even if you personally didn't vote for the bozo) and he or she wouldn't be there if not for the votes of his or her constituents. You have the right to know what is being done on your behalf.

If you are in the state capitol, you can make an appointment to see your elected representative. You may not be able to see the congressman or senator, but you will have an opportunity to meet with an aide. You don't have to have a big agenda—it's enough that you want to shake the person's hand, express some concerns that you have, and listen to him or her explain his or her position. Don't make a nuisance of yourself or you'll get written off as a crank. But it doesn't hurt to let your elected representatives know that you're watching them.

All that gives you a start in political activism on the state and federal level. Aside from that, you have tremendous opportunities to hook up with charitable, religious, and benevolent organizations that are working to improve conditions in a number of areas: public health (organizations like the Lung Association,

Heart Fund, American Cancer Society); relief (American Red Cross, Little Brothers of the Poor); evangelism (Billy Graham Association, Young Life, Campus Life); housing (Habitat for Humanity, Neighborhood Housing Service); child welfare (Boys Clubs of America, Girls Clubs of America, Make a Wish); education (Parent/Teacher Association, National Literacy Campaign); the handicapped (Special Olympics, Easter Seals Society, Muscular Dystrophy Association); peace issues (Nuclear Freeze, Americans for Peace, Fellowship of Reconciliation); justice (Mothers Against Drunk Drivers, Victim Advocacy, Legal Aid Society); the arts (National Endowment for the Arts) . . . almost everything you can think of.

Keep your eyes open, and your ears too. Read the paper and see who's doing something about the concerns that you have.

"People who develop the habit of thinking of themselves as world citizens are fulfilling the first requirement of sanity in our time. . . . More and more, the choice for the world's people is between becoming world warriors or world citizens."
Norman Cousins

Planet Earth and Beyond

If your concerns are global, you know by now that you can have an effect on world problems. A hundred years ago someone living in New Orleans, Louisiana, had no way of knowing—much less doing something—about problems in Africa, or Europe, or the South Pacific. But now our advanced system of communication and transportation have annihilated distance. We know about natural disasters minutes after they occur and can get direct aid to victims within days; we know about wars and invasions almost before they happen; we know of famines in time to send money to agencies that will purchase food and distribute them on our behalf.

So there's no excuse for not getting involved in world problems if you've a mind to. Politically? Maybe that seems a little bit tougher, but in reality it probably only takes more imagination than most of us have. For goodness sake, the Russians have named the world's largest diamond after Samantha Smith, the little girl who got it in her head to write to Andropov. She became a sensation all over the world: a little girl who cared enough about the world to write a letter and, later, take a trip to Moscow. It's more than most of our elected leaders have done.

Most denominational mission boards and parachurch mission organizations have short-term programs in which people like you can take part. They typically involve one in a three-month to two-year stay on a mission field here or overseas, preceded by a brief training period. Most in demand are people with skills in medicine, agriculture, and teaching. Some organizations have even shorter-term opportunities; they organize workers for a week or two, and all that is usually required of participants is airfare to get themselves where they're going and the ability and willingness to work like a son-of-a-gun building a clinic or school or church, digging a well, or terracing a mountainside.

The Peace Corps is still operating, and volunteers can make a big difference with that program. Some service clubs, like the Rotary, sponsor trips for individuals who are willing to go on fact-finding missions all over the world, and then do speaking in the States on their findings. Even traveling on your own to foreign countries can get you started making progress on the "world situation"; any American who has traveled abroad knows that he is instantly transformed into a mini-ambassador who will be called upon to explain his country's activities to the natives of the country he is visiting. (Take it from someone who was in Europe during the Watergate fiasco: traveling Americans are made to answer for their country.)

If you're not inclined to leave this country, but still are concerned about others around the world, you have the opportunity to give money to any of the thousands of organizations that are involved in global concerns: World Vision, World Relief, C.A.R.E., UNICEF, The International Red Cross, Amnesty International, Church World Service, and many more will represent you to the world.

This country is still receiving refugees from Southeast Asia. When they come to this country, they need sponsors who can help them learn English, find a place to live, get employment, and integrate themselves into American life. You could, with your church, help these people get resettled.

You can do anything! There is no limit to the depth of involvement that you can have in world issues. No excuses, now—get out there and go to it.

"Each time a man stands up for an ideal, or acts to improve the lot of others, or strikes out against injustice, he sends forth a tiny ripple of hope . . . and crossing each other from a million different centers of energy and daring those ripples build a current that can sweep down the mightiest walls of oppression and resistance."
Robert F. Kennedy

EPILOGUE

And now, fair reader, we come to the end of this book. I'm done writing, and you're nearly done reading. We've covered everything from pest-proofing to political activism.

That's because one is probably as important as another when it comes to dealing successfully with the challenge of establishing yourself as an adult in the world. As time goes on, it's going to get harder and harder to find someone who will kill your spiders for you, just as it's getting harder and harder to find someone who will ignore your mistakes or jolly you along when you're down in the dumps. These things are done for children almost always, for adolescents to a certain degree, but almost never for adults.

Some people spend their whole lives clinging to old ways and old habits, trying to remain children while the rest of the world grows up around them. But they never have any fun at it. Aside from occasional pampering, it isn't much fun to be in your twenties, or thirties or forties and still not know how to balance your checkbook or get a grape juice stain out of a white shirt.

Maturity comes with responsibilities; to the extent that responsibility is accepted, maturity will develop.

And maturity is a wonderful thing. For me, maturity means that I don't get embarrassed anymore when I receive a compliment; I'm not afraid to strike up a conversation with a stranger; I take a more philosophical attitude about politics (having lived through a few Presidential administrations and upheavals); I am more at peace with myself spiritually, because I've had a chance to observe how God sees me through any number of tough situations; I am less convinced that money and popularity will make me happy, and am—in my growing maturity—finding happiness in unlikely places; I like people more because I understand them better; I allow myself to indulge in reminiscing. And I have the most unmistakable mark of impending maturity: a persistent fantasy in which I return to Lincoln Southeast High School as a senior, knowing about life all I have learned since leaving there.

So here's to you, to your growing maturity, and to your life —the final frontier.

BIBLIOGRAPHY and RECOMMENDED READING

* Cited in this book.
** Especially recommended reading.

** Ammer, Christine, with Nathan T. Sidley, M.D., *The Common Sense Guide to Mental Health Care*. Brattleboro, VT: The Lewis Publishing Co., 1982.

* Ball, Rick and Paul Cox, *Low Tech: Fast Furniture for Next to Nothing*. Garden City, NY: The Dial Press, 1984.

** Belsky, Marvin S., M.D., and Leonard Gross, *How to Choose and Use Your Doctor*. New York: Arbor House, 1975.

Bolles, Richard N., *The Three Boxes of Life, and How to Get out of Them*. Berkeley, CA: Ten Speed Press, 1978.

Catalyst, *Making the Most of Your First Job*. New York: G. P. Putnam's Sons, 1981.

Chisary, Francis, M.D., Robert Nakamura, M.L., and Lorena Thorup, B.S., R.N., *The Consumer's Guide to Health Care*. Boston: Little, Brown and Company, 1976.

Comer, James, *How to Survive a Roommate*. New York: Frankin Watts, 1980.

** Coutts, Robert L., *Love and Intimacy*. San Ramon, CA: Consensus Publishers, Inc., 1973.

* Cox Wesley, *Crime Stoppers*. New York: Crown Publishing, 1982.

Friedman, Bruce Jay, *The Lonely Guy's Book of Life*. New York: McGraw-Hill, 1976.

* Graman-Barber, Lynda, *The Kit Furniture Book*. New York: Pantheon Books, 1982.

* Halpern, Howard, *Cutting Loose: An Adult Guide to Coming to Terms with Your Parents*. New York: Simon and Schuster, 1976.

* Hennessey, James and Victor Papanek, *Nomadic Furniture 1*. New York: Pantheon Books, 1973.

** Howell, Barbara, *Don't Bother to Come in on Monday: What to Do When You Lose Your Job*. New York: St. Martin's Press, 1973.

** Kahaner, Larry, and Alan Green, *The Phone Book*. New York: Penguin Books, 1983.

** Kantrowitz, Walter L. and Howard Eisenberg, *How to Be Your Own Lawyer (Sometimes)*. New York: Perigree Books/Putnam's, 1979.

Kughoff, Robert, *The Complete Guide to Lower Phone Costs*. Washington, D.C.: Center for the Study of Services, 1984.

** Lebowitz, Fran, *Metropolitan Life*. New York: E. P. Dutton, 1974.

** Lebowitz, Fran, *Social Studies*. New York: Random House, 1981.

* LeMaitre, George D., *How to Choose a Good Doctor*. Andover, MA: Andover Publishing Group, 1979.

Linde, Shirley, *The Whole Health Catalogue*. New York: Rawson Associates Publishers, Inc., 1977.

** Lopate, Phillip, *Bachelorhood: Tales of the Metropolis*. Boston: Little, Brown and Co., 1978.

** Martin, Judith, *Miss Manners' Guide to Excruciatingly Correct Behavior*. New York: Atheneum, 1982.

* Mazzei, George, *The New Office Etiquette*. New York: Poseidon Press, 1983.

* Phillips, Gerald M., *Help for Shy People*. Englewood Cliffs, NJ: Prentice-Hall, 1981.

Poriss, Martin, *How to Live Cheap But Good*. New York: American Heritage Press, 1971.

** Porter, Sylvia, *Sylvia Porter's New Money Book for the 80s*. Garden City, NY: Doubleday, 1979.

* Quinn, Jane Bryant, *Everyone's Money Book*. New York: Delacorte Press, 1978.

Raymond, Dr. Ronald J., Jr., and Dr. Stephen V. Eliot, *Grow Your Roots Anywhere Anytime*. Ridgefield, CT: Peter H. Wyden, Inc., 1980.

Rubenstein, Carin and Phillip Shaver, *In Search of Intimacy*. New York: Delacorte Press, 1982.

* Sullivan, George, *Do-It-Yourself Moving*. New York: Collier Books, 1973.

Swanberg, Annette, and Leigh Charlton, *Chic on a Shoestring*. Garden City, NY: Doubleday, 1984.

** Wallace, Irving, David Wallechinsky, Amy Wallace, and Sylvia Wallace, *The Book of Lists #2*. New York: William Morrow and Co., 1980.

** Wallechinsky, David, Irving Wallace and Amy Wallace, *The Book of Lists*. New York: William Morrow and Co., 1977.

** Wallechinsky, David and Irving Wallace, *The People's Almanac*. Garden City, NY: Doubleday, 1975.

** Young, Pam and Peggy Jones, *Sidetracked Home Executives*. New York: Warner Books, 1977.